THE BOOK OF BART

To Jessica,
"Style over substance.
     Always." - Bart

Enjoy!

To Jessica,
"Style over substance,
Always." - Bart

Enjoy!

THE BOOK OF BART

RYAN HILL

This is a work of fiction. Names, characters, places, and incidents are the product of the author's imagination or are used fictitiously.

Copyright 2014 Ryan Hill

All rights reserved.

ISBN-10: 0997462825

ISBN-13: 978-0997462821

Cover Design: White Rabbit Book Design

https://www.whiterabbitbookdesign.com

All rights reserved.

The scanning, uploading, sharing, or tomfoolery of any part of this novel without the permission of the author is unlawful piracy and theft of the author's intellectual property. It would bring a thousand years of bad karma down upon your head. So don't steal the novel, okay? I worked really hard on it. Think about that before stealing this work of art.

If you would like to use materials from the novel (other than for review purposes), prior written permission must be obtained by contacting the author at ryan@ryanhillwrites.com.

Thank you for being cool about all the legal stuff.

Visit the amazing author at www.ryanhillwrites.com and sign up for the newsletter at http://eepurl.com/7wfaf

Third edition: June 2017

Also by Ryan Hill

Bart of Darkness: The Book of Bart Verse 2
The Conch Shell of Doom
Dead New World

FOR MY PARENTS

ONE

THROUGH THE FIRE

The nerve.

All the time I'd put in should've counted for something. The years. The effort. In the end, I was seemingly no better than common street trash. So what if I tried to take over the place? Getting thrown back to Earth without a reason or goodbye felt bad enough. I didn't even get a pack of smokes and some walking cash. It was the disrespect that hurt the most. This place sucked. I wanted to go back to Hell.

A demon like myself deserved better.

Curled up on my side on a stretch of damp pavement, I felt like a cancer patient undergoing chemotherapy. My stomach felt sick and heavy. Even my bones vibrated like a tuning fork. Eventually, though, I managed to roll onto my back. High above me, framed by the squalid buildings that made up the alley, the crescent moon looked like a very pale butt cheek. I coughed, getting the last bit of sulfur and smoke out of my lungs, while questions bounced around in my pounding head.

What in Heaven was I doing back on Earth?

Had my sentence been rescinded? Did I somehow escape without anyone knowing it, including myself?

And what was I lying in?

I staggered to my feet, almost falling back down onto the rough pavement. I needed to get moving. Not only did this alley stink, but what if some vagrant caught sight of my chiseled abs? He'd probably try to take advantage of what they thought was a young man.

I glanced around the alley. I saw a still-smoking arrow and my name scorched into the wall across from me. Well, the Idiot's Guide version of my name, anyway.

Bart.

The arrow pointed to a plastic bag that, on closer inspection, turned out to be a care package. Whoever left the thing clearly didn't have a clue about the class of individual they dealt with. The clothes looked like they came from Goodwill. The jeans tattered, the shoes, white. White! Only nurses and senior citizens wore white shoes. The shirt had Tony Stewart on it. There wasn't any underwear, so on top of telling the world I loved NASCAR, I was going commando in some hand-me-down Wranglers. The disrespect just kept on coming.

My skin crawled as I put on the clothes. They smelled like old gym socks and pee. I debated making the white sneakers dirty, so they wouldn't stand out in the darkness. If anyone I knew saw me in this outfit, I'd never hear the end of it.

Thankfully, the rest of the items in the bag were a little more to my liking. I found an access card—hopefully to get into a building I lived in—a key to my car, a cheap cellphone, and a wallet containing a driver's license with my mug on it. Sadly, the ID said I was eighteen. So what if I always looked eighteen? For once, it would be nice if I didn't have to pay for an ID that said I was twenty-one. I found a pack of smokes in the bag. Not even Hell bothered with that. Though, of course, there wasn't a lighter, so apparently my benefactor expected me to just sniff the cigarettes. I pulled out a water gun, which I squirted in the palm of my hand. My flesh burned. The mystery benefactor loaded the gun with holy water.

I left the alley and emerged into a commercial area. The city looked familiar; I just didn't have a clue which city. I'd raised Hell in so many, I had a difficult time remembering them all. The remaining smoke from my eviction still clogged my brain, but I'd definitely been here before. I started down the street, which couldn't have felt more barren if a tumbleweed drifted across my path. The time had to be well past midnight. I spotted a newspaper vending machine for the *Raleigh News & Observer.* Raleigh. The plot thickened.

Raleigh used to be one of my main stomping grounds. Going by the date on the newspaper, I'd been down in Hell for only six years. Though, the way time went down there, six years felt like six hundred. Normally, I'd be thrilled to be back in the City of Oaks, but things were just too confusing at the moment.

Now, where in Heaven did I leave my condo?

I had a vague memory of my home being on Davie Street, so that seemed like a good place to start. If I could only find the blessed street. I stopped in front of a bar and approached a guy wearing his hat backwards like a total douche. Only the cigarette hanging out of his mouth granted him the pleasure of my company.

I popped a smoke into my mouth. "Got a light?"

The guy fished out a lighter and used it to light my cigarette.

I took a long, glorious drag, the tar and nicotine like a breath of fresh air. "You know where Davie Street is?"

He nodded to his right. "Two blocks that way."

I exhaled through my nostrils and headed for home.

I'd barely crossed the street when the guy ran up to me.

"Hey kid, you got a dollar?" he asked. "I just got out of jail and could use some help."

I tried not to laugh at him. "Sure. Next time you break the law…" I leaned in closer, "don't get caught."

His face turned red, and he flicked his cigarette into the street. "You know, you're right."

I heard the distinctive *snick* of a blade opening. This time, I couldn't help laughing. "Seriously? You're threatening me with that nail file?"

"I'll spill your guts all over the pavement," he said. "Now give me your wallet before I make sure your mom can't identify the body."

"Look at the ridiculous outfit I'm wearing," I said, pulling on the hem of the shirt for his inspection. "Do you really think

I have any money?"

The switchblade shone under the streetlights. "Whatever you have is enough for me. Hand it over."

I hadn't been back on Earth for thirty minutes and already one of its finest... citizens wanted to mug me. I'd missed this place. I guess I should've played nice—the mystery of my return held significantly more importance than this Hell-bound soul—but I couldn't fight the urge to provoke him.

"No."

The douche swung the blade at me.

I caught his hand and squeezed. He screamed just before I heard his wrist snap. The knife fell to the ground.

"What the Hell are you?" he cried, clutching his broken wrist.

"Not someone you want to mess with," I said, glancing down at his knife. I picked it up and used my thumb to bend the blade. "It's funny. Mine's bigger than yours."

I flipped the guy off, extending my fingernail into a sharp, brown blade.

The blood drained from his face. "Oh my God."

"Wrong direction," I said with a grin.

The mugger ran away, tail tucked firmly between his legs. That would teach him to try to mug someone in white sneakers and a Tony Stewart shirt.

I walked the two blocks and found myself back home at King Towers. The building oozed pretentiousness, just the way I liked it.

The access card and key got me into my old condo. I coughed from the dust. I flipped the main power switch. Everything came on, including the TV.

A religious show blared on the tube. Watching some televangelist preach irritated my eyes and ears but, thanks to years of practice, I could watch stuff like this without any parts of my body catching fire. If my benefactor left it on that channel purposely, well, then, kudos to whomever. That would make an excellent trap for a lesser being than myself.

I turned off the TV, set the remote on the kitchen island, and hopped in the shower. I needed to clean off the stench of smoke and second-hand clothes.

I'd been hoping for some kind of instruction from my mystery benefactor, but when I got out of the shower, still no word. I had the nagging feeling this benefactor just made things up along the way.

After wiping the condensation off the mirror, I sculpted my strawberry-blond hair into place and smoothed moisturizer over my blissfully ash-free skin. There were some designer clothes in the dresser. That was a relief. If I'd had to wear hand-me-downs while up here... I'd rather go back to Hell than endure that shame. In the kitchen, I grabbed the cellphone from the paper bag and dialed Pierce, one of my former comrades. I needed answers.

Pierce did not sound happy about getting a call so early in the morning. "This better be good."

"Now is that any way to talk to a partner in crime?" I asked.

His voice perked up. "Bartholomew? That you? I thought boss man sent you down for eternity?"

"Me too. I was hoping you could shed some light on why I'm out."

Pierce remained silent for a moment. I almost asked him if he was still on the line when he finally spoke.

"No clue," Pierce said. "But I can make a few calls. Want me to come over?"

"Sure." I slid the phone onto the kitchen island and went onto the balcony to smoke.

Twenty minutes later, Pierce burst through the door and accosted me with a bear hug. We were friends, sort of, but this still infringed on my comfort zone. I normally only allowed girls to get this close to me.

"You want a kiss while we're at it?" I asked him, taking a step back.

After exchanging a few more pleasantries that only those comfortable with their deviant sexuality could exchange, we got down to business. I waited to see if any clouds of dust popped up when Pierce sat on the couch, but thankfully, none did. That would have been a little embarrassing.

"It's nice to see the crib held up during your absence," Pierce said. His dark skin exaggerated the whiteness of his teeth.

"Speaking of, why am I back?" I asked, taking my place across from him on the loveseat. "There's no way my sentence would have been rescinded, so I'm here for a reason. Have you heard anything through the rumor mill?"

Pierce shrugged. "I don't really run in the same circles anymore."

Odd. We'd been running in those circles for several millennia. "Who do you run with now? Something big going down?"

"Not that I know of," he said, shaking his head, but his body had gone as stiff and unwilling as a virgin's. He knew something.

I got up and went to stand in front of the balcony doors. Why the cold shoulder? He knew I'd be the last to put an end to a little mischief.

"Are you sure? I'd hate to stumble onto someone's nefarious plan and ruin all the fun." I laid my hand on the glass door, watching the sun come up.

Pierce's steps bounced off the hardwood floor behind me. "Don't worry. You won't ruin anything."

Before I could even see his reflection in the glass, Pierce had his hand around my throat, his nails extended into sharp knives that ripped into my flesh. Warm, black blood ran down my body and stained my white dress shirt.

Thanks a lot, asshole.

I extended my own nails and dug into his hand, trying to tear it from my neck.

"Can't have you messing up our plans," Pierce snarled. "We have such grand designs for this world."

"I...*help*." I struggled to pry his hand away. He wrapped his other arm around me. I tried in vain to twist free.

"We don't want your help." He released his grip on my throat. The sound of searing flesh tipped me off. Pierce must've gotten something holy out of his pocket. "We just want to send your pale ass home."

His reflection in the glass door showed him clutching smoking rosary beads. I threw my hand up in front of my neck as the string of beads flew toward my throat.

I didn't expect a parade welcoming me back to Earth, but this? Completely uncalled for. Pierce had the advantage, and it would only be a matter of time before the beads tore through my fingers and, eventually, my neck. I needed to think fast. I placed my foot against the balcony door and thrust, sending the two of us against the kitchen island. Pierce's grip on the beads loosened a little. I flipped us around and grabbed the remote control off the island.

I turned on the TV. That same televangelist was on, preaching the Good Word. Pierce screamed. He lost his grip on me as he rubbed his smoking eyes and ears. I grabbed his face and flung him over my body onto the floor, the beads landing at my feet. My bag of goodies sat on the other side of the island. I ran over and tore it open, spinning the water gun onto the granite counter.

Pierce got to his feet and charged after me. I pumped the water gun a few times and squeezed the trigger, shooting holy water into his mouth. He shrieked like a girl as the liquid tore through the back of his head, spilling blood everywhere.

I ran for the rosary as he fell to his knees. Covering my hands with my sleeve cuffs, I threw the beads around his neck. After a few seconds, the water and beads burned through him. His head rolled down his back and came to a stop, face up, on the floor.

Pierce's dead body disappeared in a cloud of fire, sending his spirit back downstairs. I stared at the mess his spilt blood left on my floor. Bless it all. I wished the blood had disappeared too, but only the body and whatever was inside it will do that.

Before I could think about whether the blood would stain my hardwood floor, the cellphone rang. The ringtone was AC/DC's *Hell's Bells*, a nice touch.

"Hello, Bartholomew," a female voice cooed as I held the phone up to my ear. "Raising any Hell?"

"You wouldn't believe," I said. "By the by, if you're the one who sent Pierce after me, it would be lovely if you'd come clean him up off the floor before he leaves a mark. I just got here, you know, and I've got places to see and virgins to do."

She laughed. "I didn't send Pierce, but I did leave the bag."

"That was you? We must have a chat about your horrific taste in clothes."

The girl laughed. "Perhaps. I am glad to know you can take care of yourself, though. Now we can get started."

TWO

DEMON IN A BLUE SUIT

"Started on what?" I asked, staring at the pool of black blood on the floor. That mess was definitely going to stain.

"Meet me at the Museum of Natural Sciences by the T. rex skeleton at ten." She hung up without even saying goodbye. This chick sprung me out of Hell and didn't have the common courtesy to say "bye" on the phone? I liked her already.

I spent the downtime before meeting this mystery girl cleaning up my floor. After almost an hour of scrubbing, I finally managed to wipe Pierce off. His blood left a little discoloration on the wood. As long as nobody noticed, I supposed I could tolerate it. I changed into a navy suit and clean white dress shirt before leaving.

The Museum of Natural Sciences had a massive globe out in front, part of some renovations they'd done a few years ago. I walked up to the third floor and into the Terror of the South exhibit that housed the T. rex. The skeleton hung by wires in a railed-off area, while the tail dangled over passersby. At the moment, there were only little kids running around with tired-looking teachers trying to corral the pint-sized buggers. I laughed to myself and leaned against the rails.

Looking at the dinosaur, I couldn't help but smile that some wackos actually thought these things were a hoax. I knew the truth. Even tried to wrestle a Triceratops once. Dinosaurs served as a nice distraction, but when they died out, the warring between Heaven and Hell became a near constant. I loved the fighting, but it did make an awful mess of things. The introduction of humans gave us a living chessboard with which to do battle. An ingenious idea, really. Wish I'd thought of it.

A girl of maybe sixteen with short, curly blonde hair stood next to me, admiring the T. rex. She wore a blue pastel skirt and a pink shirt. She seemed to ooze bubble gum and purity. Her goodness disgusted me. I loved it.

"Amazing, isn't it?" I said, turning to her with a devilish grin.

She glanced at me, her gaze moving up and down my body. "It is."

"I like to imagine how hard a dinosaur like this one could hit a soccer ball with his tail. I bet the ball would explode on impact."

She examined the tail. "That, or the ball would go flying through a wall."

"He'd have been an amazing soccer player. Though I wonder if eating the other team would result in a red card."

The girl smiled, revealing blindingly white teeth. "At the very least, he'd get a yellow card."

"I'm Bartholomew," I said, extending my hand.

"Samantha." She glanced at my hand, but didn't shake it. Odd.

Her voice sounded very familiar. Was she the girl on the phone?

"This may seem out of left field, but were we supposed to meet here? I'm meeting someone for sort of a blind date at"—I glanced at my Tag Heuer watch—"ten and I'm very much hoping it's you."

Samantha blushed. "Well, I—"

Something behind her caught my eye. I held up a finger. "Hang on a second."

An angry-looking teenage boy with a crew cut stared at us from across the exhibit. He'd stuffed his hands so far down his pockets it looked like he was playing with himself.

"Is that your boyfriend over there? He looks a little jealous."

Samantha turned to get a look at him. "I don't have a boyfriend."

I tried to hide my disappointment. I'd hoped to reduce someone to tears during my stay topside. A boyfriend would've been perfect, but I could work with a complete stranger. The boy walked toward us, his eyes narrowed.

Whoever this was, he seemed to have it in for me. I loved it when humans tried to act tough in front of me. It always ended poorly for them. At least, most of the time.

"You sure?" I asked. "Because here he comes."

His crew cut caught a glare from the sunlight piercing the window. He walked under the tail, then jumped ten feet in the air, ripping off part of the dinosaur's vertebrae. In one swift move, he landed and swung the bone at Samantha.

I caught it mid-swing. "You should introduce yourself before hitting a lady."

The boy snarled, drool spilling out of his mouth. "Out of my way. I want the girl."

I smiled. "Good to know you go that way, but why her?"

The boy tried to wrench the bone from my hand, but he couldn't handle my demon strength. "She's the only one who knows. She can ruin everything."

I rolled my eyes. "You kids are so dramatic. Who put you up to this? Your mom?"

His eyes glowed red. Hmm. Someone must have placed some sort of curse on Crew Cut here. Maybe the same entity that had gotten to Pierce got hold of this kid?

"Having a party? Who else is in there with you?"

"Get out of my way," he said. "I won't say it again."

"Could you repeat that? I didn't hear you." I glanced back at Samantha, who took several steps away from us. "Did you break somebody's heart or something? Please say yes."

"No." She quivered, wrapping her arms around her body. Her gaze glanced past my shoulder at the kid. "Just leave us alone."

The boy's voice turned low and scratchy. "I guess I'll have to kill both of you. Nobody will stop me from getting the

Shard."

Shard? I opened my mouth to ask the obvious question when his face turned orange, like a near-molten piece of metal.

A small group of children gasped at the sight of this boy, as if they'd never seen someone's face turn that shade of orange before.

"Boo!" I shouted at them.

The children screamed. An adult with them shouted, "Run away."

Good thing they did. The last thing I needed was a group of little tykes getting mauled by this glowing asshole.

"This world will be mine," he said.

"That voice doesn't suit you at all. You sound like a drama queen." I ripped the T. rex bone out of his hands and smashed his face, knocking him to the ground. "Use your normal voice. You won't sound so starved for attention."

The boy spit out some blood and teeth. "We'll meet again," he said.

His body trembled, as if he tried to fight off whatever possessed him. His face grew brighter and brighter, until his head exploded. At least I wouldn't have to clean up that mess. A black cloud escaped from his body, lingering above the floor for a moment before floating away. Everyone dumb enough to still be near us cowered and shook as they watched the thing drift past them. Samantha lay on the floor with her hands over her head.

I'd seen a lot of things in my day, but never a black cloud that made somebody's head explode. Before security arrived, I turned the body over and took the boy's wallet, stuffing it into my suit jacket.

"What was that thing?" Samantha asked. All the color had drained from her face, leaving a pale and hollow complexion.

"Not sure. We'll talk about it during the rest of our little date here." I reached down and took her hand to help her up. Something sizzled and my fingers burned. I jerked my hand away from Samantha.

Getting burned by this girl's touch meant only one thing. She worked for the Good guys.

Three

SMOKEY THE MONSTER

I moved Samantha out of the museum ahead of me, making sure to keep my hand on her shirt. Feeling her bra strap under the thin cotton gave me a small rush.

She looked back into the museum, eyes wide. "Are we safe?"

I rolled my eyes. "The kid's head exploded and a black cloud came out of him. Do you see a black cloud anywhere?"

Samantha looked around us and up into the sky. "No."

"Then yes. For the moment, we're safe." I forced her to cross the street, but she stopped before moving through the intersection. "Though, that doesn't mean we should stick around to see if that thing comes back."

"Where are we going?"

"My place. It's not far."

Samantha's eyes narrowed. "That's a little forward."

"Desperate times."

"My car's parked about a block over that way." She pointed. "No funny business."

I motioned with my hand in that direction. "By all means."

We passed a row of cars, none of which caught my eye. I hoped hers wasn't much farther. Her keys jingled. She stood next to an old blue Volkswagen Jetta that looked like its best days happened back in 1993. The rust bucket needed a paint job, new tires, and who knew what else under the hood.

She opened the door and halfway climbed in. "You coming?"

"In that thing? You must be joking."

Sam pulled in her legs and closed the door. The Jetta's engine wheezed to life.

I fought back the urge to projectile vomit on the car and got in, using my arm to sweep fast food wrappers off the seat. I slammed my door, hoping the window would shatter. No such luck. This just wasn't my day.

"Unbelievable. Not only are you working for the other side, now you're making me ride around in this disgusting excuse for an automobile? I *key* cars like this when I'm drunk. I wouldn't let a janitor ride around in one of these things."

She started the car and pulled out onto the street. "Sorry it's not up to your standards. We go for practicality, not show."

"You're not even going for that in this thing." We stopped at the red light at the next intersection. I rubbed my temples. "Okay. First things first. Who are you?"

"I told you. I'm Samantha."

"No shit. I need to know a little bit more than that, and I'd prefer it if I didn't have to play twenty questions to get the answer. My patience tends to wear thin after one."

The light turned green and we accelerated through the intersection.

"I need your help," she said.

A laugh escaped my lips. This just kept getting better and better. "Since when do you yokels need a demon's help? And why me? I'd just gotten used to getting my ass raped in Hell. Now Pierce is down there, probably telling everybody I've gone rogue or found Jesus or something crazy like that. I haven't been out a day and already whatever remained of my reputation has been ruined."

Samantha looked in the rearview mirror and sighed.

"I'm not sure what to tell you. I said I needed help. You're what they came up with. Are you not happy to be out? Do you want to go back to Hell and get… taken advantage of some more, because it can be arranged."

I clasped my hands together. "Could I? Pretty please?"

Reason No. 734,906 why I couldn't stand angels. So uppity and sanctimonious they can't even say the word ass. Or rape. Or any of the fun words, really. I didn't know how they got by without going crazy.

Samantha looked up in the rearview again. "Oh, gosh." She gripped the steering wheel so hard, I thought her knuckles might pop through her skin. "It's back for more."

I peered behind me and saw the black cloud approaching us, flying over cars. I dug my hand into the seat. "Just pull over. There's no way in Heaven we're getting away from that thing. Not in this soapbox of a car. Just pull over and let me out. Maybe I can sweet-talk it into leaving us alone."

"That thing will swallow you whole."

I shrugged. "And?"

The car's engine whined as Samantha tried to speed up, weaving around other vehicles on the road. "I can't let that happen."

"And why not?"

"If you go back, if we fail, you don't return to the Seventh Circle. You go down to the Ninth. That's the deal we made to get you out."

And there it was. The rub. The Seventh Circle I could handle. There, I got to catch up with a lot of demons I wouldn't normally have seen. But the Ninth? Nobody could handle that. Spending eternity with Judas the whiner, that obnoxious nimrod Hitler, and the others? Forget about it.

"And I can't go back. I'm not an angel. Well... archangel. I'm in training."

I slapped my forehead. "You're not an angel? They didn't even pair me up with an actual angel?"

The humiliation. This... peon was so far beneath me it was pathetic. The fiery blood in my veins burned like napalm.

"If this isn't proof everything is a cosmic joke, I don't know what is."

Still, she'd put a trip to the Ninth Circle on the table, meaning I needed to be part of the solution, no matter how degrading it made me feel. "Take a right here. If we don't get on the Beltline, we're done for."

The Jetta's tires screeched as Samantha jerked the steering wheel to the right. Part of me hoped she would panic and we'd crash into a hotdog stand. Chases were always more fun with hot dogs flying around. The black cloud turned the corner sharply, disintegrating the part of the building it sideswiped. I've seen all of David Lynch's films, and this cloud thingy ranked as one of the strangest things I'd come across.

Samantha steered the car onto the Beltline. She squealed as we narrowly avoided crashing through a steel barrier. The car vibrated like it was falling apart piece by piece. I would have volunteered to take the wheel if we'd had the time.

She whipped the car around a minivan, almost nicking it.

"Sorry," Samantha said. "I'm not used to this kind of evasive driving."

"I would've guessed you weren't used to driving, period."

She yanked the wheel hard to the left, making my head bang against the window. "Aren't you funny?"

It didn't matter how much Samantha's driving improved in the next few moments; we weren't going to outrun whatever chased us. This called for something drastic. I racked my brain for an idea. Then, it hit me. "There's a church right off this next exit. Go there."

Samantha's eyes grew to three times their normal size. "What? You want to go to hallowed ground?"

"I believe that's what I said, yes. The exit is up ahead. Take it."

"But won't you burst into flames?"

I smiled. Normally a Hell-bound entity like myself couldn't set foot on hallowed ground. The dildos upstairs thought the poor, pathetic humans needed a sin-free safe zone. But I had a hunch about that.

"Either I burst into flames or the cloud evacuates me straight out its anus and right down to Hell. We don't have time. Do it."

Samantha shook her head and steered onto the exit. The light at the end of the ramp turned red.

"Run the light. Just go straight for the church. Don't stop." I grabbed the Volkswagen's oh-shit handle. If I wasn't right about this plan, I'd be saying *how do you do* to Mr. Hitler in about sixty seconds.

The car's engine made a high-pitched shriek as Samantha pounded on the accelerator. Cars honked at us as we flew past them. A few drivers even flipped us off. I casually smiled and waved at them.

"I'm so sorry," Samantha said. As if the drivers could hear her. Duh.

We sped through the intersection as cars darted by in either direction, like the most intense game of *Frogger* ever. I saw the church at the right corner of the intersection. My side mirror showed nothing but black smoke. We'd be cutting this one pretty close.

Samantha shrieked as we crashed through the iron gate surrounding the church. A spike caught the rear of the Jetta, bringing the car to a rather abrupt halt. Since I didn't care about mortal wounds, I hadn't bothered with buckling up. The momentum threw me through the windshield and onto the hood of the car. The shattered glass ripped my clothes. Another outfit down the drain. The cuts across my hands and face healed quickly.

The black cloud tried to give chase, but the church's property lines acted like an invisible fence, blocking its advance.

I stood on the car's hood, unbuckled my pants, and mooned the Black Cloud of Death. "Fresh meat, come and get it."

A guttural moan came from the cloud, angry about having lost this round. I pulled up my pants as Samantha stumbled out of the car and onto the grass. She had a bleeding gash on her forehead.

She put her hand against the wound. "Are you okay?"

I chuckled at the absurdity of the question. "Of course I am."

As an added bonus, Samantha now needed a new car. Preferably not another Jetta. I fished my lighter and smokes out of my pocket, then popped a cigarette into my mouth. I lit it, and took an extra-long huff. "Don't I look it?"

"And what about when you hop off the car?"

I exhaled. "Right. Well, I have a theory about that."

"What is it?"

I jumped off the car and onto the grass. I wiggled my toes, feeling the uppers of my shoes through my socks. I didn't burst into flames, which confirmed my theory. Yes, this was a slightly better situation than being sent to the Ninth Circle, but that didn't say much. The anger rose up in me so fast my horns nearly pushed out of my head.

I glanced up at the crucifix lording over the church. "You sneaky little bastard. I'm your agent."

FOUR

WHEN THE LEVEES BREAK

This non-angel didn't need help with some run-of-the-mill quest. Nope, she was on a full-fledged mission from God. I flicked my still-lit cigarette into the bushes, hoping the bush would ignite and set the church on fire. It was the least that could go my way.

Sirens wailed in the distance. The popo. I didn't feel up to explaining to the coppers why we tried to get away from a black cloud and then I exposed myself on church grounds, so we left, making our way toward a parking deck on our right.

"Come with me."

"You are *not* stealing a car," Samantha protested.

"Like you could stop me."

"I could." She glanced down at her hands.

"That's just silly talk. You're not even a real angel." I grabbed her arm and dragged her into the deck, not even caring that my hand burned. She wasn't getting away from me. Not now. I marched her toward a stairwell and threw her inside. My fingernails extended into small knives as I wrapped my hand around her throat and squeezed.

She clutched my wrists. The smoke coming from my flesh made her eyes water.

"Don't. Please," she said.

"What kind of game is this? That jack-off at the museum talked about the Shard." I let my eyes go completely black for a second. "Is that why your boss busted me out? To go after the very thing that got me sent away?"

Six years ago, I'd had it in my hands. The Shard of Gabriel. The last missing piece of Gabriel's mirror. The idiot made it during the War for Heaven, thinking it would give his side the advantage on the battlefield. We shattered the mirror during the final battle. He'd been trying to recover the pieces for eons, but there was still one left. The Shard. Anyone who looked into it had the wisdom of you-know-who. Omnipotence. *Want to know how to travel in time? The Shard holds the answer. Need to figure out how to perfect fusion energy? It will help with that.*

I still remembered how cold the Shard had felt in my hands, how the feeling of victory blazed through me. The memory made my blood run even hotter than usual. That blasted Shard got me into this mess. I increased the pressure on Sam's neck. Her face turned a light shade of purple. Part of me wanted to see if her eyeballs would pop out if I squeezed hard enough, one-way ticket back to Hell be damned.

She tried to speak, but nothing came out of her mouth except a phlegmy coughing sound.

I shook my head. "This isn't an oral exam. Just nod if your boss is the reason I'm up here."

Samantha nodded.

I screamed and released her, fighting off the urge to smash my head through the cinder block wall. "This is… I have to hand it to the old man. I never thought he could be so sadistic."

"I'm sorry." Sam coughed. "I didn't know you and the Shard were so… personal."

"Come on. You knew," I scoffed, pulling out a cigarette and tapping the filter against my hand.

"I asked for someone with knowledge of the Shard. That's all."

I opened the door leading out to the parking deck.

"Well, congratulations. You won the jackpot on that front." I motioned for her to leave. "Coming?"

Walking down the sidewalk in search of a cab, I lit my cigarette and inhaled half of it in one breath. The smoke felt refreshing and calmed my nerves a little.

"Since I clearly have zero choice in the matter, why have I been tasked by the All Crappy to help you?"

Samantha wrapped her arms around her body. She tucked in her chin. She looked like she tried to keep from shaking, probably because I scared her so much. I half-smiled. The goody two-shoes deserved it.

"Someone, we think on your side, wants the Shard. I tracked whoever it is to Raleigh, but it wasn't long before I knew I needed help. Because if whoever wants the Shard gets it—"

"Yes, I know. He who holds the Shard holds the world in his hands. Where do I fit in?"

"None of the fallen will speak to me."

I laughed. The fallen. Got to love the old school names. "And you think they'll talk to me? You think my comrades will see me walking around topside and welcome me with handshakes and Oriental massages?"

Samantha stopped. "I don't know. I asked for help, I got you." She didn't look up as she spoke. "You can help, or go down to the Ninth Circle. Your choice. These are the conditions that were laid out."

Of course they were.

"Where's the Shard now?"

"If I knew, do you think I would tell you?"

I doubted that. If I tried to force her to tell me, she'd bounce around the truth until I got angry and made a stupid mistake. "What about Pierce this morning? Was that some kind of test? Make sure I was up to the task?"

Samantha played with her fingers. "No. I think he got turned by whoever wants the Shard. Makes sense they'd try to send you back to Hell."

This stunk. A lot. If whoever sent Pierce came from my neck of the woods, there would be a whole lot of Hell to pay when I got my hands on them.

"Bless it all."

"What?"

"Bless it all."

"Don't you mean *damn* it all?"

Great. To top it off, nobody brought this sugar cane up to speed on the lingo. "No, I mean *bless* it all. I'm a demon. I live in Hell. Why would I say damn it all? Damning is a good thing to me. Try to keep up."

Samantha seemed to shrink a few inches. "Oh. I didn't know."

"Clearly." I finished the cigarette and flicked the butt onto the hood of a parked Chevy. Sam rushed over and blew on it. I watched it roll off the hood and onto the ground.

"That's dangerous," she said.

"Is it? I had no idea." I pulled out the kid's wallet. The Velcro screeched as it opened. I found a sales receipt inside and handed it to Samantha. "The kid went here this morning."

Sam read the receipt. "The House of the Rising Sun? I thought that was just a song."

"Where do you think the song got its name?" This wasn't rocket science.

"But that's in New Orleans. According to the song."

I sighed. "I guess they franchised."

Samantha and I found a cab, then went back to my place to pick up my ride. I yanked the blue tarp off and smiled. My baby. A silver Mercedes SL-Class. She still looked as beautiful as the day I'd bought her.

"Do you have any idea how stupid we're going to look riding around in that?" she asked from behind me.

"Stupid?" My jaw hit the floor as I turned to her. "How dare you. Nobody looks stupid riding around in an SL-Class. You're stupid. This is classy."

"We look like teenagers. You think this won't draw attention to us?"

I looked at her for a few seconds before saying anything. "It's a Mercedes. That's the point. To draw attention and say, 'Look at us. We're awesome.' Now get in."

Ten minutes later, after driving at an average speed of eighty-two miles per hour, we stood in front of a rundown storefront with green storm shutters around the windows. The House of the Rising Sun.

"And to think, if we'd taken your Jetta we'd have had to ask for directions instead of using my baby's built-in GPS."

"Yes, yes… and the Jetta doesn't have seat warmers, Dolby Digital audio, cruise control or any other fancy toys. I know," Samantha said with a sigh.

"It's okay to be envious."

"Not for me."

I opened the door for Samantha and let her enter in front of me. Demon or not, manners are still manners.

The strong smell of funky incense hit me like an unwilling co-ed as I walked into the store.

"Wow, this place smells great," Sam said.

"That's one way to put it." I took shorter breaths, trying to keep the stench out of my nose.

"Welcome to The House of the Rising Sun," the man behind the counter said. An African-American in his late thirties with closely-cropped hair, he wore a faded blue wife-beater that showed off his athletic arms, and had one entirely white eye. "It's been the ruin of many a poor boy, but hopefully you two won't be one."

"I hope they make you say that," I said, looking around the store.

The man scowled at me.

I searched for a shrunken head section but didn't see one. Must be in the back. "You have a shrunken head section? I want one for my office. I think it would make a hilarious paper weight."

"What do you think this is? Some silly tourist spot?" the man asked. He smiled at Samantha. "What brings you youngins around here anyway? I know you ain't lookin' for no shrunken heads. I don't get too many of your type, especially you," he said, winking at Sam.

I didn't like the look he gave her. "You mean white girls?"

The man focused his icy glare on me. His Casper eye made me shudder. There had to be something special about it. Nobody walked around with a Ping-Pong eyeball like that for the fun of it.

"No. I get plenty o' them. Talkin' 'bout young ladies like this one, so righteous and pure. Now, what do you two want?"

I peeked at a row of different types of bird bones. "Love the selection, by the way. Do you have that one trick where you make the quarters disappear?"

"This ain't a magic store, man. We sell mystical items. Magic ain't real. It's just shit we don't know how to do." His forehead flattened as he narrowed his gaze. "Last time I'm askin'. What do you want?"

I slid the receipt across the counter. "I found this on a kid who exploded into a black cloud a short while ago. What did you sell him?"

The man slapped my hand away. "Get that out of my face. You ain't a cop. If you ain't here to buy somethin', you best leave before somethin' bad happens. Got better things to do than waste my time with you."

Anger pushed my horns against the inside of my skull. Any angrier, and they would start to peek out of my forehead a little. Demons hid their true appearance well enough, but if we ever got angry, things became a bit more iffy.

"I love it when they don't cooperate." I kept my hand behind my back as the claws extended.

Sam gave me a pleading look. "Maybe we should just go."

I turned to her, steeling my jaw so she knew I meant business. "No."

I looked back at the clerk. "Tell us what the kid bought or

I take that tongue of yours. Maybe your freaky eye, too."

"Think you can scare me? I know what you are," he said, pointing at his blank eye. "I see your true nature."

"Then you know I'm not joking." I reached for him, but the man sprayed a foul-smelling mist in my face, freezing my body. I fought to break free, but this guy had used some potent and disgusting stuff.

He pushed me down onto the brown carpet.

Samantha leapt out of my peripheral vision toward the man, who sprayed her with the mist, freezing her mid-stride. She fell to the floor in an awkward, tangled position.

The man laughed as he disappeared into the back. When he returned, he held a foot-long Bowie knife in his hand.

"Best thing about this store? We get most of our stuff on consignment." He lightly traced two circles on my forehead with the knife. "Like demon horns." The turd's gaze fell on Samantha. "And angel hearts."

The man took out his cellphone and dialed a number. "Hey. Yeah, it's Marvin. Get on over here. A nice shipment just came in." He closed his good eye. "Got ourselves an angel and a demon. Yeah, together. I know it's crazy."

I tried to listen to the other end of the conversation, but I couldn't understand the garbled audio. All the while, I fought to regain control of my body. If I didn't find a way out of this, not only would I be back in Hell, but hornless to boot. A demon without horns is like a quarterback without an offensive line. He had the skills, but no back-up, making it possible for who-knows-what to wreak havoc. Screwed with a demon's equilibrium too, from what I understood.

My body tingled a little, telling me that whatever Marvin used on me finally began wearing off. He sat on top of the cashier's counter, picking at his fingernails with the knife. When I regained movement, I might have to use that knife to remove his fingernails one by—

A bell behind me dinged. Someone entered the store. All I could make out as the person walked past me were black sneakers, thin blue jeans, and a Drew Brees Saints jersey. Tacky. Very tacky.

Marvin smiled as he hopped off the table and shook the stranger's hand.

"Remy," he said.

"Nice haul, Marvin," Remy said with a slight Cajun twang.

Did I mention he also had a peppery beard, wavy black hair, and big muscles? I'm sure the girls in Raleigh found him dreamy when he made an effort not to dress like a bum. They certainly did back in New Orleans.

I tried to speak but only muffled grunts came out.

Remy moved to stand over me. "This one's the demon?"

"Yeah," Marvin said. "Got some lip on him, too."

"Well, once you take his horns he'll be as limp as a ninety-year-old without Viagra."

I tried to speak again. "Wha?"

Marvin knelt down and laid the knife sideways across my mouth. "You give me any lip and I'll take that as an invitation to cut them off. Got it?"

I looked over at Samantha, who was also paralyzed. Her terrified wide eyes spoke for her. I raised my eyebrows at her, trying to calm her a little. Instead, it only confused her.

Remy grabbed my feet. "Grab the other one," he said to Marvin. "Did you clear a table in the back?"

"Course I did."

Remy dragged me into the storage area of the store.

"What…" I said, trying to get out what I needed to say. Next time, Marvin would be wise to wait before shooting that mist in someone's face. "What street… you got… shoes on?"

New Orleans residents loved messing with tourists by asking that question. The correct answer was always "this street." Say that, and they believed they were talking to a local and not some tourist begging to be made a fool of.

Remy stopped dragging me. "You know New Orleans?"

I shook my head about an inch in each direction. "Know… you."

He dropped my feet and stood over me. "Who are you?"

"Katri… na."

Remy narrowed his gaze as he looked at me.

"Bartholomew?" Recognition spread across his face. "That you? Unbelievable. That *is* you. You look completely different when you're not covered in feces."

Um, yeah. I don't look like shit.

Marvin pulled Samantha past us. "You coming? You can fool around with him later."

Remy held up his hand. "Stop! I know this one."

I looked at Marvin, forcing a smile. "Ha. Ha."

Marvin threw the bottom half of Samantha to the ground. "Fine. We still got the angel. Not a total loss."

"With me," I said, not taking my eyes off Marvin and forcing myself to show off as many pearly whites as possible.

Remy seemed to think over the idea for a moment. Angel parts were very valuable. Way more valuable than anything on my person, except for my privates.

"Leave her," Remy said. "I owe him that much."

"Hell no," Marvin said. "You know how long it's been since I've had an angel heart? One bite adds fifty years to your life."

Remy balled his hands into fists. "I'm not asking."

"Yeah, Marvin," I said, mustering the strength to sit up. "Do what he says. Or, you know, freeze us again with that stupid spray," I said with just a little sarcasm.

"Shut up." Marvin waved the knife inches from my face. "Remy, why you owe this cat so much?"

"He's the reason New Orleans didn't get overrun by zombies during Katrina."

Marvin's eyes went wide. "Huh? The city flooded, man. You know that. You were there. There weren't no zombies."

Remy pointed at me. "Who do you think flooded the city? If he hadn't, there's no way the zombie outbreak would've been contained."

It was true. My hunt for the Shard eventually led me to New Orleans. Unfortunately, Hurricane Katrina followed a few days after and, somehow, a zombie outbreak happened right as the hurricane hit. Someone caused the outbreak by deflowering a witch doctor's daughter, angering the mother, who then went on a bit of a rampage. No idea who did the deflowering, though. Wink wink.

Faced with no other choice, I flattened the levees to slow the zombie infestation to a point where they could be killed faster than they could kill people. Remy was part of the group that helped stem the outbreak. The whole Saving-New-Orleans-From-Zombies thing might seem a little contradictory—what with me being a demon and all—but no way I'd let a bunch of mindless corpses kill people I could kill. Or maim. Or corrupt. Or, at the very least, reduce to tears.

"Damn it all." Marvin grabbed an empty glass jar, then flung it against the wall.

I glanced at Samantha. She mouthed, "*Thank you.*"

I gave her a slight nod.

What she didn't realize was that, like Remy back in New Orleans, I had her in my pocket now.

FIVE

WHEN POSSESSING A HUMAN GOES BAD

Remy Broussard might have looked twenty-six years old, but in actuality he was more like ninety-six. The son of a white doctor and a black voodoo priestess, Broussard acted as a sort of middleman in matters of "anonymous dealings" between humans and us otherworldly folk. Trafficking in the body parts of said otherworldly folk wasn't exactly condoned but, hey, the man had to make a living. He used to own this exact type of store in New Orleans. Same name and everything.

He helped Samantha sit down in a chair next to a box of voodoo dolls. "You okay?"

She gave him a thumbs-up.

"Can I get you anything? Water? I can whip you up something that will put you in a state of euphoria for an entire week." Remy kept his gaze on Sam a second too long. I reminded myself to ask him if he felt awkward hitting on girls almost eighty years his junior.

"I'm fine. Thank you, though." Samantha smiled weakly. Guess she'd taken getting shot in the face by Marvin to heart as well.

"I'd say the lady deserves an apology from Marvin. Wouldn't you, Remy?" I asked, leaning against the wall. I stretched my arms so my muscles could loosen up.

Marvin walked into the back room, holding the receipt. I saw his jaw move, an obvious attempt to keep his temper under control.

"I think you owe the girl an apology," Remy said. He rested his hand on a skull next to him.

Marvin laughed. "No. You wanted to cut into 'em much as me, 'til you realized you knew the demon."

"True, but I do know him, so apologize."

Marvin waved him off. "Forget this. I'm outta here. You can fire me if you want."

He stormed toward the main area of the store.

Remy moved lightning fast and stood in front of him, blocking his way. "You're not leaving here with your head attached to your body if you don't."

Marvin stood for a moment, his chest heaving. I guessed he'd never seen Remy move like that before. Eventually, he turned to Samantha, though he kept his gaze on the floor, as if too ashamed to look her in the eye.

"I'm sorry."

"For?" I prompted.

"I'm sorry I wanted to cut you up and eat your heart." His voice sounded soft and meek, a far cry from the offensive attitude he'd taken earlier.

Samantha tucked a strand of hair behind her ear. "Apology accepted."

Remy clapped his hands. "Great. Now let's get down to business."

Marvin clenched the receipt as he leaned against a storage case holding several bottles of snake poison. "Okay. This kid came in here this morning."

"Duh," I said. "That's why we're here. What did he buy?"

"He was real nervous. Pale. Shaking a lot, like he was trying to hold somethin' back. I thought maybe the dude was going through withdrawal or—"

"Don't need a literal blow-by-blow here," I said. "What did he want?"

Marvin sighed. "He bought a potion called Shah Babette, which rids someone of a powerful spirit."

"Like if they're possessed?" Samantha asked.

"Right. It's supposed to be like Ipecac for the supernatural."

Remy put his hands in his pockets. "Guess it didn't take. Up here, the ingredients just aren't as good as they are in New Orleans."

"So you're selling knock-off voodoo products?" I raised an eyebrow at him and *tsk*ed. "Remy… you're better than that."

"Hey," he said, his body stiffening. "I stand by my products."

I snorted. "Shame you had to leave after that whole zombie mess."

Remy scowled and flipped me off. I smiled. To save a nurse he cared about during Katrina, he'd broken a few rules… and lost everything. Including her. The voodoo people he ran with disapproved of him risking his life to save a Christian. They also didn't approve of his association with me, and exiled him. Why else would someone practice voodoo in Raleigh?

"Anyways," Marvin interrupted, "if the kid blew up or whatever, the spirit that possessed him had to be mighty strong." He glanced at me. "It'd take someone stronger than you to do that."

"That's preposterous," I said with a condescending laugh.

"Did he say anything?" Samantha said.

Marvin shrugged. "Said he had to get this bitch out of him. That's it really."

My ears perked up. "So he said it was female?"

"I said bitch, didn't I? He was shakin' and sweatin' like he needed a fix. He was in bad shape."

Remy paled. "That is bad."

Samantha glanced around at us, a confused look on her face. "What's bad?"

I walked over to her. "You know that saying, Hell hath no fury like a woman scorned?"

"Yeah?"

"Where do you think that saying originated?"

SIX

COME AT ME, BRO

Samantha burst out of The House of the Rising Sun, trying to catch up to me. "Wait. Where are you going?"

I waved her off. "You're on your own, kiddo."

"Where are you going?"

"Wherever the day takes me. Disney World. The moon. I don't know and I don't care." I lit a cigarette and took a drag. "I'm not messing with a female demon, or whatever it is," I said, exhaling through my nose. "You think I'm bad? I at least have fun when I'm working. Those harpies just… they take things way too seriously."

Female demons are the *worst*. So insecure. One look at another woman and next thing you know, the Titanic is sinking. Believe me, I know from experience.

"How can I stop one of them from getting the Shard?"

I stopped and turned around, moving within inches of her face. "They probably already have it. Why else would Pierce have attacked me? Why do you think we got jumped at the museum?"

Samantha shrugged. "I'm not sure."

"Right," I snapped. Lies. Or as angels call it, distortion of the truth. Anger boiled in my veins. I considered letting my horns out to play. It would be nothing to ram them through her chest, ruining her perfect C-cups. "So tell me, little miss angel face, why should I help you when you won't tell me what *you* know?"

Samantha bit her lower lip, like she carefully considered what to say next. A wise move. I wanted to impale her like a matador.

"Well?" I pressed the button on my keyless entry to unlock my car. "I don't have all day. I'd like to deflower a virgin or two before sundown."

Her expression became stolid. "I can't believe you're scared. You. A demon. Afraid of a girl."

She laughed and laid a hand on the roof of my Benz, adding to her offense.

I'd have removed her hand from her body, but she'd called out my demonhood, and addressing that took precedence. Nobody accused me of being afraid.

"Scared?" I spit out my cigarette. "I'm not scared. I'm just smart enough to know when to close up shop. You don't have any idea what you're talking about."

"Maybe you're right." Samantha's lips curled upward. "Maybe they did send me the wrong demon. Next time I'll make sure they send me someone who knows how to finish the job."

Oh, that burned. This girl was good. And I bought into it, because to be fair, why should I stand idly by and let somebody else succeed in my stead? I wanted to pat her on the back for such a fine manipulation, but thought better of it.

"Fine. I suppose I'll help."

I pulled out the boy's wallet. The driver's license had the name Casey Testerman on it. That was a name, all right.

For a girl.

This kid must've gotten all kinds of grief from his classmates.

Since The House of the Rising Sun hadn't given us much of an idea of what we were up against, we decided to go to Casey's house. By now, the police must've taken a look at the security cameras at the museum and identified Casey as the dead body. They would then notify his family, meaning people would be going in and out of his home all day, offering condolences while secretly thanking you-know-who their child was still alive, because people could be selfish that way.

Truth be told, the whole thing really was rather sad. Poor Casey hadn't lasted long enough to live a truly sinful life. Now he was stuck in Heaven with no sex, no booze, no drugs, and no fun. Just a whole lot of clouds and harps. A hundred dollars said he was already bored.

Casey lived in a two-story brick home near Crabtree Mall, with a line of cars parked up and down the street. I maneuvered my baby into a spot between a MINI Cooper and a Toyota.

"Tell me again why we got an onion?" Samantha spent the entire car ride bugging me about why I wanted to pick up an onion. She'd even asked the cashier at the grocery store if buying an onion and nothing else seemed strange. The cashier, being a woman, agreed with her.

"Because, my intellectually challenged cohort, we need to appear heartbroken at the tragedy of a child being snuffed out before he even finished puberty. Can you cry on cue?"

Samantha shook her head.

I ripped the onion in half, handing one piece to her. The sharp odor stung my nostrils and my eyeballs. "Neither can I. Now sniff."

Our tears were free-flowing by the time Casey's mom opened the door.

"Come here sweetie," she said, grabbing Samantha and pulling her in tight.

"I'm so sorry," Samantha said, closing her eyes and embracing the older woman.

"She means it," I said. "Quite an angel, that one. Her heart bleeds for the world."

Sam shot me a perturbed glance. Probably worried I'd blown her cover... Which I hadn't.

"Is that a tray full of free deli meat I see?" I tried to sneak past the two huggers to eat some, but Casey's mom got hold of me and yanked me in for a group hug. *Not* awkward. In the least. I tried to wiggle out of it, but his mom only clung to me tighter.

After a minute of faking sadness and tears, I tore myself

away from the two and helped myself to some salami and crackers. The empty hutch against the wall and the delicate bone china under the finger food on the oak dining table meant Casey's mom had probably laid out the spread herself.

The only TV I saw was a puny twenty-four-inch flat screen tucked away in the corner of the room. Weak. A huge portrait of Casey and his mom hung on the wall opposite me. I rolled my eyes. Few things bothered me more than oversized family portraits. Casey's father wasn't in the portrait, probably because he dumped them and ran off to live the high life with some trophy wife.

Beautiful.

Taking my attention away from that abominable picture, I scanned the dining room for any potential talent. Most of the people there were kids who looked like they'd come straight from school. I noticed Casey's mom still hugged Samantha by the door. Hilarious.

An attractive redhead in a V-neck sweater strolled past me, a wry smile on her lips. I returned her grin as I swallowed some food. Felt nice to see someone recognize the talent my good looks brought to the table.

A small circle of teens stood on the other side of the oak. Eyes closed, they held hands while they prayed. I chuckled and took another bite of salami.

"What's so funny?" Samantha stood next to me, having finally broken free from the elongated hug.

"Them," I said, nodding at the kids.

"Why? Because they're praying?"

I stuffed some salami in my mouth. "Why else would I laugh at them?"

Sam hit me on the arm. "Jerk. They're trying to mourn."

I swallowed the salami. "True mourning involves lots of alcohol and anonymous sexual encounters." I set my plate of meat on the table. "What they're doing is just sad."

"Not everyone is as depraved as you are," she said.

"They should be," I said.

Our conversation died down as I waited for Sam to come up with a retort. She didn't have one. The praying kids huddled closer, touching their heads together. This powwow of theirs almost made me feel bad for them. Almost.

"So how do you want to do this?" Sam asked, breaking the silence. She leaned against the table, facing the main area of the house instead of the kids.

"You walk around, mingle, eavesdrop, see if you can pick up on anything." I pulled out my pack of cigarettes. "I'm going outside for a smoke."

One of Sam's eyebrows arched. "That's it?"

"Pretty much."

"You're a big help." She sighed.

"You get what you pay for." I tucked the cigarette in my mouth.

I stepped out into the fenced-in backyard and lit my lifeline. I saw three other kids out here. The two large oafs wore varsity football jackets, in warm weather, with cringe-inducing pride as they stared down the third one who screamed *nerd* with his slight frame, awkward bowl cut, and Darth Vader shirt. To my trained eye, it seemed pretty obvious the two football players were bullying the nerd.

"Is now really the time for this?" the nerd asked defensively, his voice a full octave higher than the others'. His head barely cleared the chins of the bullies.

"Have any more of those?" a sultry voice asked behind me.

I turned and saw a beautiful brunette in her mid-thirties with big blue eyes and sharp cheekbones.

"Absolutely." I handed her a cigarette. She took it from me using nothing but her lips, which stuck out like two roses in bloom, and I lit the cig without her asking. She looked too young to be a parent. Maybe a teacher? One of Casey's, I'd bet. She reeked of sex. Being around pubescent guys who spent all day trying to get a look down her cleavage probably amped up her confidence to a colossal degree.

"Shame about Casey, isn't it?"

"Yeah, it really is. It's always a tragedy when a life ends before its time. It really makes you question things." Like, why didn't Hell get a chance to corrupt his soul? I took a puff on my cigarette and exhaled. "What do you think he was doing at the museum?"

The woman exhaled. "Learning about bugs and sharks, I'd

imagine."

"Fair point." I sucked on my cigarette, letting the smoke billow out through my nostrils. "I don't think many people would cut class and go to a museum. Kind of seems counterproductive to the entire idea of skipping."

"I know. You'd think he'd go the mall, or see a movie." The woman extended her hand. "I'm Miss Evans."

I shook her hand. "Miss Evans?"

"Sorry. I teach English. Old habits…" She laughed, wagging her cigarette between her fingers, jiggling certain parts of anatomy. Her eyes made their way downward toward my crotch. She let out the slightest *hmm* under her breath. "My name is Stephanie Evans."

"Nice to meet you." Forget Stephanie. She would forever be Miss Evans to me, especially if she bent me over her knee and administered some corporal punishment. Every move she made felt calculated, like the way she curled her hair and how she pressed her arms to her sides to push out her bosom. Maybe she wanted to try out potential poses for *Playboy*, or better yet, *Penthouse*. Regardless, I wanted to bend her over the fence and show her a thing or two about yard work. "Did you teach Casey?"

"I do. Well, did." She finished off her cigarette and stubbed it out with her four-inch black stiletto. "Thanks for the smoke."

I waved and watched her hips sway from side to side like gently rolling waves. I felt myself falling into a trance, at least until the situation with the three guys got more volatile.

"We're not asking you again. Help us, or it's your ass," one of the mongoloid football players demanded. He poked the nerd in the shoulder with two fingers, knocking him back a few feet. The two players brushed past the nerd.

I exhaled smoke in their direction as they tried to go back inside.

"What's your problem?" the other football player, this one with a buzz cut, asked. He wafted the smoke out of his face.

I looked behind me, like I thought maybe they meant someone else. "Who? Me?"

"I don't see any other homo with a suit on out here."

"Oh, good one," I slapped my leg. "Make fun of my suit, which doesn't look at all silly next to some *high school* varsity jackets that you'll never wear after you graduate from the local annex... with a GED."

"Hey, asshole," the first mongoloid, who had long red hair, said. "Our friend died today, and you want to step up? What's your damage, bro?"

"Damage?" I laughed, letting some smoke trickle out as I did so. "I'm just out here enjoying a refreshing smoke and watching a couple of jerkoffs engage, and poorly I might add, in the old, time-honored practice of bullying."

"Did you even know Casey?" the second mongoloid asked, holding his arms out by his sides. It looked like some sort of ritualistic dance before a fight.

I inhaled deeply.

"Probably better than you ever did," I said as I exhaled. After all, I had seen the kid's head explode.

"That so?" It was Thing One's turn to speak, apparently. "You know what he used to do to pricks with us?"

"Take turns getting down on all fours in front of them?" Sometimes it was just too easy. Even the nerd had to choke down a laugh on that one.

Thing Two took a swing at me. I easily dodged the punch and grabbed his arm, pulling it behind him. Thing One threw a punch at me while I tried to decide if I should break his friend's arm. I dodged his fist and my cigarette fell to the ground in the process. A massive party foul.

"You made me drop my cigarette." I let go of Mongoloid Two's arm. "Now I'm upset. I suggest the two of you go inside before something bad happens."

"Like what?" Thing One asked.

"Use your imagination." I smiled, and let out a low demonic growl.

Their eyes grew as wide as their mouths and they tripped over themselves running into the house. I missed scaring people. I picked up my cigarette and took one last drag before flipping it out into the yard.

"What did you say to them?" the nerd asked.

"I just let them know there's always a bigger fish in the

pond. What did they want with you? Your lunch money?"

"The usual. Do their homework, help them cheat on tests, keep them eligible to play." The nerd gave me a funny look. "Are you a friend of Casey's? I don't think we've met."

"I am. Also just moved into the area." I extended my hand. "Bartholomew. Not Bart. Don't ever call me Bart." What was I doing? Rambling?

Get yourself together.

I made my face carefully blank, trying to hide my annoyance.

"O… kay. I'm Kyle." He shook my hand.

"Are you behaving yourself?" Samantha asked, emerging from the house. "I heard some football players saying weird things about a boy in a suit."

"Of course I'm behaving. I wouldn't cause a ruckus here, of all places," I shouted in a mocking tone.

Kyle's face turned red. "I better get inside. Nice to meet you," he muttered and rushed into the house.

I held Samantha by the arm, wrapping my hand around her sleeve. "Find anything?"

"No. You?"

"Just a potential geek to corrupt. And a teacher to embroil in a sex scandal."

"You're such a… a sinner." She scowled.

"You love it." I walked inside, Samantha in tow. I held her arm gently as we maneuvered past the crying mourners and into Casey's bedroom. They all wallowed in their own pity, too busy to notice us. I closed the bedroom door. Clothes covered the floor. A Carolina Panthers poster hung on one wall, and another had a framed collage of different models showing off bikinis. Classy. Very classy.

"I'm not making out with you," she protested.

As if.

"Please. We need his computer. Phone. Anything he might have left a clue on." I figured this would be easy enough. The laptop sat on his desk. I opened it and pressed the power button. "Look for his phone. That's probably going to be our best bet."

"What if he had it on him?" Sam asked.

"Just check," I said without glancing back at her.

"Where?"

I pointed at all the clothes lying on the floor. "The pants."

"Gross." Samantha knelt down and started poking through the pockets.

I turned back to the laptop and went to the browser, whose default page led to his Gmail account, which didn't ask for a password.

"I'm going to throw up," Sam cried.

I whipped my head around. "Pipe down, will you? It's just dirty clothes. Although, I would mind any pairs of boxers you come across. Especially if they're a little… crusty."

The almost-angel held up a condom. "So much sin." She let the rubber drop out of her hand.

"Stop whining. It's still in the package. Keep looking." I scrolled down the list of emails, which didn't have anything of interest. Neither did his browsing history, which read like a Who's Who of porn sites. "Nothing. When did kids get so secretive about their lives?"

Samantha looked at me cross-eyed.

"It was a joke." I slammed the laptop shut. "This is worthless. Not one item of use here. I'm going back outside, talk one of the weepy virgins into a sympathy bang."

"Wait." Samantha leaned back against the bed. "Maybe Casey's got a girlfriend."

"Or he's overly optimistic and carries the rubber around in his wallet just in case, even though I thought people stopped doing that in 1995." I picked up the prophylactic. "Either way, we should get on top of this."

The bedroom door flew open. Sam gave a small shriek. Casey's mom stared at us, mouth plastered to the floor as she gasped.

Sam and I looked up at her.

"Get out," Casey's mom shouted.

"Oh, no, we weren't—" Samantha tried to say.

"Yeah we were," I said, with a grin.

"Get out of my baby's room."

SEVEN

SCHOOL DAZE

Mrs. Testerman's screams chased us out into the yard, followed closely by the lady herself. I kind of wanted to tell her that Samantha and I hadn't been getting it on, that getting burned by holy flesh tended to interfere with my libido. But mostly, I wanted to tell her to shut up. I didn't mind a woman screaming at me, especially during more *intimate* moments, but not so much in this instance.

I slammed the door of my Mercedes. "We need to find out who Casey was banging. Or at least hoping to bang."

Samantha treated her door a bit gentler, which I appreciated. "What if he *did* just keep it hoping it might come in handy?"

"That kind of thinking doesn't get us anywhere. No, we need to talk to his friends. And since Casey's mom went bat-shit crazy, we can't go back in and ask, can we?"

Samantha shook her head. "Probably not."

"I did strike up a little rapport with his English teacher. She might be able to help."

Samantha looked a bit concerned. "So we have to go to school?"

I laughed. She was right to be concerned, if that happened.

"I'll pay her a visit after class tomorrow. If you go in, you'll probably come out with a scar or two." Literally.

Samantha sat up straight, as if she'd taken offense. "If I had to, I could handle myself. I've been in high school before. I was sixteen when I passed."

Death. Another topic Sam's kind liked to be sensitive about. You never heard one of them say they kicked the bucket, bit the bullet, went tits up, any of that. They always said, "I passed," or "I moved on," or some New Age term like that. "Well, now you work for the man upstairs. There's a reason high school is torture for normal kids and turns so many sweet, innocent souls into heathens on a regular basis."

Samantha furrowed her brows. "Why is that?"

The poor girl. She didn't follow.

I tried to break the whole thing down for her.

"As the world has gotten bigger, an individual demon's impact on the world has gotten smaller. Because of that, some of us decided to start playing the long con, tainting souls while they're young and letting them do the rest while they're alive. Schools are the logical conclusion of that game. Teenagers' brains are like sponges." I made a squeezing motion with my hand. "So easy to twist and manipulate. It's brilliant, really, even if it is a cop-out. Personally, I like the challenge modern society presents."

"So high school is—"

"Literally Hell on Earth. Because it's overrun by demons." I started the car. "And they would sniff out your purity and innocence from a mile away."

"Did you see any demons in the house?"

"No. Believe it or not, I don't know every single demon in Hell." And it wasn't like they wore signs announcing their presence.

The next day, I put on a Brooks Brothers charcoal suit and

went to Casey's high school after classes ended. The ID in his wallet said he went to Frady-McNeely Christian Academy. I smirked. This kid never stood a chance. Public schools naturally sucked—demons didn't need to go there to make the experience worse, though they did anyway. The big boys came to play at private schools, since they provided more bang for the buck. Kids who came from money were more likely to have a greater influence later on in life, making them perfect targets for Hell's finest.

Once it seemed like most of the students left, I casually walked inside, only to be greeted by cream-colored cinder blocks on all sides. The evil bounced off the walls like a rubber ball. It felt like a home away from home. Except at home, I at least knew my way around.

It took twenty friggin' minutes to find Miss Evans's classroom, and that was because I broke down and asked a janitor for directions.

Posters of famous authors like Faulkner, Fitzgerald, Hemingway, and, for some reason, John Grisham hung on the walls. She sat at her desk, grading papers.

I knocked softly on the open door. "Miss Evans?"

Miss Evans looked up from her papers and smiled. She had her hair up in a messy bun and wore black, thick-rimmed glasses. I normally didn't go for the experienced type, but a part of me very much wanted to throw her up against Hemingway's poster and show the old man how we did things here in the 919.

She pulled off her glasses. "Well, hello there. I didn't think you went to school here. I think I'd recognize someone who roamed these halls in a designer suit."

I smiled. It's always a pleasure when someone appreciates fine tailoring. "What is it they say? Dress for the job you want? Or in my case, the grade you want."

"That's adorable," she said with a laugh. "So, how can I help you?"

I sat down in front of her desk. Being this close to her

made my senses go into overload. She smelled of waterfalls. I wanted to take her and leave her in ruin, begging for more.

"I wanted to talk about Casey."

She leaned back in her chair. Her breasts pushed out against her tight shirt. Even demons as appealing as me didn't command this much sex appeal.

"I'm not sure how much I can help. I was only his teacher."

"Well, you'd be surprised. The main thing is, I'm pretty sure he was seeing somebody, but we can't seem to figure out who. Maybe you've heard something? I know kids like to talk."

Demons, too. We loved to gossip. The worse the rumor, the better.

"Kids do like to talk, which is why I'm surprised you haven't heard anything, being a kid yourself," she said in a knowing tone of voice.

I gulped. Did she suspect that underneath this virile exterior lay a millennia-old demon? "True, but I don't go to *this* school. Have you heard anything?"

Miss Evans held her hands behind her head and leaned back, pushing her chest out even farther. I tried not to stare, but who was I kidding? This woman had me hooked. One day, the two of us would make beautiful music together.

"Why so interested in Casey's love life? If you were a good friend of his, I'd imagine he'd have told you."

I smiled. Not just a pretty face on this one. "Just kind of doing the family a favor. They heard rumors, and if true, they wanted to talk to the girl, get to know her a little. That kind of thing."

Miss Evans set her hands on her desk and leaned forward. The shirt hugged her body. "That's very sweet of you…"

"Bartholomew." I blurted my name out like a horny teenager. I resisted the urge to cover my mouth with my hand and vomit out my shame. How could I let my libido get this out of control?

"Bartholomew," she said. "Such a strong name. I'm sorry, I haven't heard anything. Maybe you could give me your phone number, in case I do? Or should I just call the family?"

My face felt hot. Which didn't happen. Ever. I'm from Hell—my face felt hot to begin with. I loosened my tie and unbuttoned the top button on my shirt.

Miss Evans stood and walked in front of me, her hips swaying back and forth as if they moved to the beat of a drum. "You okay? You look like you're about to burst into flames."

I laughed nervously. "I might be. I'm sorry. I don't usually get flustered like this. It's just kind of an awkward thing to talk about, I guess."

Miss Evans smiled and licked her lips. Oh, baby. She reached back across her desk, giving me a side view of her wonderful breasts. This woman knew exactly how to work it. She handed me her phone.

"Give me your number, so I can call if I hear anything, or need the name of a good tailor." She gave a small, delicate laugh, as if she'd checkmated me.

My hand shook as I keyed in my number.

"Thank you." She took the phone from me. "I hope I get to speak to you again."

"Yes. Me too."

I forced myself to stand, hoping she wouldn't see my, erm, *excitement*. I said goodbye and rushed out of the room.

Being so close to Miss Evans had me at the boiling point. A girl wearing a cheerleader outfit with blonde hair and an athletic body walked toward me. Our eyes locked.

"Hello," I said.

"Hey," she said, her eyes narrowing.

Poor girl. I'd hoped all the students had gone home already, but I'd forgotten kids participated in a sickening amount of afterschool activities to make sure those transcripts made them look like saints so they could get into a good school and begin the long march toward mediocrity.

I stopped in front of the cheerleader. Her shoulders moved up and down when she breathed. I took her in my arms and kissed her, trying to release some of my pent-up tension. Our tongues explored each other. She ran her fingers through my hair and pulled me close. I'd missed that.

Somebody grabbed my shoulder from behind and yanked me away from the girl, slamming my face into a locker. I tried to keep my cool and not let my horns come out. This asshole had no idea who he was dealing with.

"What the Hell are you doing?" a guy said behind me. "That's my girlfriend."

"Tyler," the cheerleader said. "Please, Remember what happened last time. You don't want to get kicked off the team."

"Yeah, Tyler," I said. "Or you might get so hurt you couldn't play, oh, *ever again*."

Tyler smashed me into the locker again. "Think I'm afraid of some homo in a suit?"

"Homo? Did you not see what I was just doing?"

I used my supernatural speed to break free from his grip and whip around before Tyler had a chance to inflict more damage. He hesitated for a moment, blinking as if he didn't believe I'd moved so fast. I grabbed his throat and hoisted him a good foot off the floor, then drove his back into the lockers on the opposite side of the hallway.

This felt more like it. Holding some kid's life in my hands. I'd missed this rush of power.

"I do so love it when the tough ones turn out to be anything but," I said. Tyler struggled to break free. He made a sick, gagging noise in his throat. Hopefully he wouldn't pass out before I finished speaking. "Not much fun when you're not the biggest, baddest guy on the block anymore, is it?"

"You should know," a guy behind me said.

I lowered Tyler to the floor, and then turned around. The two mongoloids from yesterday loomed in the hallway. They looked so angry, I wondered if smoke would rise from their bodies. "Thing One and Thing Two. How great to see you two again."

Thing One grabbed my tie, pulling it out of my jacket and toward him. "Messing with us is one thing. But messing with our quarterback? We're going to fuck you up, man."

I laughed. "I'm scared. Really. Terrified beyond belief." I yanked my tie out of his hands and tucked it back inside my jacket. "This tie cost two hundred dollars, so have some respect, will you? Some of us have taste in clothing."

Thing Two punched me in the stomach. I acted hurt for a couple of seconds, bending over and moaning, then I stood up and stretched. It had the desired effect of confusing them.

"That tickled," I said.

Both Things moved in, fists raised. I tried to contain my excitement.

"Clayton, Darrel, leave him alone," Tyler said. "This one isn't worth it."

He moved between us, creating some breathing room.

"Sure I am," I said.

"Tyler's right," the cheerleader said. "Leave him alone."

"This gay boy needs to be taught a lesson," Darrel said, pointing at me.

I rolled my eyes. "Again with the homophobia. What is it with you all? Quick bit of information. There's nothing wrong with being homosexual." I straightened my tie. "We just made you think there was."

Clayton tried to push past Tyler, but the quarterback held him off.

I waved to him. "You boys keep your buttholes bleached, you hear?" I left the three of them alone with their anger, but stopped at the cheerleader. "You… are an absolute heartbreaker."

"I know," she said, her eyes lingering on my lips.

I winked as I walked away from the scene, reveling in the train wreck of hormones and frustration I'd created. I lit a cigarette before throwing open the front door and heading for my Mercedes. Some kid stood by the car, his back to me. He had a silver hoodie covering his head. Little shit looked like he was breaking into my baby.

"You won't find any Katy Perry CDs in there," I said. "So

move along."

I stopped directly behind the kid, who ignored me. Bad idea. I had no problem snapping his neck, especially at this moment. "Last chance. Step away from the car or—"

The kid turned around, then spat holy water in my face.

The asshole.

EIGHT

PLAY THAT FUNKY (MONK) MUSIC

My face burned as the holy water tore through my flesh like acid, revealing my true form underneath. The scaly, monstrous one hardened by several millennia living in the fires of Hell.

"You son of a—"

The kid kicked my feet out from under me, knocking me to the ground. If my melting face hadn't already ruined my suit, being smeared over the pavement certainly would. I wanted to scream, but I refused to give my attacker the satisfaction. He bound my hands with plastic cuffs, took the car keys from my pocket, then popped the trunk.

"Unholy heathen," the boy snarled as he yanked me to my feet.

I wanted to say something witty in return, but my face hurt too much, throbbing like an exposed nerve. He pushed me into the trunk, and slammed the lid.

The engine kicked over and the momentum of the car shoved me against the side as the boy began driving. His jerky steering hurt more than my dissolving skin. This nincompoop had no idea how to handle a powerful luxury vehicle like my baby. Whatever heart I had would be destroyed if he wrecked it.

After a few minutes, my face stopped melting and the pain died down enough so that I could think clearly. I pulled my hands apart, breaking the cuffs. I wanted to tear through the back seats and remove my captor's head from his body, but decided against it. My assailant's life would be snuffed out soon enough; my Benz would last forever.

My cell phone rang. I fished it out of my pocket. "Oh. Hi, Sam," I said.

"Hey. How did everything go at the school?"

"Swimmingly. I learned absolutely nothing, then got holy water spit in my face. Now I'm locked in my trunk while some ne'er-do-well is driving me somewhere, probably so he can finish what he started without anybody seeing."

Sam gasped. "Heavens, no."

I rolled my eyes. Drama queen.

"Do you know where you're going?"

I stuck my finger in my mouth like a practicing bulimic. I'd thought her smarter than that.

"Oh, sure, let me pop my head out of the trunk and take a look." I shook my head. "Are you crazy? Of course I don't know."

"Sorry. Can't you just, you know, tear yourself free?"

"You're insane if you think I'm hurting my baby."

"Okay, okay. There's an app on your phone called *Find My Friends*. Turn it on and I can follow you."

Say what?

"That's a bit Big Brother-ish, don't you think?" George Orwell had to be turning over in his grave.

"Do you want to get sent back to Hell by this person?"

I stuck out my lips. "Not really. He spit holy water in my face like I'm common street trash. It's insulting."

"Then turn it on. I'll be there as soon as I can."

I turned on the app and watched as an overhead view of the Beltline appeared on my phone. My blue dot moved along with the map. I had no clue where we were going. After a minute of watching the dot move, I got bored and put the phone back in my pocket. I'd know our destination soon enough.

After a few more minutes of driving, I felt the car make a

sharp turn and pull to a stop. A tennis shoe slid into my face. I let my nails sharpen and wiggled around until I got myself into a good position to lunge at this kid and rip his head clean off.

The trunk popped open. I flew out, arms extended, ready to grab the sneaky little shit by the throat.

He wasn't there. I landed face first on the asphalt of an empty parking lot. I sprang to my feet and looked around for him. No way that clown disappeared into thin air. Unless…

I whipped around and found a sword pointed at my chest. I raised my hands and inspected the sword. Its onion-shaped pommel looked familiar.

"You know this weapon, don't you?" the kid asked. "Foul creature."

I shrugged. "Seen one sword pointed at you, seen them all."

He had a messy mop-top of brown hair, deep brown eyes, and still looked to be growing into his frame. He placed the tip of the sword against my throat, making my flesh burn.

He sneered. "Built from steel blessed by Pope Gregory the Thirteenth in 1577. The sword's been in my family for five generations. It passed to me fifteen years ago, when my father was killed."

"Seeing how you turned out, he must've been a real gem."

He pressed the blade deeper into my neck. The cold steel made my skin bubble.

"Do you think this is the best time to run your mouth?"

"I can go either way."

He applied more pressure to the sword.

"Okay, okay," I said. "I'm sure he was a wonderful human being."

Hidden sarcasm. Wonderful human beings existed only in people's imaginations. Even Mother Teresa had more than a few skeletons in her closet.

"You sure you don't recognize the sword? My father tried to kill you with it. His name was Joshua Rivers. Senior."

Now I remembered. Pops hunted me for several months in 1997 while I tried to throw a wrench into the United Kingdom's transfer of Hong Kong to China. Thanks to him, I'd failed. Even the best of plans somehow managed to have a monkey wrench thrown in them. In 1999, I caught up to him in Portland, Oregon where he'd tried to impale me. I snapped his arm off and plunged the sword through his heart. Technically, he'd stabbed himself, because his arm still held the sword. Semantics, I know.

"Ah. I think I remember it. Demon hunters aren't supposed to hold grudges, are they, Junior? Makes it too easy for emotion to cloud their judgment." His father wouldn't have made that kind of mistake.

Josh smiled. "There are always exceptions."

I narrowed my eyes. "Yes, there are."

I was on a mission from God. The sword hadn't yet caused as much damage as it normally would, so I figured I might as well try my luck.

I swallowed my apprehension and grabbed the weapon. Pain seared my skin, but I didn't burst into flames, which is what should've happened. I yanked the blade out of his fist, then flipped it in the air. I grabbed the thing by the handle in mid-air. By the time I could pierce Junior's chest with it, he had a bottle of holy water ready to throw at me.

Tires screeched to a halt next to us. Sam emerged from another crap car, this time a Hyundai. She'd actually managed to do worse than a Jetta. Heaven really needed a bigger budget.

"Stop," she shouted.

Junior glanced at her and froze. I didn't bother to look. Nobody spat holy water in my face and lived to brag about it. I slapped the bottle out of his hand and the glass smashed on the ground. Little Junior's eyes went wide with fear as I raised the sword, ready to take the turd's head off.

"Do it, you Hell beast." Junior spat on my shoes. "Go on. Kill a kid."

I glanced at the glistening saliva on my shoes. Unbelievable.

"These are New & Lingwood. You don't spit on five-hundred-dollar shoes, you little shit." My horns tried to poke through my forehead.

"Bartholomew, don't," Sam cried. "You know what will happen if you do."

I forced myself to stop. She was right.

"Murder is a mortal sin," Sam said. "You commit a mortal sin and it's a one way ticket to the Ninth Circle."
Just like everything else that's fun.
I sighed. This parole, or gig, or whatever, sapped the fun out of everything. I grunted and threw the sword across the parking lot. It lodged in a light pole.
"This isn't over," Junior said.
I balled my hands into fists. "How did you find me?"
"You have your sources, I have mine."
Sam moved over by my side. Her eyes went wide. She seemed terrified by the scales she could see underneath my molten face. "What happened?"
"Holy water."
"He got the drop on you?"
"You bet I did," Josh said.
I kicked at the ground. "I'd rather not talk about that."
"Put this on your face." She pulled a small vial out of her pocket and handed it to me. It contained a thick, clear substance.
"What is it?"
"Just do it, okay? It'll help."
I pulled the cork out of the vial and rubbed the ointment all over my face. Everywhere it touched, I felt a soothing sensation as my skin healed. That substance had to come from Heaven. Not many things could heal that quickly.
Sam moved to stand in front of me. Did she think she was protecting me?
"You don't want to mess with Bartholomew here. Believe me."
Junior's face turned red. He pulled out a pendant he wore around his neck. It showed two knights riding on one horse—the symbol for the Knights Templar.
"My name is Josh Rivers. As a Templar, like my ancestors before me, I am sworn to destroy evil in all its forms." He pointed at me. "He's evil. He also killed my dad. So revenge is just icing on the cake."
"Yap, yap, yap," I said, making a quacking motion with my hand at the same time.
"You really want to snuff out evil?" Sam asked. "Then help

us. Bartholomew is here because I need his help."

"Hey, whoa, I don't think so," I said, holding up my hands. "This clown just tried to kill me, and now you want him to join our little outfit?" I belted out an obnoxious, "Ha."

Sam took me by the sleeve of my jacket and pulled me off to the side. "He can help us."

"And how helpful will he be if he buries a crucifix in my back like I'm some lowly vampire? It's all I can do to keep my claws off him now." I dabbed at my still-healing face, then looked at the mushy flesh on my fingertips. Nasty.

"Doing this can only help with your sentence," she said softly.

"Give me your word on that."

"You have it."

I held out my elbow in lieu of a fist. "Bump it. I'll consider the matter settled."

She bumped my elbow and turned toward Josh. "So? Will you help us?"

Josh narrowed his eyes. "Help you do what?"

"Destroy evil," she said.

"I look at it more as a fight evil with evil situation, but you get the point," I said, standing behind Sam.

Josh crossed his arms, sizing up Sam with his eyes. "And who are you?"

Sam seemed to think taking us for ice cream at Cold Stone Creamery would make for a nice peace offering, not to mention a neutral place to explain everything. Not making that up. Cold Stone Creamery. I so needed a fake ID.

Alcohol, how I miss thee.

One of these days, I would have to get this country to lower the drinking age back to eighteen. Sometimes, America just couldn't hide from its Puritan roots.

With my face healed, we sat outside Cold Stone. Sam ate her Birthday Cake Remix with the glee of a little kid, while Josh nursed his Turtle Sundae. I went through three cigarettes as Sam got the Templar up to speed on our holy mission. Sam wisely didn't give away too many details of our situation. If Josh knew about the Shard of Gabriel, he'd probably try to use it to destroy me. Because that was what shit birds like him did.

"So what can I do to help?" Josh asked between bites.

Samantha twirled a spoon in her ice cream. "We need you to go to Casey's funeral tomorrow, see if you can find out anything about this mystery girlfriend."

"Why can't you two do it?"

Sam pursed her lips. "Well, we kind of… ah…"

I flicked my cigarette away. "His mom thought she saw us fooling around in Casey's bedroom."

Josh seemed unhappy.

I shrugged. "What can you do?"

Josh looked back and forth between us. "But you guys didn't do anything, right?"

"No," Sam said, a little too quickly for my tastes. "Heavens, no."

Josh smiled. "Good."

I lit another cigarette as I glared at Sam. "Please. If you just met me on the street and had no idea about my true nature, you'd be all over me like the world was ending and you wanted to go out with a bang. Don't even."

Sam snorted. "Who says you're even my type?"

I pulled my Ray-Bans down my nose. "Look at me. I'm everybody's type."

I huffed on my cig and blew an o-ring at her. She closed her eyes and waved the smoke off, like the smoke would blind her if it touched her corneas.

"Do you have to do that?" Josh asked.

"Yes," I said, sucking on my nicotine-drenched treat. It was so sweet, watching Josh acting chivalrous for Sam. Would he keep up the act if I told him the truth about her?

Josh peered up into the sky. "That's a weird rain cloud."

Sam and I both checked out the cloud in question. A dark cloud rushed toward us. I yanked off the Ray-Bans. The Black Cloud of Death had returned.

"We'll take my car this time," I said. The metal chair screeched across the pavement as I bolted for my Benz.

I didn't bother to look back at the death cloud as I fished

the keys out of my pocket and used the keyless entry to unlock the car. I slid into my baby and turned it on, the engine's hum giving me a small kick of adrenaline. When I heard Sam and Josh slam their doors shut, I hit the gas pedal and we sped out of the parking lot.

Being stuck in a massive strip mall with a gaseous form intent on sending me back to Hell blew. Stopped cars and red lights blocked every entrance onto the main road that led to the Beltline. Each time I thought I'd gotten out, I had to throw the Benz into reverse, tires screeching, and find another means of escape. The cloud, or whatever it was, passed just over the top of the car.

Sam screamed.

"Get us out of here," Josh said.

I slammed on the brakes and put the car in park. I turned to Josh, who sat in the back seat. "Do you really think I *want* that thing to get us? If you're going to shout ridiculous stuff like that the entire time, I'm going to rip your tongue out or let that thing do it for me. Got it?"

Josh looked at me blankly for a moment, then nodded.

"Good." I threw the gear back into drive. All the entrances were still blocked and the cloud took up the entire rearview mirror, so I did the only thing possible.

I jumped the curb.

"I'm sorry, sweetie," I said to my car. The bottom of the bumper scraped against the cement and the car shook like a bomb had gone off. I hated to do it, but no way would I let this deadly fart send me to the Ninth Circle.

I weaved through the traffic and merged with the Beltline. I pushed down on the gas and whipped the car between two tractor-trailers.

"If anybody has an idea how to lose this thing, let me know," I said, seeing the cloud break apart as it moved among three lanes of traffic. "Because I am *not* crashing my ride into a church."

Crashing Sam's Jetta was one thing. The Mercedes fell into a completely different category.

A car in front of me merged into my lane. I drove so fast I didn't have time to brake and avoid hitting it. Instead, I swerved hard to the right and ended up taking the Western Boulevard exit. The cloud flew past us and disappeared behind some trees.

"Did we lose it?" Josh asked.

I laughed. "You think that gassy asshat will give up that easily?"

Sam looked through the rear windshield. She nudged my shoulder. "It's right behind us."

The cloud moved through tree branches, disintegrating them. It left a circular hole through the top of the trees.

I had an idea. I didn't know if it would work, but that had never stopped me before. This plan would've worked on me, so I figured it would do the same to our pursuer. I jerked the steering wheel and made a U-turn, heading straight for the cloud.

Sam gaped at me. "What are you doing?"

I smirked. "Trust me."

I turned on the stereo and twirled the dial around, looking for a certain satellite radio channel.

"Is now really the best time to listen to music?" Josh asked.

"Yes, it is." I stopped channel surfing when I hit the Catholic station. I turned the volume down to nothing, then opened the sunroof and all the windows. "Sam, when I tell you, max out the volume and grab the wheel."

"I hope you know what you're doing."

"Me too."

The black cloud, now thirty feet away from us, quickly approached, flying over the tops of cars.

Sam squealed.

"You're insane," Josh said.

"Trust me," I said.

"Oh, man, I'm going to die," he said.

"Now." I covered my ears as she turned the volume up all the way and took hold of the steering wheel. The channel played some kind of music involving monks chanting. Even with my hands over my ears, the noise pollution violated me. My head shook. My skull rattled. The monk music wanted to destroy me.

The black cloud was only a few feet away. As it neared the

front of the car, the cloud broke apart into little clumps as the monks' chanting ripped through the entity like a starving person at an all-you-can-eat buffet.

Once we passed the gassy Cloud of Death, I looked in the rearview. All clear.

"Turn the music off."

The pounding in my head disappeared once Sam silenced the monks. I took back the steering wheel, relieved my gambit worked.

"How did you know that would happen?" Josh asked.

"I didn't." Hymns, psalms, Amy Grant… any stuff like that typically had a pretty nasty effect on demons, so I'd acted on a hunch. Josh didn't need to know that, though. "Got lucky."

Josh sat there, probably trying to think of an answer. "Okay. Whatever you guys are into, I'm in."

NINE

THE HE-MAN LOOK

After the encounter with the Black Fart of Death, Josh decided to go all in, regardless of his hatred towards me. He did promise that after this quest, he would have his vengeance, but in the meantime, he'd put that on hold. Whatever. I'd kill him before then anyway.

Josh agreed to crash Casey's funeral to see if he could catch wind of the mystery girl. Sam and I, knowing his mom wouldn't be around to stumble upon us this time, decided to break into the kid's house to see if that ever-elusive cellphone had somehow appeared. Josh would also let us know when Mrs. Testerman left the funeral, just to be safe. Neither of us wanted her to catch us in her home again.

The day of the funeral, I parked the Benz around the corner from the Testerman house and we walked the rest of the way. I wore black leather gloves on top of my usual outfit. It felt appropriate. Stealthy.

"How are we getting in?" Sam asked. "I'm not comfortable just breaking into the place."

I stopped. Had she really overlooked that detail? "You're

joking, right? How were you expecting we get in? Hope that she forgot to lock the door? Say 'knock, knock, Avon calling'?"

Sam tensed up. "I don't know. Spare key, maybe?"

"And if there isn't one?"

Sam looked down at her feet. "I don't think about things like that. I'm an angel."

"No you're not," I huffed. "And even if you were, angels can do stuff like that if it's necessary. You're just making excuses. Don't forget, I used to be a real angel. I know all about your stinking rules."

An old man stood in the front yard next to us while his Yorkie relieved itself.

I glared at him. "What do you want? A pooper scooper?"

The old man didn't react. He walked back into his house with the dog. I returned my attention to Sam, who looked pale.

"That was really mean," she said.

"Hello? Demon?" I closed my eyes for a moment. Yelling at Sam in the middle of the 'burbs didn't help anybody. "I get that you're so goody two-shoes you don't want to get your hands dirty. I'm assuming that's partly why the Shard decided to pull me into this three-ring circus. But don't use that as an excuse. It makes you look dumb, and I don't get the impression you are."

"Let's just check for a spare, okay? It'll make me feel better."

"Fine."

Neither of us said a word until we reached the house. We searched around the front porch for a spare key that might be hidden under one of the plants or—no joke—a three-foot-high gnome. If they had a spare key outside, we couldn't find it. We tried the back of the house next, jumping the fence and walking to the door. I tried the handle just in case, but no dice. Locked. A metal rooster stood guard next to the door.

"That's about the biggest cock I've ever seen," I said. Sam didn't say anything. I picked up the cock, running my hands over it. "You want to get in on this? It's big enough for two."

She glanced at the rooster and stuck her tongue out at me in disgust before wandering off to resume her search.

I looked under the cock for the key. Nothing. This was stupid. My patience reached its end.

I broke a pane of glass with my elbow as I heard Sam call out triumphantly, "Found it."

Oops.

Seconds later, Sam held up the key, scowling indignantly at me.

"Look at that. You found the key. That's great." I reached through the broken window and opened the door. I motioned for Sam to enter. "Ladies first."

Sam walked past me, glaring. "Patience is a virtue."

"Mind the glass." I stepped inside.

Except for the air conditioner running, I didn't hear a sound in the house. The faint smell of deli meat still hung in the air.

Sam scanned the books in a bookshelf. "If you find the phone, we have to check it here. We can't take it with us."

I sighed. "Let me guess. Thou shalt not steal?"

"Something like that. I didn't make the rules."

I patted her on the head. "No, you just follow them like a good little girl."

I had to get out of this situation. The way Sam kept our hands tied, we would never find who wanted the Shard. And even if we did, we didn't stand a chance in Heaven of stopping them.

"You check the kitchen. I'll check her bedroom."

Sam gave me a funny look. "The bedroom?"

"You never know." What I did know was that with no Mr. Testerman, chances were good I could find something incriminating lying around. Mostly for giggles.

The bedroom looked so messy you'd think Casey lived in this room, not his mother. Clothes all over the floor, the bed hadn't been made, and tear-soaked tissues lay on the nightstand. Pathetic. I scanned the top of the dresser. Not one damning item among the bottles of perfume, lotions, makeup, whatever else women used to keep time from destroying their looks. I dug into the drawers. The top right had the *coup de grâce*: Mrs. Testerman's vibrator.

I smiled and turned it on, listening to the electronic hum.

Laughing, I removed the batteries and stuffed them in my pocket. Just a little gift from me to her. "Throw me out of your house." "Bart," Sam called out.

"Did you find the phone?" I asked, meeting her in the living room.

She waved the phone around.

"Wonderful."

Sam turned the phone on and waited for it to load up. She turned to me and took a breath, like she wanted to say something, but instead said nothing.

I tapped my hands to Johnny Cash's *I Walk the Line* to kill the time. I almost went outside to have a smoke when Sam spoke up.

"That was an awful thing you said earlier," she muttered. "About me."

"What? The whole goody-goody angel thing?"

"Yes."

"Well, you're not exactly making this a real treat for me, you know."

"It's not supposed to be a treat," she said, glancing up at me. "This isn't my idea of a good time either."

I leaned against the couch. "Then why bother? Let's just give up and call it a day."

She narrowed her eyes. "Because I *care* about finding out who's after the Shard."

Whatever hurt I'd inflicted on her appeared to be turning into anger. Most angels acted like Vulcans when it comes to anger, pushing it deep down into the depths of their soul. Seeing Sam's boil to the surface was a welcome change.

"Do you even know how to care about something?"

"Sure I do."

"What do you care about?"

"I care about wrecking lives. Making the best-laid plans of mice and men go awry. Taking people's hubris and using it to destroy them. And virgins. Sweet, luscious virgins. That count?" I raised my eyebrows. "And smoking. I love smoking. But that one is a given."

"I shouldn't have asked." Sam threw her arms up. "Can't you just apologize?"

"I'm a demon. Do you get that? I don't apologize." I probably did need to apologize, actually. Otherwise, this argument might never end. "I'm not trying to make you feel bad, all right? I do it to everybody who isn't from Hell." I paused and considered that statement for a moment. "No, I do it to everybody. Even those from Hell. It's just the way I am."

If she wanted an apology, it wouldn't get any closer than that.. Period.

Samantha slapped me. Guess my apology didn't do the trick for her. A searing pain soon replaced the sting of the hit and I rubbed my face, knowing she'd left a nasty mark. I found a mirror in the hallway and looked at the damage. Just as I'd feared, my cheek had a nice, deep, burgundy handprint on it.

"Great," I said. "Appreciate that. I left your little healing semen stuff at home."

With the cell up and running, Sam went to work, using her thumbs to navigate the menu screen. "You deserved it. And you're forgiven. Come here."

"Why? So you can inflict more domestic abuse on me?"

She glared at me. "So you can look at this."

I moved next to her for a look. She navigated to the text messages. Most of them seemed to be from guys—presumably Casey's friends—his mom, and a mystery number that had Vixen as the contact. I pointed at it. "Bingo."

Sam gave me the stink eye. "*You think?*"

She touched the name, bringing up the contact information. Just a phone number. No e-mail, Facebook or any other personal information. "Dial it?"

I shrugged. "Sure. Maybe it will freak her out, make her think a ghost is calling." The idea of messing with this Vixen's mind felt too enticing. "Definitely call her."

Sam hit dial and held the phone up to her ear as I waited. After a few seconds, she ended the call. "Disconnected number."

"Of course." Things would be too easy, otherwise. "Check his photos. Maybe she's in there."

Sam went to the main menu, then over to photos. We both screamed at the same time. The first picture featured Casey, completely naked and posing like a weightlifter for the camera.

The catch? Casey probably couldn't lift a toothpick. His blotchy skin needed a tan. He reeked of nerd. Why did the football idiots like him? Probably pity.

Sam dropped the phone and covered her eyes. "That's disgusting."

I picked the cell up. "Your virgin eyes can't take the sight?"

"No. It's inappropriate. Just please look for me?"

I laughed and pointed at her. "You admitted you have virgin eyes." I flipped through the photos. "You need to see this one."

I shoved the phone in her face, showing her a picture of Casey dressed like He-Man, blue thong underwear and all.

"Gross." She ran into the kitchen. "I'm not coming back in there until you're done."

"Fat load of fun you are." I could hear her whispering a Hail Mary to herself. What a weenie. "There's no need for that. You're not going to Hell because you saw a picture of a kid in a He-Man outfit."

"So you say," she called out from the kitchen.

I scanned the photos, but didn't come across anything we could use. Back at the picture of the kid doing his best Masters of the Universe imitation, I noticed a hand on his leg. Wrapped around the thumb was a black ring in the shape of a snake. "Interesting."

"What?" Sam asked.

"Either come in here or go outside. I'm not talking to you through a wall or while you're chanting Hail Mary."

She walked into the room. I covered the part of the image of Casey with my fingers. The last thing I needed was Sam running out of the house screaming like her hair caught on fire.

Sam studied the image. "Is that all we have? A ring?"

I nodded. "The thumb might not belong to the mystery lady, but chances are it's her. I don't know who else would be taking pictures of Casey like this."

"Maybe it's a special ring?"

"Yeah. Or maybe she got it out of a cereal box." I snorted.

Sam pointed at the cell. "Send the picture to your phone. Maybe your friend Remy will recognize it."

"It's a start." I texted the photo to myself and tossed the phone on the floor.

Sam rushed to pick up the cell. "We need to put this back where we found it. I don't want his mom knowing someone broke into her house during her son's funeral."

I pointed at the broken window in the back door. "Did you forget about that?"

"Fudge." Sam dropped the phone on the floor.

We met Josh at a Starbucks to find out what he'd learned.

"Not much," he said.

I rolled my eyes. "That figures."

Josh glared at me. "It's not like I didn't try, you Hell spawn. The kids pretty much just texted each other back and forth after the service. Some even did it during."

Speaking of which… I showed him the photo we'd lifted from Casey's phone. "Did you see this anywhere?"

Josh looked away and stuck out his tongue, disgusted. "C'mon, man. It was a funeral. Nobody walked around dressed like He-Man."

"I'm talking about the ring, smart guy. Did you see that anywhere?"

Sam took a sip from her coffee. "We think it belongs to our mystery girl, or at least someone who may be able to point us in the right direction."

Josh took the phone from me and studied it. He used his hand to cover Casey's crotch area. "No, I didn't see it."

"Did you at least talk to people or eavesdrop? Do you have *anything* of use for us?" I asked.

"I didn't get any names. One of his friends did mention Casey seeing someone." Josh took a bite from his lemon pound cake. "But they didn't have a name or anything. Just that whenever he talked about her, he'd refer to her as Vixen."

"Do you know who said that? Did you get a name?" Sam asked.

Josh shook his head as he swallowed some coffee. "I guess if you showed me his Facebook picture I could point him out, but that's it."

I leaned back in my seat. I hated wild goose chases. Tracking down leads one by one? Following the trail of bread crumbs? Boring. If this Vixen indeed wanted the Shard of Gabriel, chances were she'd have it in her possession by the time we found her.

"We need to go to school," I said. "For real. Not just for a visit. Like undercover."

Sam and Josh looked at me, each with one eyebrow raised.

"I just graduated last year," Josh said. "Took me four years to get out of there. You think I want to *go back*?"

Josh actually finished high school in only four years? Interesting. Truly an astonishing achievement.

Sam held up her hand. "I second that. Especially after what you told me."

"What did he tell you?"

Sam waved him off. "You don't want to know. Trust me."

"Well, chances are Vixen is at the school, so if we play a little game I like to call common sense, that's where we should look for her." I ran my hand over my tie. "Besides, she might seek out someone as attractive as myself on her own to fill the void left by Casey."

Josh spit his coffee out on the table.

"It's true," I said. "Aside from the obvious good looks, I'm new, seemingly don't know anybody there… it would be easy for me to get in good with her and find out if she's the one after the Shard."

"What about me? She could come after me," Josh said.

"Please. A giant, bald, toothless whore wouldn't come after you."

"I don't know," Josh said, taking a sip from his coffee. "I think your mom would like me just fine."

I mock-laughed at him. "That's original."

Sam played with her coffee cup. Clearly, the gears in her head were churning. "You're right."

"I know I am. Nobody with an IQ above three would touch him."

She glared at me. "Not that. We need to go to school."

TEN

LADY MACBETH WAS A FREAK

I called the only person I knew in Raleigh old enough to pass as my father to enroll us at Frady-McNeely. My henchman, Quincy. He also hadn't tried to kill me yet, which I considered a plus. At fifty-seven, he'd served me for over thirty years, and maintained my residence here in Raleigh when I got put away. A long, skinny fellow with thinning hair and glasses, Quincy and I came to our arrangement when he fell in love with a woman way out of his league and needed help landing her. The guy knew enough to make sure the deal wouldn't blow up in divorce a few years down the road, but not enough that I didn't get to make sure his kids wound up a couple of first class screw-ups.

"So… How are the kids?" I asked as he met us in the faculty parking lot in front of the school. We'd been waiting fifteen minutes for him. Sam, ever the good girl, picked us up well before school began.

He shook his head. "Terrible."

I laughed. I assumed that meant they were either into drugs, in jail, or both. I lit a cigarette.

Quincy glared at me, but didn't protest. "I want you to fix them. Call it an even swap for getting you three into this school."

I exhaled. "I'll see what I can do, but you know I'm in the doghouse with the powers that be right now, don't you?"

"That's never stopped you before. I have faith."

Faith. Having faith in me was about as misguided as having it in the man upstairs.

I raised my head, then took a big whiff of privilege. The odor felt raw against my nostrils. Usually it takes years of glad-handing to get into a place like this, but thanks to a generous bribe in the amount of one hundred thousand dollars, courtesy of me, we were admitted in the middle of the school year with zero red tape.

"Remember, you'll try to do something about my kids?" Quincy asked.

I nodded. "Sure. I'll at least see if I can get them off the whippets and Valium. Not sure I can do anything about their deviant sexual behavior, though."

"Just do your best," Quincy said.

The bell rang. Time for school. So exciting! The rush of meeting new people to corrupt, hoping for popularity so life would be easier... this place brimmed with souls to corrupt.

"Thank you for helping us, Quincy," Sam said. "I'll make sure your children are okay."

I wanted to hug Sam. She'd just filled Quincy with a sense of false hope, especially since any request to "straighten out" his kids would be met with mockery and ridicule by my cohorts downstairs. Probably upstairs too, since the kids were born from a contract Quincy made with Hell.

Quincy thanked Sam, then drove off. We were quickly swarmed by the most detestable group of humans this side of Nazi Germany: teenagers. Throw in the demons lurking about, taking advantage of their hormone-controlled brains, and the result was quite possibly the worst human experience possible.

I loved it.

"Why don't you have a backpack?" Josh asked me.

I glanced at him sideways. "You think I'm wearing a backpack over this suit? Don't be ridiculous."

Sam pulled out her schedule. "Okay, I have history. What do you two have?"

"I have history, too," Josh said. "With Kowalski?"

Sam nodded. "Same class."

She waved goodbye and wished me luck as they disappeared into the swarm of moving bodies.

Looking at my schedule, it seemed I had... oh hello. English with Miss Evans.

I walked down the hall and into her classroom. She wrote notes about *Macbeth* on the chalkboard while I entered. "Et tu, Brute?"

Miss Evans glanced at me and smiled. "Hello, there. This is certainly a nice surprise."

A nice surprise, indeed. I double-checked my schedule. "Seems I have the pleasure of being in your class."

A kid behind me snickered. I ignored him and focused on Miss Evans.

She turned to face me, her breasts heaving up and down as she breathed. What made this woman so ridiculously hot? Every male in the classroom had the same clumsy look on his face, myself included. The last time a woman had me so dumbstruck was the fourteenth century. The girl was set to marry this asshole prince. I did everything I could to stop the wedding, which went over real well with the royal court.

"Have a seat. We're talking about *MacBeth* today. Is that all right, Mr. Shakespeare?"

"Sure. I've read it a few times." In fact, the entire play was *my* idea. The Bard beat me in a game of cards, forcing me to give him ideas for some of his greatest works—mostly the tragedies—at no charge. I still maintain to this day the piece of fecal matter cheated somehow.

I unbuttoned my suit jacket and sat down in the middle of the room—the best place to engage the entire class. From this vantage point, I could anger anyone or incite a small riot. My goal today was the latter.

Class began and Miss Evans introduced me as the new student. Most of the kids didn't give me a second look, but I heard a few of them laughing about me wearing a suit. Idiots.

"Lady Macbeth is one fascinating character, if you ask me," Miss Evans said. "What really makes her worth studying is that she had to suppress her femininity to get ahead in the world she lived in."

I scoffed. Audibly.

"You have a different opinion?" she asked.

"Lady Macbeth did what she did because Macbeth couldn't, or wouldn't, get things done in the bedroom." I knew this because I'd told William to write her like that.

Bits of nervous laughter spread throughout the class.

Miss Evans narrowed her eyes. "I'm not sure that's entirely appropriate, or correct, but please. Continue. I'd like to hear where you're going with this."

"Clearly, Lady Macbeth loved to be in control. And it's pretty obvious Macbeth himself is a bit, well, conservative in the sack, if not downright incapable. Viagra would have come in handy for Mr. Mac, if you know what I'm saying." I leaned back in my seat. Yes, that was my grand idea. Have two characters be married where one is a nymphomaniac and the other is impotent. The result? One of the most dramatic pairings in history. "It's a shame, really, because living in a castle, there were probably all sorts of torture devices Mrs. Macbeth would have loved to use during play time."

"Where are you going with this?" Miss Evans asked. Where was I going? William got the idea from me. But I couldn't say that. "If Macbeth hadn't been such a prude and taken care of business, Lady Macbeth wouldn't have had to get her dominatrix on outside the bedroom in more destructive ways and they'd all have lived happily ever after, albeit with slightly rawer nipples."

Several kids laughed when I said nipples. Silly children.

I held up my hands to quiet the crowd. Now that I had everyone's attention, I needed to put this rant to good use. "What can I say? She's a *vixen* of the highest order."

"A vixen?" A wry smile crept across Miss Evans's lips. "It's an interesting point, Bartholomew. I never looked at it that way."

The bell rang and I walked out of the class with the other kids. A girl with a ponytail rushed up to me, cradling her books. She introduced herself as Jenny McPherson. "That was so intuitive what you said in there. Just amazing. I never thought of Lady Macbeth as a sex-starved dominatrix."

"Well, I mean, why do you do what you do? It's for the

same reason, right? To get laid?" I said without looking at her.

The insinuation of sex seemed to make her squeamish. "Not really. I want to get into a good college and be successful and—"

I stopped and turned to her. "All so you can meet a quality guy to bang, right? Pass those genes of yours on to the next generation?"

The girl seemed to shrivel. "I guess?"

"*You* guess. *I* know." I walked down the hallway, leaving the girl to stand there and contemplate becoming a skank. I looked down at my schedule. I had PE next.

"You've got to be kidding me."

They issued me a ratty pair of shorts that were length-appropriate for a girl, or a guy circa 1965. The gray shirt they gave me to wear had the year 2002 embroidered on it. The thing definitely smelled like kids had sweat in the thing for over a decade. Heinous.

The best part about PE? Nothing. Demons didn't need exercise. Today, we were playing badminton. Thing One and Thing Two, aka Clayton and Darrel, took turns smashing birdies into Kyle, the geek these guys bullied back at Casey's.

Clayton overhanded a birdie at Kyle, then sneered at me. "Look who it is. The chump."

"Chump?" I moved next to Kyle. "People still say that?"

"We'd call you worse," Darrel spat out. "But adults are present."

I twirled my racket in my hands. "Tell you what. How about me and my buddy Kyle here play you two?"

Clayton laughed. "You like losin', do you?"

"Sure." I smiled. "And to make it interesting, how about a friendly wager?"

Clayton and Darrel exchanged glances.

"You're on," Darrel said.

"Good. If you win, you can shove a racket up our asses. Whichever end you see fit."

Kyle's eyes went wide. "Are you crazy? I don't want anything shoved up there. Especially by these guys."

"Oh ye of little faith," I said, patting his shoulder. "Trust me."

"And if you somehow win? What do you get?" Clayton asked.

I grinned. "Anything we damn well please."

Darrel laughed. "Why not?" He tossed me a birdie. "You can even serve first."

Kyle and I took our spots on the court.

"You better know what you're doing," he said.

I winked and served the birdie underhanded. Clayton volleyed back, then I hit the birdie with all my strength, pegging Darrel in the eye. He fell to the gym floor, screaming like a little girl.

"Man up. It's just a little birdie," I said. "Kyle here took I don't know how many from you two and he's fine."

Kyle looked at me, pale as a ghost. I gestured with my head for him to join in.

"Yeah…Yeah! Take that, sucka," he said.

The next thing I knew, we'd pulled ahead of the Things seven to nothing. I made sure Darrel's other eye got nailed with a birdie on our twelfth point.

"Stop it," he cried out. The first eye I'd hit had swollen a little. "That's cheating. I can't see."

I laughed. "Quit whining."

"Bunch of babies," Kyle said.

We rattled off eight more points. One more and we won. I really wanted the win to mean something, so I decided to do a little experiment. I served the birdie, then Darrel tried to hit it at Kyle, but I jumped underneath, ready to strike. I swung at the birdie. It disappeared. I looked around but didn't see it.

"Point," Clayton shouted, like he'd just opened a present on Christmas Day. "Point for us."

"Holy crap, man," Kyle said. His mouth hung open at the sight of the birdie stuck in my racket.

"These rackets suck," I said, throwing that one off to the side. I went to get another. The PE coach, a paunchy middle-aged man who called himself Coach Mort, stopped me.

"Hooie, boy, how'd you do that to your racket?" he asked. "I never seen something like that before. You work out?"

I picked up a new racket. "Steroid suppositories."

Coach Mort crossed his arms. "That's not funny. Steroids

are serious business."

"Compare Barry Bond's head sizes from 1990 and 2003," I called out, jogging back to the game. "And tell me that's not funny."

Clayton served the birdie to me. He hit it high, and this time I wasn't going to screw up. I steadied myself and swung at the birdie, laying off just enough not to destroy another racket.

Clayton shrieked and fell to his knees, his hands covering his face. Turned out a person could get a bloody nose from a little old birdie. Wonders truly never ceased.

Kyle high-fived me. "That rocked."

"All in a day's work. So, what do you want them to do? Set you up with a cheerleader who'll take your virginity on the first date? Quit the football team? Make out with each other? Personally, I'd go with losing your virginity."

Kyle wiped the sweat from his brow. "I'm actually okay in the girl department."

Liar.

"I guess if they and their goon friends would leave me alone, that would be good."

To each his own. I clapped my hands together. "Consider it done."

I dragged Darrel and Clayton out of the gym.

"No deal," Darrel said as I let him go. "To Hell with this."

I laughed. "I'm going to pretend you didn't say that. Now, here's what you're going to do. First, you and your caveman friends are going to leave Kyle alone. Got it?"

They both stood there, silent.

I leaned against the gym wall. "You just saw what I could do to a badminton racket. Do you want to see what I can do to human heads?"

They glanced at each other, then at the ground.

"No," the pair said in unison.

I nodded. "Good. Second thing. That kid Casey. Apparently he was dating someone he called Vixen. Ring any bells?"

Darrel rubbed his eyes. "He didn't really say much. He said they got into some kinky stuff, but other than that he wouldn't talk about her. Like you said. He just called her Vixen."

Well, shit. I looked at Clayton. "What about you, nose job?"

"Same. He said the sex was amazing, like out of this universe amazing," Clayton said. "That's all I remember."

I rolled my head back and stared at the humming fluorescent light above me. Could this be any more frustrating? I wanted to slam my head through the wall.

"Is there anyone I can talk to who might know who this Vixen is?"

"Why do you want to know so bad?" Darrel asked.

"That's for me to know," I said. "Who can I talk to?"

"Monica can probably help you," Clayton said. "She's head cheerleader. I'll make sure she talks to you at lunch."

"How will she know who I am?"

Darrel opened the door to go back into the gym. "We'll tell her to look for the fruit in the suit."

ELEVEN

A BAD CALL

I sat alone in the cafeteria, staring at a square slice of pizza on the plate in front of me. I debated whether or not to try and eat the food. Not that the pork chops looked any more tempting. Private schools should've had better food than this.

Sam and Josh took the seats across from me.

"You two shouldn't sit with me," I said. "Not today."

Josh scoffed. "Are we not cool enough to sit with you?"

"He's eating with me," a girl with short, jet-black hair said behind them. Had to be Monica.

Josh immediately tensed up. He rose from his seat and looked at the girl. She leaned to one side and stared past him like he was nothing.

"And who are you?" Josh asked. Something about this girl obviously made him uncomfortable.

Good.

"Nobody *you* need to worry about." She eyeballed Sam.

Sam extended her hand. "Hi. I'm Samantha."

"Whatever," Monica said, not looking at her. "I'm looking for the fruit in the suit. You're much too handsome to be a fruit."

I straightened my tie. "I like to think I'm the right amount of handsome."

"You two, beat it." Monica thumbed toward the door.

Josh's face turned red.

Sam stood and laid her hand on his arm. "It's fine, Josh. Come on."

Monica slid into a seat. "So. I understand you want to know who Casey Testerman was hookin' up with."

"Pretty much." I slid my tray to the side. With half of the cheese on it almost burned, that square piece of pizza didn't deserve to be inside my belly. "I heard you could help me with that."

Monica leaned over the table, showing off her cleavage. "Why do you care? Did you even know him?"

"I did know him, as a matter of fact. The thing is, the family is pretty sure Casey had some sort of STD, like herpes or vaginal discharge. Whoever he slept with has a right to know."

Monica smiled. "Vaginal discharge? You know, you never could lie to me convincingly, Bartholomew."

I scrunched up my face. "Do I know you?"

Monica stretched. "My hair's a little shorter, but yeah. Spanish Inquisition?"

I snapped my fingers. "Yes. I remember. The way you had Queen Isabella wrapped around your finger… brilliant."

On my best day, I never pulled something that epic off. Then again, I never got the chance to, either.

She gave me a sultry grin. "That's not the only thing I had her wrapped around."

That was hot. I would have loved to see those two get it on.

"But I heard some distressing things about you. I hope they're true," she said with a wink. "It would make you so much more interesting. Especially making out with Jen Partridge after school. Very ballsy."

Ah, the cheerleader. "I never got her name."

"How did you even get out of Hell?"

"I'm out on some sort of work release program. The whole thing is stupid, but when the man comes around, what can you do?"

"Who were the losers sitting with you?"

I rolled my eyes. "My entourage, for lack of a better word." Or at least a word I felt comfortable using in front of her. "So. Can you help me?"

Monica gently licked her lips. "I may be able to. What's in it for me?"

My gaze darted around the table while I thought of something to say. Nothing really good came to mind. "Saving the world?"

Monica burst out laughing. Kids at other tables stopped to look at her. After a minute, she got her giggle fit under control with a snort. "What do I care about that? What's more, why do you? You're the one who tried to take it over because your feelings got hurt."

I rested my elbows on the table, ignoring her jab. "Then for old times' sake. Whatever. It's that or the Ninth Circle for me."

Monica's face went white. "You're in that deep?"

My upper lip curled as I nodded.

"You really are in a bad spot." Monica fished in her purse and pulled out some lipstick. She moved it across her lips. "Okay. Here's what I need. I'm trying to make sure that bitch Jenny McPherson doesn't win Homecoming Queen. *I* want to win."

"I met her this morning." I rubbed my chin. "Is she a lock to win? She doesn't strike me as the Homecoming Queen type. She seems more plain Jane to me."

Monica put the lipstick back in her purse. "You'd think so, but this slutbag has some serious tricks up her sleeve. Don't take her wholesome appearance at face value."

"So what do you want me to do?"

She looked at me with hard eyes. "Break her heart and make sure she doesn't win Homecoming. Even you should be able to handle that."

"Absolutely not," Sam said in the parking lot after school. I'd just told her about Monica's proposition. She took it about like I'd expected. A few students shot a surprised glance at her outburst. "I won't allow you to destroy a young woman. Or take her virtue. Or anything else… not good."

I threw my hands up in the air. "Come on. I've done it thousands of times before. I just love 'em and leave 'em. What's the big deal?"

"I'm with Sam on this one," Josh said.

"You shut up," I said. "This doesn't involve you."

"We didn't let you out of Hell to wreak more havoc," Sam said, pushing some hair behind her ears.

I lit a cigarette and waved it around. "I'm trying to help. You don't want it, that's on you."

"It's impossible for you not to create trouble, isn't it?" Josh asked.

"Duh." I exhaled, forming rings with the smoke.

Speak of the devil.

Jenny McPherson walked in our direction. I looked back at the two of them and smiled. "You two can stay here and argue. If you find a better way to get the information we need, then do it. I'm taking this girl's virginity regardless. You can stomp your feet and pout if you want, but it's not going to change anything."

I waved and moved closer to Jenny.

"Hey, Bart."

I tried to hide my disgust at being called Bart. "Hello there."

"How did the rest of your first day go?" She popped open the trunk of her beat-up Toyota and set her book bag in it.

"All downhill after my *Macbeth* rant."

Jenny laughed. "It was a good rant. People don't do it enough, I think. They're so afraid to speak their mind or show their true emotions. As if they'll get picked on for being human."

I don't know about you, but I pick on them because they are *human.*

I stuffed my hands in my pockets. "I agree. Everyone seems so afraid to have an opinion and be individuals. They just don't get that it's okay to go against the grain."

Jenny stopped for a moment. A small smile crept across her lips. "I couldn't agree more. Makes people so susceptible to manipulation by all kinds of things. It's horrible."

I gave her a million-dollar grin. "Indeed."

Samantha called out to me. They were ready to leave, with or without me. I said goodbye to Jenny and felt her gaze on my back as I walked away.

Monica was nuts. There was nothing crafty about that girl at all. She would be putty in my hands.

I'd told Quincy that afternoon to stock my cabinets with wine, booze, and cigarettes past capacity. I wanted to come home to a kitchen overflowing with that stuff. When I got home after school the following day, I rushed into the kitchen to see if he had done as I asked. Throwing open the cabinet doors, the wondrous vision of fine liquor, wine, and Marlboro Reds greeted me like old friends. I grabbed a bottle of Grey Goose, spun the top off, and started chugging. Sweet mercy, did that vodka go down smooth.

I sat in a chair on my balcony, smoking a cigarette and enjoying a drink, when my cellphone rang. Private number. I debated letting the call ring through to voicemail, but whatever. For once, I felt pretty good.

"Hello?"

"Hello, Bartholomew."

Well, I *did* feel pretty good. Now I felt like a jilted bride. My heart sank in my chest. "What do you want?"

"I just wanted check up on my favorite parolee."

"You are one twisted son of a bitch, you know that? Forcing me into working with the other team." I downed three shots of the Goose in one swallow. The burning in my throat felt outstanding.

"It seemed like a fitting Catch-22 for someone who had the ego to challenge my rule. Either you suffer by helping Heaven, or you suffer in the Ninth Circle. I bet you wish you'd thought of it."

I smirked. "You know me so well, Lucifer."

The man downstairs laughed. "You didn't answer my question. How are things going with the wannabe angel?

Cramping your style?"

I flicked my cigarette onto the street below and lit another. "Not really."

"That's great. Just great." The swine only called to rub this situation in my face.

I inhaled half the cigarette in one breath. "Well, hey, look, this has been a fun chat, but I really need to, you know, do something that isn't going to make my horns pop out."

"Hm hum. Just remember. The Ninth Circle is waiting for you with open arms if you screw up," Lucifer said. "Adolf can't wait for some new company, now that he and Judas are no longer on speaking terms. You've never been to the Ninth Circle, have you?"

"Can't say that I have."

Lucifer chuckled. "Well, let's just say for me, personally, it's my own little Heaven. For a demon like you? I don't think the usual punishment down there would be enough for you, so imagine the most painful, torturous thing you can. Go on. Do it. I can wait."

I considered what that would be like for a moment. There'd definitely be a mixture of Christmas carolers, an endless loop of children's television programs, and a never-ending shower under holy water.

"Got it?" he asked.

"I do."

"Ratchet that up about a million times, expand it to infinity and know that the Führer is right there next to you, chatting your ear off. That's how the Ninth Circle will be for you."

"Great. Thanks for calling. Always great to hear from you. *Auf weidersehen*." I ended the call, shaking my head. For the first time, I began to have an idea of how awful the Ninth Circle really was. I didn't desire to go there because of the rumors, but I'd never doubted my ability to hack it, if necessary. If what Lucifer said was true, I was wrong. Dead wrong. And knowing the man downstairs, whatever tinkering he'd done would also slowly drive me insane as time went on.

We couldn't fail. We *had* to get our hands on the Shard of Gabriel. And when we had it in our possession, maybe I could flip my punishment on ole Lou and give him a butt rash for all eternity.

    I finished the bottle of Goose and left the condo. I needed a virgin.

TWELVE

ROSEMARY'S BABY

Downtown Raleigh, especially on a weeknight, was not necessarily the easiest place to find my kind of girl. Most of the available females were over twenty-one, making them a bit too old for my taste. Plus, they all seemed more than willing to give it up. I preferred the challenge of virgins. I walked down the street to Rum Runners, an obnoxiously loud dueling piano bar that admitted girls under the legal drinking limit.

I paid a five-dollar cover charge just to get into the place. Was there anything as ridiculous as paying to get into a bar, aside from maybe burgers made out of black beans? They were already making money from people buying alcoholic beverages. A cover charge on top of that reeked of gluttony.

The pianists took turns playing Journey's *Don't Stop Believing* as the patrons sang along to the music. The bar was crowded and the scene so annoying, I had to fight off the urge to set fire to the place right then and there. Thanks to my ID, I couldn't even buy a drink to numb the pain. I had to get my claws on a fake ID as soon as possible.

I stood against the back wall, watching the crowd in front of me. I needed to find the right virgin: the perfect mix of naïveté and horny. Before I could get a really thorough look, the song, mercifully, ended. The crowd clapped and cheered. I tucked my hands underneath my arms.

"Hey, you don't like the music?"

I looked over and saw a gorgeous brunette in a green tube dress. She smiled. This girl looked wholesome. Uncomfortable. Unsure of herself. Inexperienced.

A virgin.

I shrugged. "It's okay, I guess."

I glanced down at her hands. Like mine, they were marked with an X to tell the bar we weren't old enough to drink.

We have ourselves a winner.

"I'd probably enjoy it more, but my friend stood me up," I said.

The girl's face dropped. "I'm sorry."

"What can you do?"

"Well, I'm still waiting on my friends to get here," she said. "Would you want to hang out with me?"

"Why not?"

Her eyes perked up. "Really? You want to?"

"Sure. Can I get you a drink? Water? Coke?" That line just did not sound right when you couldn't offer a girl some alcohol. At all.

"Water."

We made our way through the maze of people to the bar. The place was so crowded, I could probably bang this girl against the wall and nobody would notice.

"Thanks," she said, taking the water from the bartender. "I'm Cassandra."

"Beautiful name." I introduced myself and shook her hand.

After trying to chat over the sound of the dueling pianos, Cassandra and I retired to a side room where we could talk. We sat down next to each other.

"So what happened to your friends?" I asked.

She played with her water, which she'd been nursing. "I have a small confession to make."

I smiled. "Is it provocative?"

Cassandra leaned her arms on the table, smiling nervously. "I don't know if I should tell you."

I clapped my hands together. "You can tell me anything. It's okay."

She bit her bottom lip. "I didn't come here to be with my friends."

I hadn't thought so. "Did you come here in the hope of meeting a guy?"

She started to say something, then stopped. Her mouth hung open until she spoke. "Maybe. It's just... I'm nervous. I'm sorry, I feel so weird talking about this."

This girl screamed *virgin*. "You have nothing to be ashamed about. I came here to meet a guy, too."

Her face turned to stone. "Are you serious?"

I burst out laughing. Inside, however, I cringed at her lack of humor. "I'm just kidding. But regardless, your radiance and beauty would be enough to make any man worship at your feet."

She blushed. "That's... maybe the sweetest thing anyone's ever said to me."

Sweet statement from a sweet demon. "It's true." I wouldn't lie. *Honest*. "So what do you say? You want to get out of here? My place is just down the street."

She glanced down at the table. "I don't know."

I laid my hand on hers. "It's fine. We can go, hang out, and if you feel uncomfortable at any point, we'll call it an evening."

Her thumb rubbed against mine. "Promise?"

I held up two fingers. "Scout's honor. I even have some alcohol, if you want."

Cassandra went starry-eyed at the mention of alcohol. "That sounds great."

Hook. Line. Sinker. I loved being me.

I led her out the front entrance and started toward my condo. Cassandra tugged at my arm.

"My car is over this way," she said, pointing in the opposite direction. "Can I park at your place?"

"Of course."

We walked to her car, which was next to Moore Square, a small park across the street from Rum Runners, in an unlit strip of road. I debated having a smoke but decided against it. Much as I wanted one, I didn't want to risk scaring Cassandra off. Some people can be so touchy about smoking.

What happened next should've been as obvious as a girl on

a street corner trying to pull a trick.

Cassandra pulled out her keyless entry and pushed a button, making her car's lights blink on and off as the car unlocked. The vehicles on either side of hers turned on their lights and the doors opened. People stepped out, but the blinding light of the high beams hid their identities.

I *really* should've seen this coming. I'd been over-excited about deflowering Cassandra, sure, but that's no excuse. If a girl approached me, chances were she was an experienced pro. And probably from Hell. I should've sniffed out Cassandra within five seconds of meeting her.

I stopped. "You know what? It's kind of late and I have a test in the morning. I think I'm just going to walk home. Lovely to meet you and everything."

Cassandra turned and kissed me on the lips. "I wouldn't do that."

"I'm sorry to be a tease, but I'm not really in a partying mood, so I think I'll be on my way." I turned to make a run for it, but a dark figure stood in front of me.

"Stay awhile," the man said.

He sprayed something cold in my face, and the fire coursing through my demon veins literally froze. The only thing that could do that to me was Hell Water—scooped from the frigid terrain of the Ninth Circle—and only two beings in the universe could handle the stuff. Lucifer and his son, Nicholas. And I knew Lucifer wouldn't pull a stunt like this.

My body fell over, but Cassandra caught me before my face planted on the ground. A bunch of hands grabbed me, then picked me up by my feet and carried me over to a car. I banged my head when they threw me in the trunk. I had to admit to getting sick of this little routine. Some manners would go a long way toward making these kidnapping situations more tolerable.

"Been a long time, Bart. A long time," Nicholas said as he smiled above me. "If you had come willingly, Cassandra here might have given you a happy ending to our little transaction. Pity."

"He's right" she said.

The trunk slammed shut. Cassandra lied about being a

virgin, but I'd still have had a go with her, just to end the drought. Bless it all. The next entity that pulled something like this would get a horn up their ass.

The car pulled to a stop and the engine cut off. I heard doors open and close, then Nicholas popped open the trunk.

He smiled down at me, showing off his blindingly white teeth. "Sorry about the theatrics, but I knew you wouldn't voluntarily listen to me. Can you move?"

I could, a little. Enough to wrap my hands around his throat. I decided to keep that to myself for now and remained frozen.

Nicholas *tsk*ed. "I thought you were stronger than that. You must not have been exposed to a lot of Hell Water in your day. I, however," he took out the small canister and sprayed some into his mouth, "find it quite refreshing."

A cold mist escaped his lips as he spoke. The showoff.

He reached in to pull me out. Once his throat got close enough, I extended my nails and buried them in his neck. I squeezed, hoping I could reach his spine. I felt vertebrae rub against the claws, but I didn't have the reach to get a good grip.

Nicholas reached into his pocket and sprayed the Hell Water into my face, freezing me with my hand in his throat. He tried to free himself from my death grip, but because of the Hell Water, neither of us could move. Served him right.

"A little help?" he called out, his voice scratchy and gurgling, thanks to me.

Cassandra came over and tried to pry my hand loose. They didn't budge. I wished I could smile, but either way, this was awfully poetic.

"He's frozen solid," she said. "The only way to get free is to melt his hands with holy water."

I hadn't considered that before trying to rip Nicholas's throat out. That would stink. I liked my hands. I needed them, for groping virgins and such.

"No," Nicholas said.

Whew.

He glared at me. "He's going to need those hands."

Once I could move my eyes, I glanced up at him. I tried to make my look say something along the lines of *nanny nanny boo-boo*.

"Don't look at me like that," he said.

Guess he understood my look.

"What do you want to do?" Cassandra asked. The other demons with them looked on with mouths agape, as if in shock I'd done this to their fearless leader.

"Wait," he said. "He'll thaw soon enough."

I felt sensation return.

"Get the holy water," Nicholas said. "In case." He returned the look I gave him a moment ago.

Within moments, Cassandra held a two-liter bottle of holy water over my head, a depraved smile on her face. "Been a while since I've ruined a face as pretty as yours."

She should've been there when Josh spat holy water at me the other day. Considering the excited look on her face, I'd bet good money the sight would've gotten her off.

After a few more minutes, I could wiggle my hands. Nicholas tried to free himself again, but that only made things worse. Finally, one of his cronies got my hand out.

Nicholas stumbled backward. He caught his balance, then placed his arms on his hips and cracked his spine. The finger-shaped wounds around his neck healed, leaving no evidence I'd even hurt him.

"It is *not* fun leaning over like that for so long," he said in his normal voice.

Cassandra set down the holy water. One of Nicholas's henchmen helped her yank me out of the trunk and lean my body against the side of the car. We were in a parking deck and, from the glimpse I got of the Raleigh skyline, still downtown. I didn't know what street, though it couldn't be far from where they'd snatched me.

Nicholas picked up the holy water and unscrewed the cap.

"Not the suit," I said. "I already had one ruined because of that blasted stuff."

He smirked. "Beautiful piece of fabric like that? Wouldn't dream of it." Nicholas pointed at one of his goons. "Take his shoes off."

Cassandra and the henchman removed my shoes and socks, then threw them across the parking lot. I winced. They were probably scuffed beyond repair. Nicholas moved next to me and poured the holy water over my feet.

I fell down, screaming in agony. My hands also caught some of the runoff when they hit the deck. I had to hand it to Nicholas. He knew how to be sadistic as Hell. Almost like he was born for the job.

"That's for thinking you're smarter than me," he said, grabbing my hair. "Do you have any idea how much it hurts to have your claws rub up against my spine?" He threw my head toward the concrete. "Get him up."

Two of his goons picked me up and set me down on a dry spot of concrete. I tried to stand, but my feet felt like they'd been grilled and sautéed in a fine vinaigrette.

Nicholas kneeled down, meeting me eye-to-eye. "I know why you're out of Hell."

I laughed. "Who'd you rape to get that information?"

Nicholas's gaze narrowed. "Wouldn't you like to know." He grabbed my face so hard my lips puckered out like a fish. "Here's the deal. I want the Shard of Gabriel. Get it for me, and you can consider all your debts to Hell paid in full. All of them. You'll be a free demon. We'll be square. Heaven, you may even get a spot on my cabinet. Wouldn't that be something? You'd finally have that respect you crave so much."

We'd be square? After I'd screwed up his plot to have Alexander the Great take over the world, Nicholas swore up and down he'd never forgive me. "Square?"

He stood. "Forgive and forget."

"Even for—"

"Even that."

The idea of getting the respect and adoration of my peers sounded appealing, but no way he'd hold up his end of the bargain. "How do you know about the Shard?"

"My room is right next to Dad's. We have thin walls. Most of the time they're *too* thin, but hey! Something worthwhile finally came of it after all these centuries."

I forced myself to my feet, even though standing felt like

being crushed by a sledgehammer. "That's an enticing offer. Can I think about it?"

Nicholas pulled back his sleeve and looked at his watch. "Sure. You have… ten seconds. If I don't hear a yes, the rest of the holy water is getting poured on your head and you get a one-way ticket to the Ninth Circle." He took out his cellphone and wiggled it in the air. "I'll even let Dad know you're on the way, so he can be there to greet you when you arrive."

That certainly made this a difficult decision. Agree to a classic bait and switch or get sent to my own personal Hell. "How can I say no to that?"

Nicholas's face lit up. "Excellent." He looked at Cassandra and the henchmen. "Let's go."

They all started for their cars.

I held out my hands. "Can I get a ride home, at least?"

Nicholas opened the door to his Lexus and shook his head. "Afraid not. Don't want you dripping in the car."

"Come on. Don't make me roll home. Think of the suit."

"It is a nice suit," he said. "We'll be in touch."

He disappeared inside. The car door slammed and everyone drove out of the parking deck, leaving me to figure out how to get home with a pair of half-melted feet. Fun. It hurt so much, it took me ten minutes to get my shoes and socks on. Once I'd managed to drag myself out of the parking deck, I looked up at the nearest street sign. Fayetteville Street. Only three blocks from home, yet I still didn't walk through the front door until an hour later.

I needed to put an end to this tomfoolery. No more would I be treated like some black sheep. I had to get my mojo back. I decided to pay Remy a visit after school tomorrow and get myself some sort of protection from both Heaven and Hell. Something a lot stronger than a rape whistle.

Thirteen

I'M A DEMON, NOT A GEEK

School went by the next day without incident—a welcome change after the previous night's exploits—and I managed to arrive at Remy's store without being abducted, making me two for two so far today. Marvin manned the counter. I cleared my throat.

Marvin looked up at me and went pale. At least, as much as an African-American can.

"Hey boss?" he called to the back. "Your demon friend is here."

Remy emerged from the rear of the store and greeted me with a handshake. "What's up?"

He had on a blue button-down shirt today, so he didn't look quite so much like a bum.

"I need some help."

"And here I thought you just dropped by to see my pretty face."

I rolled my eyes. "I need some babyproofing. If someone's not spitting holy water in my face, I'm getting frozen with Hell Water."

Remy's mouth fell open. "Hell Water? I thought that was just a myth."

"Afraid not. And don't even think about getting your hands

on it, unless you always wanted to be an ice sculpture when you grew up."

If he came into contact with Hell Water, he'd be frozen for ten thousand years, and when he thawed, scientists would *ooh* and *ahh* at his perfectly preserved body, proclaiming it to be the Missing Link.

"So," I said, clapping my hands together. "You got something that can keep me dry?"

Remy scratched his head. "I think so. Come on back."

I followed Remy past the counter and Marvin's frightened gaze. I made a move for Marvin, making him jump.

"Come on, man," he said.

"Tough guy," I said with a hearty chuckle.

Remy stood next to a table covered by a pile of crocodile heads. He pointed at them. "For the kids."

"I'm more the shrunken head type."

We walked past several rows of vials, bones, and plants. Nothing I'd call powerful. They had small purposes, like changing someone's mind or bringing good luck, but those trinkets didn't interest me.

The last row of shelves was stocked with items I didn't even know Remy had. I saw a bejeweled knife, a wooden crucifix, even a knight's helmet.

"Here we go," Remy said, picking up a silver chain on which a large, circular pendant hung. Etched into it was the face of a woman. "I don't have anything that can protect you from Hell Water, or holy water for that matter. But this is the Charm of Agrippina. Wards off evil spirits."

I gave him a sardonic look. "How does that help me? I *am* an evil spirit."

Remy sighed. "Doin' the best I can here."

I crossed my arms. "What else do you have, Q?"

Remy shifted some items around, which made a loud bang as they fell over on the shelf. Surely the man had *something* that could help.

"Here we go," he said, holding up a very large bracelet.

I burst into laughter. "You can't expect me to wear that. I'll get slaughtered at school."

"It's the Bracelet of Saint Holos. It'll at least help speed up healing."

Accelerated healing *would* increase the chances my wardrobe would survive another attack. I took it from him and my hands burned, starting to smoke almost at once. We both stared at the rising smoke for a moment, then I tossed the bracelet back to him.

"There's got to be some kind of charm a disinterested third party created to keep Heaven and Hell out of their business. Isn't that what you deal in?"

"Not many want to ward off Heaven and its agents."

I waved him off. "You and I both know that's a load of bunk."

"I'm sorry. Since I left New Orleans, my selection just hasn't been as diverse."

"Then go back. Improve business."

"Wish I could." Remy leaned against the shelf, a blank look in his eyes. He must have been thinking. "I know of someone who collects rare artifacts. Rarer than my stuff. He may be able to help you, but it's going to take a little time to get an address. And no promises, either. He might not be interested in selling."

I ran my hand through my hair. "We both know that's never stopped me before."

"Fair enough." Remy threw the Charm of Agrippina to me. "In the meantime, wear that. Should at least help with part of the problem. I'm sure if you wear it over your clothes or something, you'll be fine."

With my hands smoking, I put the charm on over my suit. "I look like a vampire with this thing on." I shook my hand, trying to get the burning sensation to go away.

Remy chuckled. "I think it suits you. By the way, say hello to your angel girlfriend for me."

I expected school to be a struggle, wearing something as ridiculous as this necklace out in the open. I couldn't have been more wrong. School wasn't a struggle. It was an ordeal that made the Bataan Death March look like an evening stroll on a midsummer night. Okay, so maybe that was an exaggeration, but whatever.

I tried to wear the charm on top of my undershirt but that still burned a little, forcing me to wear it in plain sight over everything so it wouldn't hurt. Girls and guys pointed, snickered, and made snide comments as I passed them in the halls. This pissed me off. A demon should've owned this place, not been a punch line. The charm may have warded off evil spirits, but it didn't keep humans from making a mockery of me.

"What are you wearing? Do you *want* to blow whatever cover you have?" Monica asked. Her eyes looked a bit crossed at the sight of the charm. She leaned back against a locker. "I can barely look at that thing."

I shook my head. "Don't ask." Interesting that she moved away from me. Very interesting.

Monica crossed her arms. "Have you talked to Sam today?"

"Should I have?"

"She's trying out for the cheerleading squad."

I stopped. "She *what*?"

"You heard me."

Cheerleaders were the most attractive and cruelest girls in every school for a reason. Most of them were either demons or girls who'd sold their souls for good looks and popularity; the rest tended to be out-and-out bitches. Samantha would be obliterated on a molecular level in that group. Monica did me a favor telling me this. She had to know Sam was different, and that the pseudo-angel wouldn't be able to hack it with the cheerleading squad. She probably assumed if something happened to her, our deal might become null and void.

I tried for nonchalance. "She can take care of herself. Besides, you think she'll listen to me?"

"I'd hope so. I don't know what your end game here is, and I'm not sure I want to." Monica looked at her cellphone and began pecking away at the buttons. "I have to go. Duty calls. I just wanted to give you a heads-up. And seriously, take that thing off. It's creepy."

"Thanks," I said. The bell rang as I watched her leave. Female demons had the best rears in the universe.

I made my way to Miss Evans's class. She had her back to everyone, writing notes on the blackboard. I took my seat and tried to see past her luscious body to the board. What would the *Macbeth* discussion center on today? I hoped we would talk about whether or not Lady Macbeth liked spanking.

"Hey," Jenny whispered. She sat next to me today. "What's up with that necklace?"

"I lost a bet."

She tilted her head to the side, a sympathetic look on her face. "I'm sorry. How long do you have to wear it?"

"Who knows? Does it at least bring out my eyes?" I tried to make them look as big and wide as possible. They pressed against my eye sockets I pushed them out so far. Any farther, they might pop out.

"You wouldn't believe," she said with a wink.

Miss Evans turned and began lecturing about *Macbeth* again. I put on my best blank face and tuned her out almost immediately. I wasn't in the mood for this today. I felt so out of it I didn't even have the slightest bit of attraction toward her. Jenny didn't seem up for it either. She excused herself to go to the bathroom a few minutes into class.

"Bartholomew? You awake?" Miss Evans asked.

I shot straight up in my seat. "Yes, Miss Evans. Sorry."

After class, I threw my notebook and copy of *Macbeth* into my Fossil satchel. It turned out I really needed something to carry my stuff around in. I worried what would become of me if I kept adapting to high school, especially in the wardrobe department. The kids snickered at my satchel, which cost three times as much as their book bags. At least they didn't laugh at my suit, I guess.

"Hey, do you want to do something later?" Jenny asked. She clutched her three-ring binder close to her chest.

Score! Touchdown!

"Sure. What did you have in mind?" Some sinning behind the gym, perhaps?

"The Honor Society is going to read to kids at Wake Med hospital. You should come."

And the call has been reversed. No touchdown.

Sick kids? What the Heaven kind of date is that?

"Um, yeah, I don't know. Hospitals kind of make me uncomfortable." Not to mention reading to children constituted a *good* deed, making me predisposed to hate the idea.

Jenny touched my arm lightly. "Come on. The way you tore Lady Macbeth a new one the other day? I bet you're a natural with stories." She leaned on the balls of her feet, swaying back and forth. "And afterward maybe we can get some food or something."

Ah. Okay. I see what's going on here.

I knew my animal magnetism would draw her in eventually. I smiled. I hadn't won the game, but I'd take the tie. Do a little good now for a lot of bad later. "It's a date."

I told Sam and Josh about going out with Jenny at lunch.

Josh choked on his milk. When he finally managed to stop coughing and get himself under control, he said, "I've seen her around. She seems really nice. Don't you dare do anything to hurt her."

"I have to, numb nuts. It's the only way Monica will tell us who Vixen is." I turned to Sam. "Speaking of which, what are you thinking going out for cheerleading? If you want to punish yourself, I'm sure there are a few S&M freaks who'd love to oblige you."

Sam swallowed a bite of her salad with care. "Josh and I talked about it last night, and we agreed. You shouldn't hurt some poor, innocent girl if you don't have to, so I thought maybe I'd go out for cheerleading, see if I could find something out on my own."

I rolled my head back. "We've been through this. You want to make it in the Mob, you have to break a few legs."

"Well, that's why I'm going out for cheerleading. See if I can't find out for myself who Vixen is."

The pre-angel made me want to pull my hair out, or at least mess it up a bit. "Monica knows you're pure and innocent. She doesn't know exactly what you are, but she knows something's up." I moved close to her, hoping she would understand I meant business. "Because of that, they're literally going to treat you like a defenseless animal. They won't go easy on you, and when they're done, you'll be lucky to have the self-esteem of a crack whore."

Josh dove right into defending Sam again. "I think Samantha can—"

I shushed Josh. "Adults are speaking."

Sam took another bite of her salad. "I signed up for this. I signed *you* up for this. If I can avoid collateral damage, I will."

I sat back in my chair. "Fine. When you need a shoulder to cry on, don't come crying to me. Yeah. Don't come to me. Because… I won't be there."

I stood and marched out of the cafeteria, pissed I'd screwed up what I'd tried to say.

Fourteen

YOU KNOW...FOR KIDS

Samantha still couldn't accept my plans for Jenny. She crowed about there being a "better way" or some shit like that while she marched around her apartment. Whatever.

"Get over it." I stretched my legs across her coffee table. "It's happening. Move on."

"I want my protest officially noted," she said.

"Noted."

"So, this is real? You're actually reading to kids?" Sam asked in a calmer tone.

"Of course," I said. "I'm probably reading *Go the Fuck to Sleep*. That way it'll be fun for everyone."

Sam burst out laughing. "That's so… sweet?"

The almost-angel had a gleam in her eye that needed to be toned down a notch or two. She needed to know I wasn't trying to turn over a new leaf or anything like that.

"There's always been kind of an unspoken rule about kids," I said. "The goal is to get people to go sour over time, not taint them right out of the gate when they don't know any better."

"No sport," Josh said. "Right?"

"Amongst other things," I said, ignoring his sarcasm. "There's just no fun in tainting children. Especially sick ones." I sighed. *How did I get into this conversation again?* I glared at

Sam. "That still doesn't mean I'm happy about this. You don't get tax write-offs in Hell for volunteering."

"So, what?" Josh asked. "No gold stars in Hell for doing the right thing?"

Josh dangled the bait out there, hoping I would latch onto it like a good little fish and snap at him.

I didn't.

Sam asked if she could go. She just *had* to see me doing something good. Josh, on the other hand, decided to pass, saying he needed to do a few things around the city. At least I wouldn't have to worry about him getting in my way.

Sam drove me to Wake Med, where I met up with Jenny and the other Honor Society members. Virgins, the lot of them. Paradise. Glancing at the group of them, I saw every girl let her gaze linger a moment too long on me.

"Hey, you made it," Jenny said with a smile.

I returned her smile, showing off my sparkling teeth. "Of course. This is my friend, Samantha."

Samantha shook Jenny's hand. "Sorry to crash your party, but when Bartholomew told me about this… well, I had to see it for myself." She held up a copy of *Green Eggs and Ham*. "Is this okay?"

Jenny gave her a thumbs-up. "Perfect."

I held up *Go the Fuck to Sleep*, making sure to plaster a shit-eating grin on my face. "How about this?"

Jenny laughed. "Oh my gosh," she said in a hushed tone, like it embarrassed her to even talk about it. "You can't read that to the kids."

"Why not? You said a children's book. This is for kids of all ages," I said, acting bashful. "You didn't specify that adult language was frowned upon. This may be the *only* time these kids get to enjoy filth. In their entire life. Honestly, I feel I owe it to them." I should've snuck in an issue of *Playboy*.

"What if one of the teachers sees it? You'll get in big trouble."

"Okay, okay. I guess I'll read this one instead." I pulled a copy of *Walter the Farting Dog* out of my satchel. Sam had made me pick it up, just in case. Or as she put it, "when they say no to the dirty book."

Jenny grinned. "Much better."

Two teachers with the group led us upstairs into the children's section of Wake Med. The air smelled of death and sickness as soon as I stepped onto the floor—normally my favorite scents, but not when it came from little kids. It felt wrong on so many levels.

The teachers led me into the cancer ward and sat me down next to a boy who looked about five. All his hair had fallen out. Even his eyebrows. Someone had raised the mattress so he could sit up while I read to him.

"Hello," he said weakly.

"Hi there. I'm Bart." Sick children don't have to pronounce my entire name. Bartholomew is probably too long for them anyway. I extended my hand. He gently shook it.

His eyes lit up upon touching my skin. "You're different."

Being in life-threatening situations made mortals more prone to seeing our true nature, especially children. Their vision hadn't been beaten down by reality yet, making them doubly able to see things differently.

"I am, but don't worry about that. I'm just here to read this fine piece of modern literature to you."

I cracked open *Walter the Farting Dog* and read aloud. The little boy, Erik, smiled and laughed as best he could at the story without hurting himself. Even I found it funny. Dogs and farting really were a winning combination. When I finished, I looked up at him. His eyes beamed.

"So, you liked the story?" I asked.

"Yep. I liked the farts. And Walter."

I stood. "I'm glad. Well, I think I should go read to someone else. Get better soon, stay strong, all that stuff."

"Is there a Heaven?"

I stopped and glanced back at Erik. I'd hoped our time together wouldn't lead to a discussion about the existence of you know who. The question gave me a sick feeling inside. Truth be told, I only really cared about farting dogs at the moment.

Sighing, I sat back down. "Do you think there is?"

Erik's face lit up.

I smiled. "Well, then. There you go. You don't need me to

tell you there is if you have faith." Being this kind hurt. I'd almost rather just kiss a virgin goodnight and leave her unsoiled by my sinful touch than be nice to sick kids.

"Will I go to Heaven when I die?"

I did *not* want to go there. I liked to operate on a plane of existence that bordered on the surreal and avoid serious conversations about things like life, spirituality, and the perfect bra size. This whole thing just got way too real for my tastes.

"I guess so, yeah. If you're into that sort of thing."

"Will you?"

This kid killed me. I shook my head. "I've already been there."

Erik leaned closer to me. "Did you like it?"

"Not really, but then again I'm a little bit of a troublemaker."

"Is that why you're not there anymore? You got in trouble?"

I snorted. "When don't I get in trouble?"

"Did you at least say you're sorry?"

"I don't think they'd care if I did." I needed to get out of there. Erik was just too adorable for words. "Tell you what. How about I put in a good word for you?"

Erik coughed. "What about you?"

I patted the kid's arm. "I'll be okay. You will be too, no matter what happens. I promise."

Never in a million years had I ever thought I'd say something nice about those armpit stains upstairs. "Now get some rest, okay?"

"Okay. Thanks."

I held my gaze on the boy for a second. That was why children were off limits. They were just too innocent. Too sweet. Pissed me off how cute they could be.

I got to my feet. Sam stood off to the side.

Paying no mind to my embarrassment, I pointed at her face. "Your eyes are leaking."

She sniffed and wiped the tears away. "That was so… wow."

I walked out of the room, Sam trailing behind me. "Spare me. All I did was adhere to the previously established boundaries concerning children."

108

"Still. That... There is good in you." Sam put her hand on my shoulder.

I shrugged her off. I got so angry, my horns pressed against my skull.

"I'm not Darth Vader. I'm a demon. I'm bad. Down to my very core. You'd be wise to remember that," I said, snapping at her.

Jenny came down the hall, a content look on her face. I walked over to her, giving her a high-five.

She stared at Sam. "Is she okay?"

"I think she's a bit overwhelmed by everything. Plus she's also never really seen me in action when I'm in do-gooder mode."

Jenny perked up. "You have a do-gooder mode?"

"Sometimes, yeah." Lies. Nothing but lies.

We hung around the hospital for a little while, just long enough to say bye to all the children, then I left Sam to fend for herself while Jenny and I went to dinner at some franchise restaurant. Because, well... why not? If people only knew how awful those places were. One meal probably shaved a good twelve hours off a lifespan.

"So tell me a little bit about yourself," I said.

Jenny sipped from her ice water and dove right in. Her mother died when Jenny was seven, of leukemia. She didn't have any siblings. She had applied for early admission to UNC-Chapel Hill. I knew a few people over there, but I had no interest in the place, as they'd already sold their souls several times over for basketball success. That well ran dry a long time ago.

"I want to be a doctor, to hopefully save people from my mom's fate," she said.

"That's noble. Very noble," I said, placing my hand on top of hers. "It's rare when people your—I mean our—age have such a clear idea of where they want their lives to go."

She smiled, her eyes glowing under the soft lighting. "Thanks. It just kind of came to me, really. I feel like it's my destiny, almost. Like fate. What about you?"

I chuckled to myself. "Me? I'll probably stumble through existence as some sort of Hell-raiser."

"So you want to be an actor-slash-playboy?"

I managed to choke on a piece of ice before it melted in my over-warm throat.

Jenny burst out laughing.

I held up my hand. "No, please, don't worry about me," I said, coughing. "I'm fine." I waited until I'd got myself under control before speaking again. "Not an actor, per se. But someone who plays a lot of different roles, I guess. I like to be involved in all walks of life."

Jenny nodded and looked off to the side, like she pondered what that meant. "So… an actor?"

"Yes," I said. My phone rang. "Sorry." I reached into my pocket, forwarded the call to voicemail and set the phone to vibrate.

The waitress delivered our food. I picked at mine, since demons didn't exactly need to eat. Especially this garbage. Jenny followed suit, probably because she didn't want to seem like a pig. Girls were so insecure. My phone vibrated in my pocket. I bit the inside of my mouth, trying to hide my frustration.

"So do you have a date for Homecoming?" Jenny asked, blushing.

Now we were getting down to business.

"Nope. I'm not *that* smooth." Actually I was, but sometimes the situation called for a little false modesty. "I've been at school only a few days."

Jenny grinned. "Would you like to—?"

"Unbelievable." My phone rang *again*. "I'm so sorry, but someone keeps calling me. Do you mind?"

She pulled her phone out. "Nope. I'll just sit here and tweet about our date."

"Great." I looked at the caller. Sam. I walked around the corner of the booth so Jenny couldn't hear me lecture Sam.

"You have the worst timing, you know that?"

"I'm sorry," she said, sounding out of breath. "It's Josh. We need your help."

"That's hysterical." I rolled my eyes. "Wait. Is it life threatening?"

"Yes."

"Good." I ended the call.

Sam immediately rang back.

I didn't want to, but I answered. Otherwise she would just keep calling back until I lost my temper and jammed a chicken finger in someone's ear.

"If he dies, that's one less problem I have to deal with."

"Please? He was out hunting and got injured."

My jaw dropped. "Hunting? Now? What an idiot." I ground my teeth. "I'll be right there."

FIFTEEN

ONE-EYED JOSH

I told Jenny I had an emergency and we needed to cut our dinner short, which was sort of true. Naturally, she understood and had her food boxed up while I paid the bill. She even sped a little on the way home.

"You don't have to speed," I said. "I'd rather we just got there in one piece."

And if we happened to be too late and Josh died? My bad, guys. So sorry.

"But you said it's an emergency. We need to get you to your friend."

Oh, the bleeding hearts. I'd truly enjoy destroying this one.

"Well, he said it was an emergency, but who knows with... You know what? Keep speeding." Speeding is breaking the law, making it a minor sin. Score one for me. "I can't thank you enough. It's so kind of you to do this."

"Is he okay? What happened?"

"I'm not sure. But if it's anything less than his hair catching on fire, I'm going to be very upset." I glanced over at Jenny. "Especially since he ruined such a wonderful evening."

Jenny smiled and tilted her head away, like being complimented embarrassed her. "Thanks. I had a good time, too."

We pulled up at Sam's apartment complex. I opened the door to get out, then leaned back in. "Sorry about all this, but we should definitely see each other again. Outside of school, I mean."

She glanced at me through some strands of hair. "I'd like that."

I leaned over and kissed her on the cheek.

"And I'd love to go to the Homecoming Dance with you," I whispered in her ear.

A slight moan escaped her lips as I pulled back and got out of the car. Blessed Heaven, was I smooth, or what?

Sam's apartment looked like a Serbian death squad marched through it, leaving a path of destruction in its wake. I stepped over the bloody shirts and towels littering the floor. Josh lay on her kitchen table, a blood-soaked towel on his face.

"Did you poke yourself in the eye with scissors? While running? Please say you did, because that would be *priceless*."

"Go to Hell," Josh spat out from underneath the towel, extending his middle finger toward me.

"I'd love to," I said. As long as I went on my own terms, and as a free demon, at least.

"Finally," Sam said, walking past me with more towels in her hand.

"What did the dipshit do this time?" I asked.

"I'm right here, I can speak for myself," he said.

I folded my arms. "What did you do this time, dipshit?"

Left by himself, Josh figured he would hunt a minion he had a lead on. The moron had actually gotten himself bloodied chasing Hell's equivalent of an indentured servant. I snorted. This couldn't have been better if he *had* poked his eye out with a pair of scissors.

"I'd tracked the minion to Pullen Park when your smoke monster thing attacked me," he said. "I tried to kill it, but no luck."

"And in the process lost his eye," Sam said, switching out the bloody towel with a fresh one.

Interesting. "How did you get away?"

Josh forced a grin. "Templars have their secrets, and I'll be damned if I'm going to give them to a demon."

"He hid in a sewer," Sam said.

Josh threw up his hands. "Ruin it, why don't you?"

"So why not call 9-1-1?" I asked. "They'd at least *want* to help you."

"The ointment I gave you could save his eye," she said. "Otherwise it's gone for sure."

"It can't be that bad. Let me see." I walked over and pulled the towel off Josh's face. Sure enough, one of his eyeballs lay on his cheek. "Looks like somebody took half a bite out of a gumball."

"We don't have time for this. Give me the ointment." Sam held out her hand. "Please."

I moved back a few paces. "Now hold on a second. This pissant has done nothing but belittle and talk about killing me since he became the Short Round to my Indiana Jones and your Marion. Why should I help him now? For all I care, he can spend the rest of his days looking like a pirate."

I would like to thank the Academy and all their souls, which they sold to me for a pittance.

"We'll be square," Josh said. "Don't call me Short Round. I'm at least Sallah. Or Sean Connery."

I shook my head. "I give you your eye back and you forgive me for taking out dear old dad? For some odd reason, I don't believe you."

Sam narrowed her gaze and marched over to me.

"Bartholomew, give me the ointment. Now." She held out her hand.

I smirked. "Make me."

She placed her hand on my chest. "By the authority given to me by the Almighty, I *order* you to give me the ointment."

Her palm lit up.

A blank kind of contentment crept through my brain and everything else leaked out. Doing what she wanted was the only way to go.

I fumbled the vial out of my pocket and handed it to her.

Smiling, she took her hand off my chest. "Thank you."

She moved over to Josh, then applied the ointment. His eye instantly began healing.

My senses came back to me like a volcano erupting in my brain.

Wait. What just happened?

"What did you do to me?"

Sam hummed to herself.

I straightened my jacket. "I'm talking to you, Samantha. What kind of juju did you pull on me?"

"Nothing." She finished applying the ointment and handed me the vial. "I just have the ability to… keep you in line, if need be."

Keep me in line? Me?

My jaw hit the floor. "So you think you can keep me on a leash? I'm done. You and one-eyed Jack over there can do this on your own. I am not your pauper."

"A pauper is a poor person," Sam chirped.

"You know what I mean." I stormed out the door before my horns came out and ripped a hole in her wall.

I kicked at the air before storming back inside. "You have to drive me home first. I don't have cash for a cab."

SIXTEEN
DEVIL'S ADVOCATE

I stewed in my own personal cauldron of anger as Samantha drove me home. The horns pressed against my skull so long I had a headache. Seemed everybody wanted me as their puppet nowadays. Lucifer. Nicholas. Even the butt plug upstairs had a hand on my strings. Well, not anymore. I decided to make a run for it. Work out some other way to pay my debt to Hell and avoid the Ninth Circle.

"I'm sorry I didn't tell you sooner about my Hand of God thing," Sam said, breaking the silence. "I never thought I'd have to use it."

I refused to look at her. "Doesn't matter."

"I can't do this without you."

"Guess you're screwed, then." I nibbled at a fingernail. It itched from wanting to extend into a claw and slash Sam's throat. "I don't care how much you need me. There's nothing more demeaning than having to do *His* will. Nothing."

Sam sighed. "Fine. You're out. What are you going to do? When they catch you, you know where you're going."

"Guess I'll have to make sure they don't catch me."

The car pulled to a stop at a light one block from my condo. I unbuckled my seatbelt. Sam reached out and grabbed my arm.

"Think about what you're doing. You can have a better life," she said.

I pointed up. "What? Working for Him? That's a better life? I don't think so. Don't forget, I've worked for Him before. Red Cross workers in the Sudan have more fun than His *employees*. Now, if you'll excuse me."

I threw open the door and got out. Sam tried one of those sad puppy dog looks on me through the window. I ground my teeth together until she gave up and drove away, leaving me alone to wallow in my thoughts.

Half a block away from my condo, I caught the scent of a cigarette. A very particular kind of cigarette. Moore Tobacco smelled exactly like marijuana, and just so happened to be Lucifer's brand of choice whenever he went topside.

Hell had its own brand of cigarettes called Red Circle, but good luck finding a pack. Forged on the Third Circle of Hell, the cigs were extremely difficult to harvest. Most of the time, they caught fire before they could be hand-rolled. If a batch ever survived to production, the Circles had a taste, and buzz, that felt nothing short of divine. If a human smoked one, it would be the equivalent of a thousand Cuban cigars all at once.

Of course, when Red Circles were in supply, Lucifer hoarded most of them, if for no other reason than to make everybody suffer. The last reported crop to go into production was in 1822.

I found him standing by the entrance to my building, looking up at the night sky and wearing one of the finest suits I'd ever laid eyes on. He had a touch of gray in his black hair and a slight paunch that only added to his commanding presence. His blue eyes were even more piercing than my own.

"Beautiful, isn't it?" he asked with his gravelly voice.

"I wouldn't go that far," I said, lighting up myself. "You here to taunt me some more?"

The boss man turned his attention away from the stars and glanced at my charm. He scrunched up his face. That's probably the worst it would do to someone like Lucifer.

"You know that clashes with your ensemble."

"I hadn't noticed," I said. "But thanks for pointing it out."

Lucifer shook his head. "So much hostility. If only you'd

focused your anger in the right direction, you might have been successful enough to be in my inner circle, not the Seventh."

"You're assuming I want to be in your inner circle. That circle's a bit too brown for my tastes."

Lucifer tilted his head up and blew out some smoke in the shape of a pentagram. "I thought you loved being inside little dark circles."

"Look at you with the jokes." Of course, Lou would make a joke about ass play.

"Can you really stand there and say you never wanted to be a part of it?"

"Be a part of your little boys club? Nope. Not once." The inner circle helped guide Hell's vision and values, like a board of directors. The very idea entailed so many of the things I hate. Rules. Projects. Red tape. Team-building exercises. I'd rather be a lone wolf, prowling the countryside for some action.

He glanced at me, his eyes burning red as he drew on his cigarette.

"I understand you're quitting, so I'm here to escort you to, um," he pointed at the ground, "the Ninth. You sure you don't want to take a look at the stars? It'll probably be the last time you ever see them."

I blew out a cloud of smoke. He'd never shown up this soon to collect someone, even a demon. Hopefully, that meant I'd pissed him off.

"I wanted to talk to you about that. See if we couldn't come up with some sort of deal."

Lucifer laughed. "What could you possibly offer me? I already own you."

"Did you know your baby boy paid me a visit the other day? He must be planning another coup against dear old dad," I said.

Lucifer exhaled through his nose. "You think he's smart enough to overthrow me, even with the Shard? Much like you, there's a reason he fell flat on his face when the time came for him to step up. That boy is my biggest failure and my greatest achievement."

I didn't know about me, but he was right about his kid.

When Lucifer took a vacation five hundred years ago, he gave Nicholas the reins in his place. Before anyone knew what happened, the Dark Ages came to a screeching halt and humanity ushered in the Age of Enlightenment.

"I can't believe you're making me work with you-know-who." I looked up at the Heavens. "That's low."

Lucifer grinned and ran his tongue along his lips. "It happens. I knew how much it'd pain you, which is icing on the cake." He clapped his hands. "So. You ready? Being among all these mortals gets my libido going. We better get moving before I get fresh with some young lass."

"So there's no kind of gentlemen's agreement we can come to?"

Lucifer flicked his cigarette into the street. An attractive blonde eyeballed him as she walked past. "Tell me where some gentlemen are, and I'll get them to broker an agreement."

I sighed. I really thought I could talk him out of it. Regardless, I'd rather be mad at a fake angel than get banged by this turd for eternity. "Fine. I'll stay here and finish the job, if that's what *you* want."

Before I knew what had happened, Lucifer moved within inches of my face. "Yes, you will. And you'll quit bitching about how bad you have it. All the mistakes you've made, your little coup, I've given you one, this *one*, chance to get your act together and it's the only one you're going to get." He used his *I am the devil and I will swallow your soul* voice. Mortals pissed their pants when he spoke, but not me. I'd heard him speak a million times. "Do we understand each other? If I have to come back up here for you I *will* drag your sorry ass back down with me."

"I understand."

He beamed. "Excellent," he said in his normal voice. "Now, if you'll excuse me, I'm going to have sex with that blonde who walked by."

The next morning, I texted Sam, to let her know I'd changed my mind about quitting. I stood on the sidewalk, smoking a cigarette while I waited for her. When she pulled up next to me, Josh sat shotgun, his eye completely healed. I knocked on his window.

"What?" he asked as the window rolled down.

"In the back," I said, jerking my thumb in that direction.

"Why?"

"Because there's not enough room back there for me and my Johnson."

"Gross," Sam said.

Josh glared at me as he opened the door, then got in the back seat. Sitting in Josh's seat, I wondered if he'd farted before getting up, since the seat felt pretty warm.

I didn't give Sam an explanation for my change of heart, and fortunately, she didn't ask for one. She probably believed the inherent good in me won out. We rode to school in silence. I kind of wanted to rip Josh's eye back out and shoot it with a slingshot.

Walking into school, Sam decided to break radio silence.

"I have cheerleading tryouts today," she said, like nothing happened.

Forgive and forget. That was one of the angels' mottos. I preferred to revenge and remember, but that's just me.

"Can you put in a good word with that Monica girl?" she asked.

"Why don't you just mind rape me again?" I said. "Get me to do it that way?"

"Don't be a jerk," she said. "I'm trying to be nice here. You put me in a corner last night and forced my hand."

"True, but you probably don't want me to talk to her," I said. "She'll see it as a sign of weakness and insecurity."

Josh held the door open for her. She thanked him.

"Then let her see it that way," she said. "I *know* how to cheer. We were so good, we even went to nationals. I just want to make sure I've got all my bases covered, and if we know someone who can put in a good word for me, all the better."

I moved in close. I could smell her apricot body wash.

"You want my advice? Quit." I turned to go to class, then stopped. "If you go through with it, don't blame me if you get eaten alive."

I hoped she didn't make the team. I wanted her to fail. She really didn't seem to grasp the reality of the situation. And, more than ever, I wanted to get something for myself out of this little deal. Speaking of which… Miss McPherson sashayed her pretty little self down the hall, her innocence begging to be taken from her right there in the hallway.

I grinned. "Hey, Jenny."

She cradled a science book in her arms. "Hey there. How's your friend?"

"He's fine. A watermelon seed flew up, poked him in the eye, and for some reason he thought his eye would fall out. He was just being a drama queen."

I scowled at Josh as he strolled past us.

She grinned. "That's good about his eye, at least. What time do you have lunch?"

"A few minutes past noon. You?"

"Twelve-fifteen. Save a seat for me, okay?"

I widened my eyes, trying to make them look inviting. "Absolutely."

"Great."

When she leaned back against her locker, I slid myself next to her so we both could see the hallway. "Quick question. Did you know Casey well? The kid who died?"

"Not much, but some. Why? Did you know him?"

I moved closer, so that our arms touched. "A little. I'm more curious about him than anything."

"Like a morbid curiosity?" Jenny asked, eyes wide and her mouth open.

"That's a good one."

"Thanks," she said with a laugh.

"Bartholomew," Kyle called out.

He held out his fist for me to bump. I obliged him.

The bell rang. All of the kids scurried about as they went to their first class of the day. It looked like an organized ant farm.

"I'm off to class," Jenny said. "Bye."

"Okay." I told her goodbye as she disappeared into the wave of students.

"Cockblock much?" I snapped at Kyle.

Kyle's face went pale. "Sorry."

I waved him off. "It's fine. What's up?"

"I wanted to thank you. For helping with… you know. I can't tell you what a relief it is not to have to worry about Clayton and Darrel. If there's anything I can do for you, let me know."

I pushed myself off the lockers and entered the current of moving bodies. "I'm going to hold you to that."

The morning came and went about as quickly as possible, which is to say not very fast at all. In normal time, it took four hours for lunchtime to roll around, but today, it felt like about four months. I walked into the cafeteria, which served fish filet sandwiches as today's featured item. Josh and Sam walked toward me with their lunch trays, then moved right on past, wisely giving me room to breathe.

I picked at my fish sandwich. Looking up, I noticed Jenny sitting across from me.

"I did some thinking earlier," she said. "About what you asked me."

I leaned forward. "You did?"

Jenny opened her Diet Coke and took a sip. "Yeah. What all do you know about Casey?"

I picked up the sandwich, then dropped it on the tray, landing with a squishy thump. "Not much. I know he'd been dating someone, but not much beyond that. I really want to find out who that was."

Jenny opened her water bottle and took a sip. "Why? If you didn't really know Casey, you don't owe him, or this mystery girl, anything."

This conversation went around in circles. I needed to give her something bigger to get anything of use out of her. "I know what happened. I was there. At the museum. He didn't die from some random heart attack, or whatever excuse the doctors laid out."

Jenny's jaw dropped. If the jaw hadn't been securely fastened to her head, it would've fallen off and landed on the table.

"Are you *serious*? Why haven't you told anybody? Why haven't you told the police?" She put a hand to her mouth. "Did you... did you have something to do with it?"

"No," I said, shaking my head vehemently. A chair a few feet away from us screeched as some girl got up to take her tray to the trashcans. I hoped she hadn't overheard anything.

"Then for God's sake, tell me what happened."

I forced myself to take a bite of the filet-o-fish, to give myself some time to mull over what to say. The filet tasted like someone forgot to fry it and hoped some breadcrumbs would mask the rank flavor. "It's... difficult to explain. I don't really believe it myself. And unless you're the one he'd been seeing, I don't feel comfortable telling you. I'd like her to know first." I took another bite of "fish."

"Okay. I am the girl."

I spit out my bite, which landed on her tray. She looked at the piece of food, shocked, then burst out laughing. "Nice distance."

"Are you really her? Casey's mystery girl?"

Jenny picked up her fork and dug into her salad. "Sorry, no. I don't know who she is. I just wanted to see what you'd say. The whole thing does sound... intriguing."

"That's one word for it. Hey, don't tell anybody what I told you, okay?"

She crossed her heart with her index finger. "And hope to die."

I kept getting weird looks from everybody the rest of the day, like I'd silently farted, but everyone still knew I'd dealt it. One girl with pigtails stopped in front of me. I almost walked right through her.

"What?" I asked.

"You're an attention whore," she said. "You monster."

I mock gasped. "You've found me out."

A hand burst out of the crowd and grabbed me, pulling me in the opposite direction from where I'd been heading. The next thing I knew, I stood in the women's bathroom, with a very hot and bothered Monica staring at me. I couldn't tell if she wanted to bang me or hang me.

"Did you tell Stacy Parker you *killed* Casey?" she asked, her breathing so heavy it gave her bosom a nice little heave-ho.

"What? I don't even know who that is."

"Apparently, she heard you spouting off about the whole thing in the cafeteria." Monica sauntered up to me, then took firm hold of my privates with her hand. Being this close to me, the charm did its work. Her face turned a sickly white before she took a few steps back. "Big, bad Bartholomew. Snooping around, trying to keep people off your scent when all the while you killed Casey." The color returned to her face. "You want to kill this mystery girl too, don't you? Not that I have a problem with that. I'm just sad you didn't include me in your little scheme."

Maybe I'd been spending too much time with Sam, but Monica's audacity took me by surprise. Even more surprising, I didn't flush the charm down the toilet and knock out a quickie with her.

"Don't you think killing Casey, then making it a point to ask about him is a bit… obvious? Give me some credit. I have been doing this demon thing a few millennia longer than you." Monica became a demon shortly after a Roman Caesar had her executed for refusing to marry one of his older friends. In exchange for revenge, she became what she was now.

"And yet you're the one in the dog house." Monica moved closer to me, then took one look at the charm. She stopped her advance. "Tell me how you killed Casey. Did you take your time? I *love* it when they take their time."

"I didn't kill Casey. I don't even know how that rumor got started. Wait… does Stacy have lunch the same time as me?"

Monica arched her eyebrows. "I think so. I've seen her around in the cafeteria some."

The screeching chair. That must have been Stacy, running off to tell her friends a juicy bit of gossip. Freakin' high school.

"Interesting."

"Wait. So you really didn't kill him?"

I threw out my hands. "No. Don't you think I'd be

bragging right now if I had?"

Monica sighed. She looked at herself in a mirror, fixing her hair. "Pity. I'd have told you who the girl is. Guess you'll have to fulfill the terms of our agreement after all, you tease."

In that case. "Why didn't you say so? I did kill him. I was only joking before."

Monica smirked as she straightened her hair. "Now I know you're lying."

I pointed at the door. "Can I go now?"

Monica reached into her purse and pulled out some lipstick. "You may."

I left before she could try to blame me for something else, like the Lincoln assassination. If I spent much more time with Monica, we were liable to fight, screw, or both. I hadn't taken three steps out of the bathroom when a hand drenched in holy water wrapped around my neck.

The hand belonged to Frady-McNeely's star quarterback, Tyler Haxall.

SEVENTEEN

THE WRONG KIND OF RUBBER

I tried to fight off Tyler, who again had good old Clayton and Darrel at his side. He dragged me out into the parking lot. This at least reminded me to call Remy about the progress on a protective charm against these kinds of shenanigans.

"You killed our friend," Tyler snapped. "Payback time. We know what you are."

"Your kind isn't welcome around here." Clayton punched me in the stomach.

I laughed. "That doesn't hurt, you moron."

"Yeah, but this does." Tyler grinned as his grip around my neck tightened.

The smell of burnt flesh seared my nostrils.

"Why'd you do it? Why'd you kill Casey?"

"I didn't. I don't know where you heard that, but it's not true." I began choking. At least I had that vial of Sam's super healing ointment in my jacket pocket.

Tyler punched me in the face with his free hand. It felt like he'd dented my left cheek. He must have dosed both of them with holy water.

"How do you know what I am?"

"Doesn't matter," Clayton said. "We know."

"Darrel, bring your car around." Tyler pulled out a plastic

water bottle, probably full of holy water, and tossed it to Thing Two. "Put that on one of the front tires. I want to show this damned thing what we do to douches who mess with us." He grabbed my charm. "What the Hell are you wearing? One of your boyfriends give that to you?" He yanked it off and threw it across the parking lot.

Great.

Darrel ran to get his car. If they were dousing a tire in holy water, they must be planning on running me over. I'd normally survive that kind of thing, but a tire covered in holy water? That was a scary proposition.

"Think about this for a second," I said. "You don't want to do this. You guys aren't killers."

Tyler's eyes narrowed. "Killer? The only killer is you. We're just doing what the good Lord intended. Sending you right back to Hell where you belong."

I coughed up some nasty black bile. At least it got on Tyler's hand and not my suit. My blood ran hot and had been known to burn human skin. Not as much as the acid blood in *Alien*, but it'd do the trick. Tyler flicked it off before any damage could be done.

I had to think fast to get out of this mess.

"I have a fake ID coming, I can buy you guys some alcohol," I said. "Whatever you want. My treat." The sniveling tone of my voice disgusted me. "Just name your price."

That's the best you can do, Bartholomew?

I couldn't remember the last time I'd had so much difficulty coming up with a reason not to be destroyed. At the least, I hoped my awful idea would stall them until a good idea decided to make an appearance.

Tyler and Clayton laughed. "We play football. All we have to do is snap our fingers and we get whatever we want," Clayton said. "Girls, booze, drugs... you name it."

Tyler snapped his fingers. "And right now I want to see what happens when you run over a demon's head with a car."

He grabbed the back of my neck and threw me down on the asphalt, right next to a cigarette butt.

Idea.

"Can I at least get a final smoke before you... you know?"

I asked.

Clayton chuckled. "Why not?"

Tyler glanced up at his friend. "You do it. I'll keep holding him down."

"Great. They're in my jacket pocket."

The jacket pocket in the suit you just ruined, turd face.

Clayton kneeled down and pulled out my pack of cigs. He tucked one in my mouth.

"Light?" I asked.

Tyler wrapped his fist around a chunk of my hair. I felt my scalp begin to rip. "Can't you just light it with your fire and brimstone breath?"

Have I breathed fire and brimstone so far? I haven't? Well, then. You're an idiot.

"I'm not a dragon. So would you?"

Tyler took the lighter out of my pocket and lit the cig. At least I'd go out smoking.

Out the corner of my eye, I saw Darrel's car pull up. Wonderful. They wanted to send me to Hell using a late model Nissan Altima. An *Altima*. How embarrassing.

"Do either of you have a nicer car than that? I'd prefer to go out in style," I said.

"Nope," Tyler said. "You're not good enough for American."

I watched Tyler motion for Darrel to pull the car up. The front driver's side tire came to a rest against my face, burning me with the holy water. I wished I had some sort of telekinetic or Jedi powers to call for help. Failing that, I settled on the next best thing.

"Help!" I cried out as loud as I could. "Help me! Fire! Rape! Fire!"

"Shut up," Tyler said, punching my face as he held me down.

"Please! Somebody! Fire! Help! There's a kitten stuck in a tree!"

Please let someone hear me.

"You're going to die, demon," Tyler said, pushing down on my face with his hand.

"Please! I'm a virgin! Damsel in distress! Get your fresh,

juicy hot dogs!" I screamed so loud my throat started to feel scratchy. Although, the constant smoking probably didn't help with that, either.

"Hey, what are you doing over there?" a voice called out. I looked over and saw Kyle.

"Kyle," I shouted. "Help. Go tell somebody on these assholes for me."

"Bartholomew?" he called out. "What are you doing?"

"Get these meatheads off me."

More students emerged from the school to check out the commotion. Even Miss Evans came outside to investigate the hullabaloo.

"Hey Ty. Man, let's bolt," Clayton said. "There's too much heat."

"You lucky demon," Tyler said, an inch from my face. "Next time you won't be able to cry for help like a little bitch."

He jumped up and got into Darrel's car, along with Clayton. The car sped away before anyone could tell who'd tried to end me. I sat up and dusted myself off. Thankfully, my suit didn't look any worse for wear, so I quickly applied the healing ointment to my neck and pulled up the collar to hide whatever spots I'd missed.

"Bartholomew?" Miss Evans asked, running a hand through my hair. "Are you okay? What happened?"

Miss Evans wore a tight navy top that showed off just enough cleavage to let the world know she knew she had a fantastic rack. I hadn't noticed how hot she looked earlier in class, but I did now. I wanted to take her then and there.

"I'm fine. I left a book in the car and some undesirable accosted me. He knocked me down, called me names I'd rather not repeat, stuff like that."

Miss Evans patted my shoulders, getting more dirt and muck off. Just feeling her touch made me want to show her a Hell of a good time. "Well, it's a good thing you've got such a powerful set of lungs on you, otherwise who knows what would have happened."

"Yeah. Sorry to cause such a stir." So embarrassing. A demon crying out for help? Simply inexcusable. If anyone from down below knew what I'd done…

"We're just glad you're okay," Miss Evans said, giving me a hug.

I wrapped my arms around her, making sure my fingers brushed the top part of her rear. Being so close to her felt intoxicating. I had to think of a naked, overweight nun with a massive, hairy mole on her face just to keep myself in check.

Miss Evans released me and gave me a warm smile. "I think we should get back to class now, don't you?"

"Yeah."

Sam rushed up to us. "What happened? You okay?"

"Yeah. I'll tell you about it later."

She pointed at my body. "Where's your, um, thing?"

I patted my crotch. "Still there."

"Your *charm*," she said with a droll look on her face.

I laid my hand on my chest. The charm wasn't there. "In the parking lot somewhere."

Miss Evans said goodbye and walked back to school.

I found the charm under a pickup truck and slid it over my head. I instantly felt at peace.

"Who was it?" Sam asked. "The Black Cloud of Death?"

"No. Tyler and the two Things." I strolled past Sam and out of the parking lot, fuming.

"At least you're okay," Sam called out from behind me.

I didn't answer. If not for the holy water, I could have easily handled myself with Tyler and the two Things. Someone tipped them off about my true nature, but I couldn't worry about them right now. Their day would come. Nobody would believe them if they ran around telling people about me being a demon. No, the more pressing matter concerned that rumor about me killing Casey. That one could ruin everything. Monica wouldn't rat out a fellow demon, but somebody else might have put the pieces together and spilled the beans.

Jenny.

I knew Jenny had Latin at the end of the day, so I moved as quickly as possible through the hallway in that direction. I found her talking to a friend of hers outside the room. Her friend saw me, did a double take, and quickly vamoosed. Smart girl.

Jenny turned to me. "Before you say anything—"

I grabbed her arm and pulled her into a corner of the commons area, where hopefully nobody would hear what I had to say.

"You're hurting me," Jenny said, trying to wiggle free.

"It'll hurt a lot more if you lie to me right now."

"I didn't tell anyone. I promise."

I narrowed my eyes. "The entire school thinks I'm a murderer. Care to explain how that little ditty got started?"

Monica said Stacy Potter spread the rumor, but I needed to be sure.

Jenny's eyes went wide. "Not by me. I can't believe you'd even accuse me of such a thing."

"I didn't tell anybody else about it. I mention to you that I saw Casey die, then all of a sudden some of his football buddies try to run me over with their car. A bit of a coincidence, don't you think?"

I laid my fist against the cinder block wall and pushed. The white paint cracked from the pressure.

Jenny leaned forward. "Is that what happened to you outside? Are you okay?"

"Messed up my suit a little but otherwise, yes. I'm fine. Thanks for asking."

"Good." Jenny brushed past me, giving me a furious look, her face flushed with blood. "I can't believe you would think I'd do something like that to you."

She shook her head and rounded the corner into the hallway.

Okay, so maybe it *was* that Stacy girl from the cafeteria.

Or maybe Josh was the guilty party. Only one way to find out…

I looked all over school for that little shit. He had to be here somewhere.

I walked past Kyle making out with some Goth-looking chick with dyed purple hair and an eyebrow ring. Her leather jacket topped off the "I hate you, dad" look she obviously aimed for.

Good for him.

At least he tried to sin. I'd have given him a high-five if he wasn't still enjoying first base.

I found Josh out by the bleachers, watching the football team practice.

"Well, well, well," I said, sitting down on the row of bleachers behind him.

"I played linebacker in high school," he said. "A headhunter. I loved it. If an opponent did anything to piss off our team, it was my job to retaliate against the offense." He leaned back against the row behind him. "Break a finger in a pile, late hit the QB, whatever. Defend the team at all costs. Then high school ended. No more football. But I'm still a headhunter for the Knights Templar. Funny how some things stay the same, no matter how much changes."

"That's great," I said. "Very moving monologue. Am I to believe you're still defending your team?"

"I just want you to know I've stuck to my word. I heard about your run-in today. Sorry that happened, especially since I had nothing to do with it. Whatever problem I have with you, I promised I would wait until after we got the Shard of Gabriel, and I meant it. Particularly after saving my eye."

"Honor is such a turn-on." It was high time for a cigarette. I lit up, offering the cig to Josh.

"No thanks."

We sat in silence as I smoked a few more cigarettes. Tryouts should be over soon. Josh's cell rang.

"Hey," he said softly, in that universal voice guys use when they're talking to a girl they like. Josh sprang up. "I'll be right there."

"What's up?" I asked.

Josh ran for the steps. "It's Samantha. Something's happened."

EIGHTEEN

JALAPENO STYLE POPCORN

Samantha sat on the floor outside the gym, clutching her knees to her chest and weeping. I couldn't tell if she'd been physically hurt or not. She didn't seem to be bleeding anywhere. At least she cried quietly and didn't draw attention to herself.

Josh rushed over to her, taking her in his arms. "What happened?" he asked. "Did somebody hurt you?"

Okay, jerk, be the real gentleman here. See if I care. "Are you okay?"

Sam nodded. "It was horrible."

I told you so.

"What was?" Josh asked, rubbing her arm. "Tryouts? Did you get cut?"

"No." Sam shook her head. "That's the worst part. I got in."

Hmm. I crossed my arms. "So what's the problem? That's what you wanted."

She looked me in the eyes, tears making her face glisten. "You were right. They are the most awful collection of monsters. All they want to do is torture and manipulate anything that's in their way. And I have to be part of it now."

"You didn't notice when you were a cheerleader before?"

Josh asked.

She shook her head. "No, why should I have?"

Sam lowered her head again, a new stream of tears pouring down her cheeks.

I had warned her about this. Sam's breakdown had to be due, in part, to her trying to become an angel. For whatever reason, the transition sort of mutated a person's DNA, making the individual want to do good. Some people are born with addiction in their genes. Angels are born with the desire to be good. As such, when surrounded by something as horrible as cheerleaders, that impulse ran up against a brick wall, which could be a bit… upsetting for the angel.

"It gets worse," she said, her voice cracking. "It gets so much worse."

"How's that?" I asked, lighting another cigarette. "Should we get a doll so you can point to where the bad girls touched you?"

Josh gave me a disgusted look. "Come on."

"It's the coach," Sam said. "He's the reason I died."

I drove Sam's crappy Hyundai back to her apartment. Inside, Josh continued doting over her while I ordered a pizza. Sam took some time to compose herself before getting into the story, as she apparently had to wade through years of conflicted emotions about the entire thing. She set a bottle of red wine on the kitchen counter.

"Why do you have wine?" I asked. "That kind of seems like a no-no."

"It is the blood of Christ," she said.

Whatever. Wine is wine. I uncorked the bottle and poured its contents into the three wine glasses. Josh passed on his, stating he preferred beer. The heathen. I poured his wine into my glass. After Sam finished her wine, she dove into the story.

Coach Mort was a senior at Samantha's high school when she was a sophomore. Tall and athletic, all the girls wanted him.

"Even the teachers noticed him," Sam said.

"I bet they did, the catty hoes."

Sam glared at me. "Can you not joke right now?"

"Seriously," Josh said with pizza in his mouth, the disgusting brute.

I took a sip from my glass and nodded.

"I met him one day late in the school year. We'd both volunteered in an adopt-a-highway program through some after school group."

I stifled a yawn. This story sounded like *loads* of fun.

"During the clean-up, Coach Mort struck up a conversation with me. He said he'd recognized me from the cheerleading squad. Sophomores normally don't get to cheer varsity, but I did." She held out her glass. "Can I get some more wine?"

I grabbed the bottle and poured her another.

She took a sip. "I was so naïve."

Apparently, they talked about gymnastics, school, and some other boring stuff. I tuned out once I got the gist that they'd really hit it off.

"I found him so charming and funny. And mature. I remember really being bowled over by his maturity," Sam said.

He sounds like an absolute dreamboat. But I digress.

She blew her nose. "We were together for… eight months. I couldn't believe it. Nobody like him had ever taken an interest in me. Ever. He made me feel… special. Like I mattered."

I knew exactly how this story would end. Next time I saw Coach Mort I might have to give him a cookie.

"Then he got into college down in Georgia." Sam's eyes watered again. "And that was it. He ended things the day he found out. He said the distance would be too much and he didn't see the point in prolonging the inevitable."

I could feel the catch in the story coming. Taste it, almost.

"Go on," I said.

"Well, it turned out he lied about going to school in Georgia. We lived in Charlotte, and he was going to school just down the road at Clemson," she said. "With some skank named Viola. Who runs off with a girl named *Viola*?"

Apparently Coach Mort.

"It seemed that he and Viola were sleeping together the *entire* time he was with me. I gave him everything."

I perked up. "Everything?"

She looked down at the floor. I took that to mean she *had* given him everything, including her virginity. Finally, this story was getting good.

"I thought we were going to get married."

And there's the catch. Sixteen and she thought she'd found her soul mate?

Ah, young love.

Cupid can be a sneaky little bastard sometimes.

"I didn't know how to handle everything. First, I stopped eating. Then my grades started to drop. I fell into a deep depression. When my parents went away one weekend, they left their medicine cabinet full of pills. You can figure out the rest."

"I had no idea," Josh said, laying a hand on her back.

"Now you know the truth," she said.

I sat down in the chair diagonal to them. I'd heard this kind of story so many times before. Seeing that my favorite hobby had always been deflowering virgins, a lot of those times I played the role of Coach Mort in the story.

"Suicides almost always go straight to Hell. Yet here you are. They offered you a way out, didn't they?" I asked. "That's why you're in training."

Sam glanced over at me and nodded. "Because of my age and the circumstances, they offered me a certain kind of clemency. They said I could earn my redemption by serving Heaven and one day become an archangel, or go straight to Hell and burn."

I tried not to snort.

Burn.

Saint Peter and his hooligans are some of the sneakiest salesmen around. They make car dealers look like amateurs. Sam probably would've had fun in Hell, at least after the brass tired of torturing her. At some point, they'd have given her the option of becoming a demon so she could somehow get revenge on Coach Mort and advance through the ranks of Hell, like Monica.

"I know what you're thinking," she said with a knowing look. "That I made the wrong choice."

I held up my hands. "I didn't say a word."

"You didn't have to. I can see it on your face."

I paced around the room, trying to improve my poker face. "Do you think he recognized you?"

Sam went pale. "What?"

Josh glared at me. "Have some compassion, you hellion. You're talking to an angel."

I frowned. I really didn't think our relationship would be able to get past this whole me-offing-his-dad thing, which was just petty on his part.

"Josh, if Coach Mort recognizes Sam, the gig is up. We're blown. Do you understand what that means?"

I paused for a moment to see if he would answer. He didn't.

"Of course you do. You're a *smart* guy," I said with a *slight* hint of condescension.

Josh looked like he bit the inside of his cheeks to control his temper, a smart move on his part. Maybe the kid had some intelligence after all.

I sat on the arm of the couch next to Sam. "I understand if you want to pull out."

"No," Sam said, shaking her head. "Absolutely not. I let him get to me once. He won't do it again."

Steely resolve. I didn't think Sam had it in her. "Good girl. But you've got to minimize contact with him. Don't look him in the eye, give short answers, that kind of thing."

Sam impressed Coach Mort and the cheerleading squad so much in her tryout that they asked her to go on and cheer at the football game tomorrow night. Josh and I were going to the game to mingle, see if we could find out anything about Vixen. Sam would do her best to stomach being a cheerleader and see what she could learn through that group.

I offered to drive Sam and Josh to the game in my Benz. Josh said he had things to do afterwards, so he'd go separately. I wouldn't have even bothered showing my car around school, but I figured the kids would assume it belonged to a grownup and leave my baby alone. Then, when the kids realized the car belonged to me, they would be so awestruck by my majestic stallion of a luxury sedan they would strike up a conversation that would either lead to a clue about Vixen or a virgin being deflowered. One guess as to which one I preferred.

We got out of the car. Sam wore her cheerleader outfit, which showed off enough of her legs and cleavage to make her look awfully provocative. She stared straight ahead at nothing in particular.

"Nervous?" I asked, waving my hand in front of her face. It broke her train of thought.

"What? Oh. Yeah. I mean, a little."

I popped the trunk and buttoned up my overcoat—finally covering up the stupid charm—then called her over.

"Here. I want you to have a shot of this." I pulled back a towel to reveal a bottle of vodka.

She stood back, shaking her head. "I don't think that's such a good idea."

"One shot isn't going to get you drunk. It's just going to calm your nerves, make it easier to be around those people." I spun the bottle in my hand. "The best part is, this is unflavored vodka. People won't be able to smell it on your breath, so one shot will literally do nothing but settle you down. Just trust me on this one."

"Fat chance."

"You don't think it will help you relax?" I unscrewed the cap and had a shot myself. This wouldn't be easy to say, but if I didn't, Sam probably wouldn't take the vodka. "You know that thing when you do something for somebody else that isn't out of spite or malice or a personal desire to see them fall flat on their face or have their spirit broken by epic failure?"

She squinted, like she tried to figure out what I meant. "Do you mean a good deed?"

I had a few more swallows of vodka and pointed to her, nodding. "That thing."

Sam gasped. "Wait. Are you trying to do something nice for me? Is that what this is?"

"You don't need to get all worked up over it. Either you take the shot or you don't." I tipped the bottle up and downed about two more shots.

Sam took the bottle from my hand and drank. Her face tightened as she forced some vodka down her throat. "It burns."

"That means it's working." She gave me the bottle and I took another swig "You've got this."

I walked Sam to the locker room. Coach Mort paced back and forth outside, probably waiting for the cheerleaders to arrive. Sam's gaze darted to the floor. I decided to run some interference. The less time he had to possibly remember her, the better.

I said hello to the paunchy, balding man slouched in his windbreaker and shook his hand. Nothing about his touch said demon. Coach Mort was human. Being face-to-face with him after learning what he'd done to Sam left me feeling disappointed and let down. I expected more out of our meeting. I wanted to be proud of him, to slap his butt and tell him he'd done a good job. But there'd been no duty in his actions, no desire to see the world crumble one soul at a time. He was just a selfish piece of dung. I respected what he'd been able to pull off, but I still didn't like him.

"Hey, it's the badminton pro," Coach Mort said.

I bowed. "I understand you're pretty impressed with my friend here."

"She's got some moves."

If anyone knew about that, it would be Coach Mort. "Yes she does. Hey, be good to her, okay? She's a little nervous."

Coach Mort gave me a faux salute. "Yes, sir. I treat all my girls with the utmost care."

I walked outside and down behind the bleachers, where most of the students hung out during the game. Jenny had her hair up in a ponytail with a bow in green and white—the school's colors. How precious. I smiled and waved.

She returned my smile weakly, then resumed whatever conversation she'd been engaged in. It took me a moment to notice, but the kids seemed very aware of my presence. I got a handful of repulsed looks. A few guys made sure to shove their shoulder into me as they walked by. Worse, not one girl gave me an interested look. Not one.

I saw what was going on here.

I smirked at the crowd. With one rumor, I'd been excommunicated from the entire student population. Usually I would've been the one spreading lies and ruining other people's popularity, but not at this silly bizarro school.

To Heaven with them. I popped a cig in my mouth and lit up. Some kid from my English class tried to look menacing as he got in my face. Too bad the *Angry Birds* shirt he wore under his jacket kind of undercut his intimidation factor.

"You should go," he said. "Nobody wants you here."

I blew smoke in his face, hoping he would retaliate so I could show everyone who they were messing with, but he didn't make a move, the coward.

"Yeah, that's what I thought," I said, pushing him aside. I needed to find Josh. I scanned the crowd and finally spotted him hanging around a group of kids by the concession stand.

"What's up?" he asked.

"I'm no good here. That rumor has everyone spooked. Let's meet up after the game so we can go over anything you learned."

Josh shook his head. "We'll have to do it tomorrow. I'm taking Sam out."

I swallowed my surprise. He probably would have loved to see me look shocked, but no way would I give him that satisfaction. "Really?"

"She was pretty shaken up yesterday, so I told her I'd take her out for ice cream after the game tonight. Give her a chance to get away from everything and have some fun."

That girl and her ice cream. Ridiculous. "Where are you two going?"

"A place that serves ice cream."

"No shit." Like I cared anyway.

Josh and Sam were going on a date? I didn't like that one bit. I bet they just wanted to collude against me or, worse, they actually liked each other. The thought of those two blissfully happy together made the fire in my veins run cold. The idea in general disgusted me, but Josh didn't deserve Sam. Period. I had to stop this… Or at least make sure the date didn't go well.

Kyle stood by himself, playing with his iPhone by one of the light poles. I put my hand on his shoulder, making him jump.

"Don't do that, man, you scared me," he said. "Which is not a smart thing to do, considering the rumors going around."

I rolled my eyes. "Yeah, thanks for bringing that up. You busy later? I need to call in that favor you promised me."

"I'm in, so long as we're not, you know, disposing of any bodies or anything."

I mock laughed at Kyle. For all I knew, it might come to that. "I'll be in the parking lot. Come find me after the game."

Scanning the crowd of students, I noticed a lot of them buried their faces in popcorn and soda, leaving zero eyes on me. Good.

I snuck around to the back of the small concessions building behind the bleachers. A large tin of jalapenos sat on the counter, open and halfway used. I peeked inside and saw that they needed to empty out the nasty juice. Since none of the concessions people were looking, I took it upon myself to do it and dumped part of the juice in the bin holding un-popped popcorn and the rest in the ice for the drinks.

That would teach them to mess with me.

NINETEEN

VOMIT COMET

I cracked a window so I could listen to the radio while chain-smoking outside the Benz, waiting for the game to end. The longer I waited, the fewer cheers I heard. Clearly, tonight featured another sterling performance from the lowly Frady-McNeely Eagles.

When the PA system announced the end of the game, the crowd started filing out of the stadium. I got a few more angry looks, but most people seemed too distracted by my awesome car to notice me.

"No way, is that your ride?" Kyle asked, standing on the other side of the car.

"Yeah, man," I said. "Hop in."

I opened the door and slid in, followed by Kyle on the passenger side. He gawked at the interior, running his hand over the dashboard. "Unreal. Why don't you drive it to school every day?"

I laughed. "You know how many idiots would key this thing if I did that? Especially with that rumor about me going around?"

I let Kyle play with the radio while I waited for Josh and Sam to appear. After a few minutes, they emerged from the gym. I turned on the engine.

"So, what are we doing?" Kyle asked.

"Following Sam and Josh. I want to make sure they stay out of trouble."

They got into Josh's car and drove out of the parking lot. I made sure to keep a comfortable space between us.

"Okay... Why do you care what they do?"

I didn't have a good answer off the top of my head. If I said I didn't want them to have fun on their date, he might get the wrong idea about my intentions. "I don't trust them together."

"All right."

I don't know if he bought my excuse or not, but he didn't say anything else about it, so I didn't either.

We followed them to Goodberry's, a locally owned frozen custard place. I parked in an unlit spot across the street. A lot of high school kids hung out there, only instead of drinking beer they ate custard. The whole thing felt rather silly.

Since Kyle was a high school kid, he also wanted to hang out there. "Can we get some? My stomach is raging and could use a little Goodberry's."

"We're on a stakeout, we're not here to get some ice cream, or custard, or whatever they serve. If we go up there to order something, they'll see us, which goes against the entire point of a stakeout." Sheesh. "Tell me about that twisted sister I saw you making out with after school."

Kyle slunk down in his seat. "You saw that?"

"Everyone in the commons area saw it. Who is she?"

"Just a girl I mess around with sometimes. It's not serious or anything." Kyle laughed under his breath. "She's trying to be part of my harem, I guess."

"Look at you." I held out my fist and Kyle bumped it. "Good job. I didn't take you for a player."

"Th... thanks," he said with a bashful look on his face. "The ladies love my lanky frame."

Josh and Sam sat next to each other on a low brick wall, eating their custard.

The Templar put his arm around Sam. I hoped he didn't try to get too physical with her.

"Josh is making his move," Kyle said with a chuckle.

Better not be.

Kyle laughed. "What do you think they're saying?"

"Josh is probably consoling Sam about some guy she likes who doesn't like her while at the same time trying to work up the courage to tell her the shocking truth about his chronic bedwetting, and that he tends to suck his thumb when he's anxious." I turned to Kyle. "It's all a bit sad, really."

A hunched, hooded figure limped past us and across the street. The figure didn't exactly come across as the type to frequent a *custard* shop on a Friday night. I sat up.

Kyle noticed him too. "Who is that guy?"

Before I could say anything, the figure ripped off the hoodie and screamed. It sounded demonic in nature, a growl I felt in my bones, complete with a screeching that made my eardrums ring. The man stretched his black arms out. The right arm ended in razor-sharp claws, like mine. The other was nothing more than a stump. This had to be the minion Josh attacked.

Josh and Sam jumped up. It looked like the three of them exchanged some words. I couldn't make out what Josh said to the beast, but it didn't seem pleasant. He threw his custard at the minion, who slapped it away.

Effective weapon, Josh. Really. Not just saying that.

I started the car. "Get in the back seat."

"What?"

I grabbed Kyle by the arm and threw him into the back. The tires screeched as I made a U-turn. I pressed my foot down on the gas, quickly closing the distance between us and the minion until I ran him over. I hoped the suspension would be okay after such a violent hit. I rolled down my window.

"Look at this. What are the odds of seeing you two here?" I asked.

"Bartholomew?" Sam asked. She seemed disoriented.

"In the flesh." I grinned. "Need a ride?"

The pair wasted no time getting into the passenger side of the Benz, with Sam taking the front seat. I hit the gas pedal and we were off.

"Good job with the minion," I said to Josh.

"Thanks."

I tried to smack him, but he was out of reach. I tried again, hoping I could somehow overcome that last inch or two separating his body from my hand. No luck.

"You moron. How could you let him find you?"

He slapped my hand away. "I don't know."

"You suck at your job. The Templars only let you in because of your dad, didn't they?"

"I didn't purposely let him find me."

I rolled my eyes. "I know. That's why you suck at your job."

"Shut up."

Something didn't feel right with the car. I turned the wheel side to side, checking the Benz's maneuverability. The car felt a bit sluggish. "Something's wrong," I said.

"What?" Sam asked.

"I don't know. It's like we're—"

Sam screamed. The minion crawled onto the rear of the Mercedes, digging its claws into the trunk to keep from falling off. Son of a bitch.

If Sam's scream was loud, Kyle's was earth shattering. "Oh my God. What is that thing? What's going on?" He grabbed my shoulder. "We're gonna die."

"Calm down," I said, shrugging his hand off. "Nobody's going to die. I think."

"You *think*?" he shrieked.

The minion smashed the rear window. Josh and Kyle thrust themselves forward and down, trying to evade the monster. Kyle sounded like a banshee. The kid had some serious lungpower.

If this kept up, somebody might really die.

"Of course, accidents do happen." I jerked the steering wheel to the left. The minion slid off the side of the car, but its claws remained embedded in the trunk, keeping him from falling. I heard each claw scrape against my baby. Add a new paint job to my To Do list.

"Stop ruining my car," I shouted at the thing.

A claw pierced the roof as the minion moved forward. I swerved to the right, but the claw didn't budge.

"Everybody buckle up. This is about to get… scary," I said, smirking.

"It's not scary now?" Kyle shrieked.

I moved across the yellow lines and into the oncoming traffic. Sam fumbled with the seatbelt while praying buckled up and began praying. I couldn't tell if the two yokels in the back buckled up. Cars honked and swerved to get out of my way. I weaved around them as best I could, hoping the minion would either lose its grip or accept defeat and give up the chase. It did neither.

"You're going to get us *all* killed," Sam said. "Even you."

"Ha."

Kyle and Josh both screamed in the backseat as I barely missed a car that flew by us. The side mirror ripped off, I came so close to a collision. I glanced at Sam, her eyes wide and frightened, breathing so fast her heart might explode. I'll admit it, chances were more than fair I'd get us killed.

"Fine," I said. "We'll try it your way."

I steered back onto our side of the street. The claws disappeared from the roof, but I didn't for one second believe the minion had gone. Things were never that simple. The sunroof shattered, spraying glass all over us. A black hand reached down and buried itself in my shoulder.

So much for my charm protecting me from evil.

Thanks a lot, Remy. You Cajun greaser.

"I only want the Templar," the minion growled. "The rest of you can go."

"Then get your hand out of my shoulder. You're ruining my coat." I shot a glance at the minion, with his black skin and short hair.

Wait a second.

I looked up at him again.

Marlon!

"Marlon, you old dog," I said. "What are you doing here?"

"Who is that?" Marlon leaned into the car. His face lit up. "Bartholomew? That you?"

Josh must've thought now would be a good time to do something stupid, because the next thing I knew both Marlon and I got a nice dose of holy water. The minion screamed and pulled his head out of the car. I groaned through clenched teeth. The holy water melted Marlon's claws into my shoulder, as if the holy water on its own didn't hurt enough.

"Smart guy," I said. "That burns me too."

"Sorry," Josh said.

Marlon ducked his head back into the car. "Just let me kill the kid, Bart. Please?"

"Right now, I don't care who kills who. Just stop ruining my suits, okay?"

"There's a monster on the roof and you're worried about your *clothes*?" Kyle asked. "What the Hell is wrong with you people?"

What's wrong with me is that this ensemble cost well over a thousand dollars.

"Not now, Kyle," I said, too occupied with Marlon to argue with the kid about the merits of wearing nice clothes. I tried to pull the minion's arm out of my shoulder. His claws tugged against bone and muscle, refusing to budge. The holy water fused us together, which made swerving the car to get him off us nothing more than an exercise in torture at this point.

"Come on, Bart. Just give me the hunter," Marlon said. "You know you want to."

"Don't call me Bart." I glanced over at Sam. "Wrap your hands around his forearm."

She narrowed her eyes. "You want me to *what*?"

"Do it," I said.

Sam hesitated for a moment, then closed her fingers around Marlon's flesh. It sizzled and burned at her touch. The minion screamed bloody murder, but she held firm.

"Now what?" she asked.

"Hold on until you can break it off," I said. Marlon's claws wiggled back and forth in my shoulder, which didn't hurt. At all.

And I thought a gallon of holy water to the face hurt.

Sam's hands sunk into Marlon's molten forearm until I couldn't tell where she began and he ended. Glancing down, the mess looked like someone threw up Brunswick stew all over my shoulder. Bits of Marlon's arm dripped onto the middle console between Sam and me, which only caused more damage to my car.

"I'm sorry, sweetie." I patted the steering wheel.

Kyle stuck his head between his knees. "I'm going to be sick."

"Don't you dare," I said. "This car has had enough damage tonight. Swallow that shit back."

Marlon's arm looked ready to break off. I nodded at Sam. She pulled, ripping the minion's arm from his body.

Sure would've been nice if she'd gotten it out of my shoulder, too.

I slammed on the brakes. Marlon flew twenty feet in the air, then crashed face first into the asphalt. After rolling several feet, he stood, clothes torn to shreds, face scuffed and bloody. Since he didn't have any fingers to flip us off with, the minion made a *fuck you* motion with his arms.

What a jerkoff. I tightened my grip on the steering wheel and floored the gas. Marlon stood his ground as the Benz sped toward him. We slammed into him, making a large dent in the front hood. He bounced over the car and landed on the road behind us.

I turned to Josh. "Now you can holy water his ass."

Josh fumbled to get his door open, shock making him even more useless. Sam had to reach back and help him. He stumbled out of the car, ran over to Marlon and poured the holy water on his face. The minion convulsed with pain and Josh sauntered back to the car, making a gesture like he washed his hands of the situation.

"Easy enough," he said, getting in. "So, that wasn't so ba—"

Kyle threw up all over Josh, who stared at him for a moment with wide eyes, then vomited as well.

I closed my eyes and rubbed my temples. "Anybody else need to hurl?"

"I'm okay, thanks," Sam said.

When I worked on my own, I never, ever had issues with my car getting messed up. Now the blessed thing was probably totaled, and we had to drive the rest of the night with the interior reeking of throw-up. It was expected some items of clothing would be damaged, but that didn't make the pain any easier to deal with.

"Can somebody please explain to me what just happened?" Kyle asked. "Are we going to jail for killing that thing? We are, aren't we? I can't go on the run, man. I can't. I'm not built for that life."

Kyle's rambling mercifully ended when he passed out, his head plopping down into his own vomit. One problem solved. However, I still had the issue of Marlon's arm being stuck in my shoulder and Sam's fingers in the middle of it all.

Sam pulled, trying to wrench her fingers free from his molten forearm. My shoulder exploded in pain as she yanked and yanked.

She gave me a knowing look. "This isn't good."

"It's *not?*" I snorted. "Look, stop trying to get it out all at once. All you're doing is hurting me. Try going one finger at a time."

I tried to pry her fingers out of the forearm. That might have worked, but my fingers burned when they touched her, which just made an even bigger mess of things as my flesh began to melt into theirs, creating an odd, gross sort of three-way of gunk.

"Maybe if we got out of the car first," Sam said.

"That's too much trouble," I said. Grabbing the forearm, I tried to wrench it away from Sam. "Josh, go around and pull on Sam. Maybe we can pry it loose."

Josh got out and opened Sam's door. He wrapped his hands around her shoulders.

"Do it," I said. Sam and Josh yanked in their direction, while I pulled in the other direction. Her fingers slowly broke free.

"This is so gross. I can feel the goo bubbling between my fingers," Sam said.

"Don't stop." They tugged so hard parts of my shoulder moved with them. That's all I needed—an entire chunk of my shoulder ripped out. "Come on. Put your back into it. Your ass. Anything."

Josh and Sam audibly strained as they pulled. After about a minute of tugging, Sam's hand broke free from Marlon's forearm. The change in momentum made Josh fall backward. Sam stared at the black and red mush all over her hand.

"This is so disgusting," she said, wiping her hand on the floorboard.

"Sure. Why not mess up the floorboards?" I sighed. "It's not like the rest of my baby isn't dead."

"Sorry," Sam said.

I waved her off. "Whatever. Can we just get this thing out of my shoulder?"

Sam leaned in close, inspecting the wound. She dry heaved. "Oh my gosh."

I rolled my eyes. "Just don't do it on me. I can take only so much."

Josh got to his feet outside. "Um, guys."

"We're a bit busy at the moment," I said.

"The minion is gone."

Sam's gaze darted behind the car. She moved so fast her hand bumped against Marlon's forearm. I winced.

"Sorry," she said, patting my shoulder.

"Can you take care of Marlon?" I asked Josh. "I'm kind of stuck at the moment." I touched Sam's shirt. "If you'd do the honors."

Her fingers hovered over Marlon's hand, like she tried to figure out where to begin. She touched one of the claws with her thumb and index finger and pulled gently. His hand melted some more.

Holy Heaven that hurts.

"I'm sorry," she said.

I opened my car door. "Josh. Come yank this thing out. Sam's got too physical a touch."

"But I haven't found—"

"Don't care. Do it now."

"Fine." Josh ran over and took Sam's seat in the car. She stood outside. The Templar took a deep breath, grabbed the claw and tried to wrest it free. It barely moved.

"Seriously, I'm going to start crying if you don't hurry up," I said. I couldn't stand the pain.

"I wouldn't mind seeing that," Josh said.

I was in too much pain to come up with a proper comeback.

Sam moved around outside, looking for Marlon. "Josh, I

don't see—"

The minion flew out of the shadows, tackling Sam. Josh's attention immediately went to the fake angel. I tugged on his arm.

"Me first," I said. "Let her do her thing. She'll be fine."

Josh continued trying to get the claws out of my shoulder, but all he succeeded in doing was torturing me. My eyes watered. After another minute of pain, the likes of which I hadn't felt since taking a cannonball to the gut at Gettysburg, Josh freed up Marlon's hand enough to where he could peel the fingers out of me, then the rest of the arm.

"This is the nastiest thing I have ever done," Josh said.

"Try being boiled in a vat of acid." I threw open my door and got out.

Sam and Marlon fell to the ground as he attacked her with flailing elbows. She covered her face with her hands in an effort to defend herself. Seeing him fight without hands was pretty impressive. They rolled over and I got an up-close look at Marlon's face, or what remained of it. Even his demonic skin looked messed up beyond repair.

"Marlon, how are you still moving around? Can't you just go back to Hell?" I asked.

The minion tried to speak, but only gurgling sound came out. The black goo that squirted out of his throat made me shudder.

Josh rushed over and grabbed Marlon. He tried to keep the minion's arms away from Sam's neck. "You going to help or not?"

"I guess." I moved to Marlon's side. I reached down, cupping my left hand around his chin. I put my foot on his back and snapped off what remained of his head. A wheezing sound came from the neck wound, like air escaping.

I dropped the head on the ground. "You two better move back."

Josh and Sam rolled away as flames engulfed Marlon's lifeless body, returning him to Hell. When the body disintegrated, the fire died out, leaving nothing but a charred spot on the road.

TWENTY

I AM A BETTER LOOKING VERSION OF TONY SOPRANO

I used the rest of the healing goo Sam gave me to fix my shoulder. Took a little while to kick in, but everything felt as good as new soon enough. "Do you have more of this stuff?"

Sam shook her head. "That's it."

I glanced off to the side. "Can you get more? I'm going to go out on a limb and say we'll probably need it."

She crossed her arms and sank into her seat.

"I'll try." Her tone suggested there was a better chance of seeing the Pope snort cocaine than getting more.

"Do that," I said as I started driving. This night had better end. And soon.

Kyle still hadn't come to when we pulled to a stop next to his car in the school parking lot. Josh tried to wake him up, but the kid remained dead to the world. I got out and grabbed him by the wrist, dragging him out into the parking lot.

"We can't just leave him like this," Sam pleaded, moving next to me.

"He'll be fine," I said.

Josh got out and joined in the conversation. "At least get him in his car."

He *would* take Sam's side in all this.

I ground my teeth together. "Do what you want. But one of you dig the keys out of his pocket. I'm not getting that close to his vomit or his junk."

Sam narrowed her gaze at me and kneeled down next to Kyle.

Josh laid his hand on her shoulder. "I'll do it."

"And they say chivalry is dead," I said.

Josh patted him down, trying to avoid the vomit-stained areas. When he got to Kyle's left pocket, he reached in and pulled out the keys. After he unlocked the door, Sam and I tossed Kyle in the back seat. Sam pushed the door's lock button, and then tossed the keys on Kyle, so when he woke up he'd be good to go.

I got into my car and slammed the door shut, watching Sam as she slid into the passenger seat. "That was so sweet of you to do that for Kyle. It's like... you're an *angel*."

Sam stuck her tongue out at me.

"You really are an attractive woman when you want to be, you know that?" I said, pulling the gearshift into drive.

After twenty minutes, we made it to her apartment. The two of them got out of my soiled car and started for her place. Sam stopped and put her hand on Josh's arm. He carried on walking and she came back to the Mercedes. Just the two of us and the wheezy hum of my dying Benz now. She made a motion for me to roll my window down. I obliged her.

"What?" I asked.

She rested her forearms on the roof of the car and kept her gaze on the ground. "I'm not sure how to ask this."

I smiled. "If it gets you in any kind of trouble, the answer is yes, I'm game."

She laughed under her breath. "No, not that." Her eyes met mine. "What were you doing at Goodberry's?"

I laughed nervously.

Damn. Damn, damn, damn. Damn.

"Saving your ass," I said. "You're welcome for that, by the way."

"Thanks. But... *why* were you there? You couldn't have known about the minion."

I glanced at the dashboard, trying to think of something. And fast. "Kyle wanted some custard, or whatever it is they serve there. I saw a shady character coming at you, so I sprang into action."

Sam narrowed her eyes, clearly not buying my story. "You followed us, didn't you?"

Busted. Ah, well. Best just go with it now. Wait. Why am I worried about what some pseudo-angel thinks? I'm a demon. We don't care about things like feelings. "Yes, I was," I said firmly. "I wanted to make sure you two weren't getting… copacetic with each other. I'm keeping my mind on the task at hand. I just wanted to make sure you were doing the same."

Sam huffed. "You've been keeping your eye on the ball?"

"Both of them."

"And how does taking Jenny McPherson's virginity play into all that? Or flirting with Miss Evans? Or anything you've done, for that matter? The only thing you've focused on is how to get *out* of the task at hand."

I huffed right back at her, putting some spit into it, which I had to wipe off the steering wheel. "That's not true. All that stuff has been in the name of finding the Shard and getting the heck out of Dodge. This little date you went on with Josh? Totally outside the established parameters of our assignment. And if you must know, yes. If things had heated up between you two, I'd have stepped in. Thrown a trashcan at Josh's head or something. I don't need you compromised by things like feelings."

The thought of her having feelings for him nauseated me.

Sam stood there for a moment.

"I don't think that's the truth." Her mouth hung slightly open. "You're jealous, aren't you?" she asked, taking a couple of steps back.

Huh? What?

I burst out laughing. "Surely you jest."

She grinned and pointed at me. "That's it. You're jealous. It makes total sense. You never had a mom to hug you and tell you she loved you, or tell you to stop acting like a brat. Now I'm here, and what do you know? The demon finds out he likes being treated this way."

I waved her off. "Hush, you. Go home. You have no idea what, or who, I am. What I've done. You can't possibly understand."

Sam laughed. "I understand. I understand men always want what they can't have. Or in your case, never had."

My horns pushed against my skull. This almost-angel talked about things way above her pay grade. "Samantha, if I wanted you, I would take you."

I rolled up the window and sped off before she had a chance to respond.

I needed a new car. Yes, the damage to the exterior could be fixed, but the interior would always have a barf-like stench from now on, which I refused to tolerate.

I called Quincy on Saturday morning to help me pick out a new ride. Without him, if I strolled into a Mercedes dealership and tried to buy a car myself, they'd probably assume I was a drug dealer and call the cops. I had the car towed to the dealership, so it would be there for trade-in, though I'd probably get twenty-five cents and a slice of bacon for the car, if I was lucky.

Quincy's face looked flushed when he picked me up. He seemed preoccupied. We didn't exchange a word as he got on the Interstate. He kept tapping his fingers on the steering wheel, like he tried to speak in Morse code.

I couldn't take the silent treatment any longer. It gave me goose bumps. "Are you okay? You haven't even asked why I'm buying a new car so soon after getting out of Hell."

He stared blankly at the road ahead. "Yeah. Um, sorry. Why are you?"

The man didn't seem to be in the same zip code as me, let alone the same car. "What's up with you? Are you on meth?"

Quincy shook his head. "Long night."

Bull. I know a crackhead when I see one.

"You and the missus have too much fun with the whippets again?"

A quiet laugh escaped him. "That's it."

Something seemed off about him. I didn't know what, but something. Quincy typically bitched up a storm when he did a job for me, trying to find some sneaky way to alter our contract to his advantage. I snapped my fingers at him. "Seriously. Are you all there today?"

"Sure," he said, glancing over at me. "Why wouldn't I be?"

It was the first thing he'd said that sounded like he had full command of his faculties.

We pulled into the Mercedes dealership. A salesman greeted us within thirty seconds of parking. His greased-back hair and deep Southern accent was typical for a car dealer in this area of the country.

"I'm Stan. How can I help you two gentlemen?" he boomed. "It's a beautiful day for a new Mercedes."

"Uh..." Quincy stammered.

My gaze locked on a black S65 AMG. "We had my dad's old Benz towed in earlier today. Some hooligans got hold of it and went for a joyride. Did some unmentionable things to it."

Things I'm going to convince myself never happened.

Stan touched his hair with the tip of his finger, like he wanted to scratch an itch without messing up his greasy hair. "Yeah, I saw. They sure tore the heck out of that thing. Did a wild boar jump on the roof or something?"

"Wish I knew." I *wished* a wild boar had done this. An animal would've been easier to dispose of, and my jacket wouldn't have been soiled by minion goo. I pointed at the S65. "Can we take that for a test drive? Dad figures now is as good a time as any for a new car."

I talked Stan into letting me drive, saying that my "father" let me drive the car as much as he did.

"So the Benz will pretty much be like both of ours," I said.

Stan cocked an eyebrow. "You must have some skills to be able to handle a performance vehicle like this."

I smirked. "You have no idea."

Stan let me take the car out on the Beltline. I drove eighty-five miles per hour, weaving in and out of the lanes. Poor Stan looked so terrified *I* could practically see his life flashing before his eyes.

"Son, you do realize you break it, you buy it," he said.

"Don't worry, I won't break it. But we're still buying it."

"Thank the good Lord in Heaven," Stan said. I glanced over and saw him cross himself. I tried not to laugh at him.

The S65 had me more excited than a room full of virgins unsure about their sexuality. With six hundred and twenty-one horsepower, how could I not get excited? So what if it cost over two hundred grand? I'd been flush with cash ever since I took part in the sacking of Rome and made off with a few tons of gold and marble statues of naked women. The statues I'd sold to museums for a nice fortune, and the gold… well, I just kept that bit of information to myself. I will say that my stash would make a pirate jealous.

I had Quincy write a check for Stan, who may or may not have wet himself during the test drive. Fortunately, I didn't come across any nasty salesman urine in the car.

After filling out all the paperwork and I officially owned the car, I invited Quincy over to my place for a celebratory drink and to discuss what kind of favor he'd like me to do in exchange for helping me get a new car so quickly. He accepted.

It took me no time at all to drive home in my new Benz, which I'd decided to name Sweet Claudette, mainly because I'd never driven a sweet girl called Claudette the way I drove this car.

Quincy still had a dazed look as he walked into my condo a full ten minutes after I did.

He slumped down on the couch, staring at the wall. I poured us both a shot of Cognac. I handed the man his and sat across from him in my loveseat.

"Cheers," I said, holding up the glass. I downed my drink in one smooth swallow.

Quincy held onto his, still staring at the wall. I could've understood his fascination if there were a nude portrait of myself hanging up there, but nothing graced that wall.

"Okay. No more games," I said. "What are you on? You chasing the dragon?"

He stood and walking over to the wall, running his hand over the plaster. "I never told you," he said, still sounding like he was away with the fairies and not in my living room. "I met your teacher."

"Which one?"

"Miss Evans. They forgot to have me sign some paperwork when I enrolled you. I went back later that day and met her."

Miss Evans. Of course. Any man who met that creature would want to talk about it. "Lovely lady, isn't she?"

Quincy smiled, like he performed some sort of automated reaction. The rest of his face didn't follow suit. It looked creepy. "Very."

What was going on with him? I stood up and moved closer to him. "Quin, you—"

He snatched up the remote and the television sprang to life.

"TV? You trying to watch a stoner movie?"

Quincy turned the television to the religious channel and thumbed up the volume, negating a good bit of my tolerance. One of the televangelists preached about a time he volunteered at a food bank and some other happy junk. The man's voice made it feel like spikes pierced my brain. I grunted. I needed to figure out a way to block that channel.

"Turn it off."

Quincy smirked as he turned the sound all the way up. At normal volumes, I can handle the onslaught of televangelism, but I still hadn't figured out how to handle high volumes. At this level, the fake preaching felt like a handful of grenades exploding in my head. My horns pushed against my skull, begging to come out. I fell to the floor, squeezing my head between my hands, as if that would ease the pain.

Quincy pulled out a wooden knife he'd been hiding behind his back as he stood above me. He got down on one knee, held the knife up, then brought it down as hard as he could. I raised my arm to shield my face and jerked my body to the side just enough that he missed my head and got my arm instead. The puncture wound burned, like he'd injected holy water into me. My entire arm went numb. That knife must've been carved out of wood from a crucifix. How had he gotten his hands on that?

I rolled across the floor away from him, the knife still lodged in my arm.

"I have to do this," he said.

My awesome ninja rolling maneuver brought me

conveniently close to the big screen. I hit the power button, bringing me instant relief from that televangelist's rambling.

"Who wants me dead? Miss Evans?" I asked, getting to my feet. That didn't make any sense. Unless... maybe we were closer to the truth than any of us realized?

Quincy lunged for me. I tried to push him away, but he grabbed the knife's handle and pulled, trying to get it out of my arm. The blade rubbed against bone. Not fun. I headbutted him before he could do it again and he staggered back, holding his head.

Quincy screamed and ran toward me. I yanked the knife out of my arm. It burned my hand. I stabbed him in the neck with it. Momentum carried his body headfirst into the wall, where his head lodged as the life drained from him.

I stared at Quincy, bent over with his head stuck in my wall. What in Heaven had Miss Evans done to make him go off the reservation like this? I pulled him out of the wall and let his body fall backward onto the floor. His face was frozen in shock, like some post-modern take on Edvard Munch.

This wasn't like Casey's possession. The Black Cloud of Death consumed his body, using it like a puppet. Someone placed Quincy under a curse of some sort, like a high level hypnotism. Quincy's blood had slinked down the wall. Great. Now I had to repaint the walls.

How did Miss Evans fit into all of this? Sure, the woman looked sickeningly hot, but that—

It smacked me in the face like an angry mother's hand.

The Charm of Agrippina. When I wore it around Miss Evans, I felt almost ambivalent to her. But when I didn't have the stupid thing on, the need to have her almost drove me mad with desire. Somehow, Miss Evans was the key to this entire thing. Could she be Vixen?

I found my cellphone on the floor and called Sam. For some reason, Josh answered.

"Where's Sam? I need to talk to her now."

"What do you need? She's busy," Josh said.

"I got the sudden urge to volunteer at an animal shelter."

"Are you serious?"

I held the phone away from my ear for a moment. "No,

you dolt. I need you two to get over here as soon as possible. No more questions. Just get in the car and drive."

Surviving all these attempts on my life made me feel like Tony Soprano, except much better looking.

Josh laughed. "Big bad demon needs some help?"

"Didn't I save your mortal ass last night?"

Josh stayed silent on the other end.

"That's what I thought." I walked into my bedroom and opened the dresser. I got an undershirt and wrapped it around my knife wound. A little sensation came back to my arm, along with a touch of excruciating pain. "Just get over here. And bring some tarp."

"Tarp? Did you kill somebody or something?"

I didn't have time for this. If I said yes, he'd probably call the cops on me. "Clock's ticking. Move it."

I ended the call and dialed Remy.

"Yo," he said. "I think I have a line on that thing you asked me about."

"Excellent." If Sam couldn't get hold of more healing ointment, Remy probably would be able to. "I need something else now, too."

Remy sighed. "I know we go back a ways, but you're pushing it, Bartholomew."

I told him what I needed. He didn't say anything for a bit.

"Let me double check, but I think you can get whatever you want at this place I'm sending you to."

I thanked him and hung up. I went back into the living room and stood over Quincy's body. I didn't want him lying around here, stinking up the place until nightfall. He had to be disposed of ASAP. I yanked the knife out of his neck.

"Have fun down below," I said.

I placed the knife in the sink and set about thinking of the best way to get him out of here. Things were so much easier in the old days. Just put an arrow, axe, bullet, whatever, through someone's head, dump them in the middle of nowhere, and people would assume Indians, barbarians, or thieves did in the person. Thanks to the invention of investigative tools, it was pretty much impossible to hide anything anymore. Sure, the new technology helped diminish people's belief in the

Almighty, which couldn't have made me happier, but that sure as Heaven didn't do me any good at the moment.

Thirty minutes later, Josh knocked at my door.

"Where's Sam?" I asked.

"She went to get the tarp and asked me to go on without her," he said, moving past me. He looked a bit shiny around the edges, like he'd been sweating. He saw Quincy's body and froze. His jaw seemed to jut out as he focused his gaze on me.

"This was your big emergency? You really did kill someone?"

"Basically, but it's not that simple. He tried to kill me first."

Josh knelt down next to Quincy and closed his eyes. He muttered some sort of prayer that made me a little nauseous. Not that it would've helped Quincy, who was probably being processed by Hell at this very moment.

"Amen," he said, finishing the prayer. "I'd ask you how it happened, but I know you'd only lie."

"You might be surprised."

"I doubt it." He ran his finger around Quincy's knife wound. "Where's the weapon?"

"In the sink." I held up my arm. "If you'll notice, he attacked me first. With a weapon carved from the wood of a crucifix."

"Maybe you stabbed yourself after the fact to hide your guilt."

"That could not be more convoluted."

Josh walked over to the sink and picked up the knife, twirling the blade around in his hand.

"So I'm thinking the easiest way to get rid of the body is fake a suicide note, then take him up to the roof and toss him off," I said. "The impact should take care of the rest."

Josh stared at the knife. "I don't think that's a good idea."

"We can't call the cops, if that's what you're thinking. I stopped paying them when I got put away." My cell rang. Sam. "How far away are you?"

"Maybe a few minutes? I got the tarp."

I glanced over at Josh, who remained fixated on the knife. The scene did not make me feel warm and fuzzy.

"Get here as fast as you can." I didn't have time to end the call before Josh rushed at me and tried to bury the knife in my gut. I jumped to the side, barely missing the blade. "And here I thought you'd promised to be a good boy."

Josh smirked. "You murdered someone. The deal is off."

He lashed at me, making me trip over the coffee table.

I grabbed his hand with both of mine to keep the knife from stabbing me and let my claws come out. I dug them into Josh's wrist, making him grunt in pain. He punched me in the face with his free hand. Laughing, I threw him off me and across the coffee table with all the strength I could muster. I got on top of him before he could react.

"You really think a normal fist can hurt me?" I straddled him and pinned his hands to the floor. If someone walked in and saw us without knowing the context of the situation, they would've wondered if we were shooting a porno.

"Get off me."

"Do you want to die?" I asked. "Do you? Because I'm more than happy to oblige you if you do."

"Go to Hell," Josh spat on my face.

"Really?" The spit dripped down my chin.

"Demon scum."

My horns pushed against my skull. When it came to people trying to kill me, I drew the line at one a day. I grabbed the knife and wrested it from his grip. The blade dug into my hand and burned. Better than it digging into my chest and obliterating me. Josh struggled to free himself, but my demon strength kept him in place. I held the knife against his throat.

Sam burst through the door, tarp in hand, a wide-eyed look on her face.

"Josh." She stopped when she saw that I'd turned the tables. I figured she also saw Quincy's dead body when she shouted "Oh, God." The tarp fell to the floor as she covered her face with her hands. "What have you done?"

I tilted my head toward Quincy. "I can explain. It wasn't my fault."

"He's lying." Josh said, with only a slight hint of venom. "Send him back to Hell."

I nodded at Josh. "This one decided to get in on the act. Clearly it didn't work. Now I'm trying to decide if I want to kill him too."

"Don't," Sam said. "Please. You know what it means."

I did, but part of me didn't care. So much bullshit flew around this whole thing, I just wanted it to end. Yes, an eternity of being Lucifer's butt-buddy would suck, and having to listen to Wolfie Hitler's chatting would grate on my last nerve, but putting a snot-nosed little kid like Josh six feet under for trying to get the better of me meant I'd at least go to my punishment with a smile on my face. I might even be able to talk Lucifer into getting him sent down with me.

Sam inched closer to me, her hands outstretched. "Bartholomew, I know you did what you did to Quincy out of self-defense. You know how I know?"

"How?"

She got down on her knees next to me. "Because nobody from Hell is breaking down your door to take you away. I'm the only one here. Nobody else. And I know you wouldn't keep a knife like that lying around. I also know that if you murder Josh, your parole, or whatever you want to call it, will be off the table."

She inched her hands closer to me.

"Do not use your little Hand of God thing on me!"

"Don't give me a reason to."

I slowly pulled the knife away from Josh's throat and handed it to Sam, who sat back and looked up at the ceiling, probably to thank the Big Jerk-off.

Josh shoved me to the side so he could stand up. He wiped the sweat from his face. "One day, demon. My father will be avenged."

"Do you listen to yourself when you say things like that?"

"Come on, Josh," Sam said. "He's got a point."

Josh's face turned a dark red. "You're taking that thing's side?"

I *tsked* him with my finger. Sam only did what Sam did best. Calming the situation. "You're done. Leave. If I see you again, I'll assume you're once again trying—and failing—to finish your father's job." I looked back at Sam. "I showed him mercy. I won't do it again. We kosher?"

She nodded. "I'm sorry it came to this."

I shrugged. "Whatever. Three's a crowd. Besides, we have work to do."

 TWENTY-ONE
THE DEMON COMES AROUND

Sam escorted Josh out to make sure neither of us tried to pull any "funny business." She actually said that, the cornball.

After sending the turncoat away, Sam and I still needed to figure out how to dispose of Quincy's body. I ran my idea of tossing him off the roof by her.

She looked at me, aghast. "No. Absolutely not."

"Come on. It's perfect. Put on your big boy pants and let's do this."

"I'm not throwing a dead body off the roof. That's disgusting."

"Your side can be so touchy." I sighed. She'd better not ask me to reimburse her for the tarp. "Fine, let's hear your grand idea. How do *you* suggest we get rid of the body?"

She shook her head. "I don't really have any ideas. This isn't exactly my area of expertise."

"I do have experience in this arena." I sat on the arm of the sofa. "Listen. Calling the cops is out. Period. I don't want to deal with the hassle, and I doubt the truth will set me free on this one. Normally I'd call one of my servants to take care of it…" I motioned toward Quincy's body. "But alas, he was the only one I had left."

"What about Remy?" she asked. "Maybe he has something

that can help?"

Not a bad idea. I'd bet Remy did have something that could make the body go *poof.*

"He might. Let's put Quincy in the tub so he won't keep leaking all over the floor. And here I thought we wouldn't get to use the tarp."

We rolled up Quincy in the tarp. I picked up my end of his body.

Sam grimaced as she wrapped her hands around the other. "They didn't tell me I'd be doing this kind of stuff when they offered me the job."

"They never do." I lifted the body, revealing a pool of blood on the carpet. Yet another stain.

We dumped the body in the tub, then set about cleaning up the bloodstains. Both of us were on our hands and knees, pouring cleaning liquid on the blood and blotting it up with towels. Like everything else I owned, this carpet hadn't come cheap.

"Should we be doing this right now?" she asked.

I gave her a stern glare. "I'm not coming home every night to a bloodstained carpet. I am not a college student, and I refuse to live like one. Got it?"

"Okay, okay."

After finishing with the carpet, I changed into a sleek ensemble that included black pants and a matching long-sleeved shirt. My suits needed a break from being destroyed. At least until I could buy some new ones.

We went to Remy's to find out where to go for something more powerful than the Charm of Agrippina. I hoped to give Remy's crazy-eyed assistant Marvin some grief, but he seemed to have the day off.

"No more," I said. I slammed the Charm of Agrippina on the counter. Looking at it reminded me of Miss Evans, and that I hadn't told Sam about her yet.

"I'm surprised you lasted this long." Remy picked up the charm. "I just got a new shipment in the back. Let me see what

I got."

"Awesome," I said, giving him a thumbs-up.

Remy disappeared into the back. He returned a moment later with what looked like a wooden tooth the size of a hot dog. "Here you go. It's a third party item, so it's safe to touch. Doesn't have the power of the charm, but it will help in the meantime."

I picked it up and felt its smooth texture. "Anything special I need to do?"

"Just keep it on you."

I stashed the tooth in my pocket. "Easy enough. Now, where do we go for that other item?"

"Charlotte," he said. "Everything you need should be there."

"Great. It turns out we need something else as well."

Remy smirked. "Give 'em an inch."

I held my hands up. "I just wondered if you had something that would, um, expedite the removal of a dead body."

Remy's face dropped. "You killed somebody, didn't you?" He slapped his hand on the counter. "Every time."

"It's not like that," Sam cut in. "It was self-defense."

Remy looked at me like I was an idiot. "You got an angel lying for you now?"

I put my hand on my chest. "She's not lying. Honest to… well… you know."

"Dare I ask if there's a chance it will get up and start trying to eat brains? I'd rather not go through that ordeal again."

The question made me grin. "Never say never."

"Let me see what I can cook up. But I want your word." He pointed at Sam and me. "Both of you. One day, I'll need you two for something. I don't know what, but something. I want your word that when that day comes, you'll be there."

I shook his hand.

"Don't see that we have much choice in the matter." I glanced back at Sam. "Do you?"

Sam sighed, like she knew we were asking for a lot of trouble neither of us wanted to deal with later. "Can't say that I do."

She shook Remy's hand.

"Good. Now. There's a guy in Charlotte who's loaded with stuff. He might be the largest private collector in this time zone. He even has some of your angel ointment, from what I understand."

"He willing to sell?"

"Not exactly." Remy set an iPod on the counter.

"What's that for?" I asked.

"The person you're seeing is a televangelist."

My chest sank into my bowels. Anything but a televangelist.

"Don't you have an easier way? I'm okay with driving out of state if it means avoiding one of those clowns."

Remy shook his head. "His name's Arthur Powell. He's the only one who has what you need. I'm surprised," he said, leaning his elbows on the counter. "You actually seem scared of them."

"No," I scoffed. "I just avoid them if at all possible. It's a personal preference, like preferring blondes over redheads."

Seriously. I'm not afraid of them. I just hate them with the fury of a massive hurricane. Being forced to watch one on TV was one thing, but in person? Forget it.

"What does an iPod have to do with a televangelist?" Sam asked.

Remy glanced at her. "It's loaded with your favorite." He eyeballed my wardrobe. "A little Man in Black for a man in black."

Sam's expression was carefully blank. "You lost me."

I sighed. "It's full of Johnny Cash songs. His catalog is like the universal language of pain and suffering. If you listen to Cash, nothing can hurt you because you're already in a dark and painful place."

"Where's that?" Sam asked.

"His soul," Remy whispered.

Sam nodded politely, like she didn't understand but also didn't want to be rude.

"The only problem is, you have to listen to it so loud you can't hear anything else," Remy said. "The music literally has to drown out everything around you."

"Otherwise it won't work," I said.

"Okay. I understand," she said. "I think."

Sam still struggled to grasp what we needed to do as we made the three-hour trek to Charlotte.

"What is the Ring of the Gods?" Sam asked.

"It's from ancient Greece. Forged from the blood of Zeus, Athena, Hades, and Apollo. The ring pretty much protects you from anything supernatural. It's one of the most powerful third party items out there."

"I thought Zeus and the Gods were just mythology."

I shot her a sideways glance. "They might say the same thing about angels one day. Even pseudo-angels, like yourself."

"But we're real."

"Just because you've never met Zeus doesn't mean he never existed."

"I guess so." Sam didn't say anything for a moment. Probably tried to wrap her mind around what I'd said. "Wow."

"Indeed."

Yep. Mind... blown.

"Are you sure he won't sell this thing?"

"Would you?" I huffed.

"So we're stealing from a televangelist."

"Pretty much. I know that's against your code of ethics or whatever, but it's not as if televangelists are the most ethical people on the planet."

"Why would a televangelist collect all this stuff, anyway?"

"Maybe to keep it away from others, maybe because he has some grandiose plan to take over the world, or it could be he likes showing them off at cocktail parties."

Sam shot up straight. "You think so?"

"No clue. That's not our concern, though." I loved cruising down the highway in my new Benz. I couldn't hear anything outside of the car. A storm siren could go off next to us and we wouldn't notice.

"You still haven't explained Quincy to me," she said.

"Right. That." I launched into the entire story of what happened, how he'd helped me get the new car, acted funny, then came at me with the knife.

"So he was possessed?"

I nodded. "By Miss Evans, no less."

"Miss Evans?"

I got Sam caught up on my theory about Miss Evans. "I don't know what she is, exactly. I've come across plenty of beings out there that use sex as a weapon, but none with the Helen of Troy-like allure she has. Long story short, I'm pretty sure she's Vixen. She wants to make the Shard her BFF."

"Have you seen the snake ring on her?"

"I haven't. That doesn't mean it's not her, though."

We pulled into some swanky neighborhood bordering Lake Norman, located just north of Charlotte. All the houses around the lake were priced in the million and up range. I parked the car around the block from the televangelist's home and killed the engine. I thought we should wait until the sun went down before heading in.

"I don't like this," Sam said.

"What's to like?" I asked. "He lives in a mansion. We have no clue where the ring is, just that it's in that freakin' castle somewhere. We don't know if anybody else is in there with the guy, and if the iPod dies on me for any reason, I'll probably explode the second he starts preaching." Voluntarily being close enough to hear a televangelist speak in person ranked pretty high on the list of dumb things a demon could do. A human, too, for that matter. Watching one on TV was one thing, but in person? Without any sort of filter? Pure insanity.

"What about the stealing? Won't that get us both in trouble?"

"Think of it as borrowing. I guess they never taught you about necessary evils, did they?"

Sam shook her head.

"Things may have changed since I've been up there, but basically, if you have to commit an evil that's necessary for the greater good, then it's okay. An example would be killing all the firstborns in Egypt." I left out the part where necessary evils can be a bit of a slippery slope. Angels could become addicted to necessary evils. The fun angels did, at least. But that slippery slope also tended to be frowned upon by the more uppity members of Heaven who refused to do what sometimes had to be done. Probably the reason they didn't tell Sam about the loophole.

"How do you want to do this?" she asked.

Anything we did, from knocking on this guy's door posing as Mormons or pretending to deliver a pizza, would raise suspicion. So we had to use that suspicion to our advantage by drawing the televangelist's suspicion away from the actual mischief happening right under his nose.

Since I had to listen to the Man in Black during this little operation, Sam and I decided to communicate with each other via text message. I would go inside and she would keep an eye on things outside, keeping tabs on him for me.

Darkness set in about twenty minutes later. We got out of the car and rounded the block. Thirty yards separated the street from this guy's front door. I hated that he got to live like a king, especially since televangelists were some of the lowest creatures around. They had the power of you-know-who at their disposal and most of them used that power for their own dirty deeds, yet never got punished for them. Made me jealous.

"We should've brought Josh," Sam said.

"No, we shouldn't have. He's been nothing but trouble. And honestly, how can I expect to be at my best when someone I'm working with is always trying to kill me? It's enough everybody else is trying to do that." I glanced at a rock on the ground. "I'm going to smash one of the front windows. That will draw him out, then I'll run around and slip in through the rear, if you get my drift."

She didn't look impressed by my double entendre. "Grow up."

"Can't. I was created this way."

I picked up the rock, and then took aim at one of the large windows. The rock shattered the glass. Sam hid behind a tree near the front door, and I rushed around to the side of the house. Leaning against the brick wall, I popped the earbuds in and turned on the Cash. *The Man Comes Around* played. One of my favorites.

The front door opened. Powell stood on the front steps.

"Whoever's out there, I called the cops, so you'd do best to get the Hell off my property. Thank you and God bless."

What an ass. I ran around to the back of the house and onto the deck overlooking Lake Norman. Most people are pretty careful about keeping their front door locked, but the back is another thing altogether, especially here. People constantly went in and out to enjoy the view, so keeping the rear locked probably seemed like more of a nuisance than anything else. I pulled open the sliding door and stepped into the kitchen. I tiptoed around, looking for some kind of study or library. I found the room next to the den.

Inside, all the crucifixes in the study almost blinded me. Big ones, small ones, old, new, gold, silver, wood, even one woven out of string. Powell had at least six different versions of the Bible in the bookcases and, naturally, a framed photo of himself with Jimmy Swaggart. I studied the picture.

Son of a bitch.

Arthur Powell was the same one I'd seen on TV when I first got out of Hell. I wished demons could excrete, because I would so take a dump on his floor. I did my best to have tunnel vision as I scanned the artifacts in the room, hoping that being near so many crucifixes wouldn't literally blind me, or worse.

Remy should've come along on this little expedition. The items in this room made his little party favors and shrunken skulls look like something out of a bubble gum machine at the grocery store. I found not one but *five* vials of the angel goo. I would've taken only one, but since I'd already suffered because of the televangelist's ranting, I figured taking all of them would make us even. I kept looking but didn't see any Ring of the Gods.

My phone vibrated. A text from Sam.

He's going back inside. I think he's wearing the ring. At least he's wearing A *ring.*

I dropped my head. "You've got to be kidding me."

My phone vibrated again. *Cutting off his finger is* not *an option.*

"Why would it be?" I said to myself. It was only the easiest solution. I glanced at the corner of the study. A green robe hung on the wall, next to a photo of Pope John Paul II wearing the same robe. I sighed. This would hurt.

I turned down the volume on Cash so I could hear, then slid the robe on and pulled the hood completely over my head, casting a shadow on my face. My skin burned where the robe touched me, and the smoke coming from those exposed areas only made me look that much more intimidating. I walked out of the room toward the front door.

Arthur Powell's white hair somehow seemed even more striking in person. His gin blossoms and paunch told me he might've spent his professional life "serving" the Holy Spirit, but he'd dedicated his personal life to drinking as many spirits and touching as many kids as he could get his hands on. To be fair, I only guessed about the kids. He clung to a glass of Scotch. Or whiskey. I never can tell the difference between the two. The glass smashed on the floor when he saw me.

"Sweet baby Jesus," he said. "Who are you?"

"Who do I look like?"

"I don't know, but you're smokin' somethin' fierce. Like a car without a muffler."

"And I'm not even having a cigarette." Though I definitely could've used one.

He held up his hands. "What do you want? I'm just a simple servant of God."

I tried not to laugh. "We both know that's not true."

"Please. That robe is priceless."

"You've been a naughty boy, Arthur. A simple servant of God wouldn't live in such a palace."

"I don't know where you've been gettin' your information, but I haven't been naughty. Hand to God."

"Quiet."

Powell bit his lower lip and nervously covered his face with his hand.

I pointed at a finger, which had a weathered silver ring on it. The Ring of the Gods. It had to be. "The ring. Hand it over."

He covered the ring with his other hand. "Ring? What ring?"

"The one you just covered up. Give it to me and I'll be on my way."

"You know the cops will be here any minute. I called them when you smashed my window."

This time, I did laugh out loud.

"Look at me." I spread my arms out. Smoke billowed from every opening in the robe. I tried not to scream from the pain. "You think I'm afraid of a few cops? The ring."

"No. It's a family heirloom. I can't. Belonged to my grandpappy."

Lies, lies, lies. What an absolute weenie. I pulled my arm out of the robe's sleeve and fished my lighter out. I lit it, and held the flame under the sleeve of the opposite arm.

"Don't do that. Please. That robe means the world to me."

I smirked. "So, which is it? The ring or the robe? Or how about I rip your hand off with just these two fingers," I made a pinching motion with my thumb and index fingers, "then burn your entire orgy of artifacts."

I heard the police sirens through the shattered window.

Powell smiled at the sound of the police approaching. "And I say now unto the Lord, that you shall be forgiven for your sins."

The drunkard preached. The Cash helped with the pain, but his rant still seared through my mind. I had to act fast or this Arthur fellow would give me a one-way ticket back to Hell. I fumbled around inside the robe, trying to find the iPod. My brain felt like metal stakes stabbed it. That piece of wood Remy gave me could be a normal toothpick for all the good it did me.

I found the iPod and turned the volume back up on old Johnny, drowning out the sermon. Much better. Stakes removed. Powell continued preaching, but I couldn't hear him anymore. With no sound, his bombastic arm movements made him look like a weird sort of mime.

I ran at him as fast as I could and clocked him in the jaw. He fell to the floor, shielding his face with his hands. I yanked the ring off his finger and slipped it on mine just as the police lights started appearing on the driveway. My phone vibrated, but I didn't need to answer. I knew it was Sam, telling me to get out of there.

I threw off the robe and ran out onto the deck. I jumped over the deck's metal railing and made a break for the lake. I stopped before jumping in to text Sam.

Go 2 car. Swmmng 4 it.

I stuffed the phone back in my pocket and dove in, ruining

whatever electronics I had on me. I hoped Remy didn't expect to get his iPod back in working condition, because... oops.

TWENTY-TWO
EVEN DEMONS SHOP AT TARGET

I swam about a quarter mile through the chilly lake until I found a small dock. I climbed up and ran for the car, water dripping from my body. I could not have been happier that I'd decided against wearing a suit for this. Sam, arms crossed, leaned her back against Sweet Claudette.

"Did you get it?" she asked.

I held up my hand, showing off the ring. "See if your Hand of God thing can work on me now."

Sam's eyes darted back and forth down the street. "Can we get out of here first?"

"Most definitely." I reached into my pocket to get my keys.

The keys.

Sweet Claudette had keyless entry. I'd fried my keyless entry, along with Remy's iPod, the second I jumped into the lake. I tried to activate it anyway. Nothing.

"I should've known," I said, fighting off the urge to kick something.

"We can't get in the car?"

I lowered my head. "Sweet Claudette's locked up tighter than a virgin in a chastity belt."

"Well. That's just great," Sam said, inching closer to me. "You really know how to plan ahead, don't you?"

"Obviously." And Powell, with his arsenal of religious gobbledygook, could be on us at any moment.

A wry smile crept across Sam's lips. "Good thing I do."

She turned and opened her door.

Huh? What?

"How? I locked the car when we left."

Sam held up the other keyless entry to the Benz. "I saw it on the table at your place and figured better safe than sorry."

Check out Sam being a cheeky scoundrel. "Did you now?"

She tossed the key to me and got in. "Hope you have some towels in the trunk or something for the leather."

Now she's worrying about the leather?

"Are you okay?" I asked as I started the car. "You're acting really…nice."

"Hello? Angel," she said, mocking me as she buckled up.

"I deserved that."

"You did."

"We'll pick up some towels somewhere down the road." I just felt happy to be in my car, driving away from Arthur Powell and his playhouse of religious horrors. I placed the five vials of angel ointment in the container of my door.

We stopped at a Target a few miles down the Interstate to get some towels. No way would my exquisite body be clothed with items from there. I'd had my fill of bad clothes with that Tony Stewart shirt I'd had to wear. Now that we were away from Powell's, a sense of safety began to take hold. I started getting more concerned about Sweet Claudette sprouting mold.

Before we went inside, I pulled off my shirt in the parking lot and wrung it out. I noticed Sam staring at my six-pack abs, so I held out my arms and did a twirl. "Like what you see? It's okay to look."

"Thanks, I'll pass."

"You want to touch? I won't bite."

"I'm good."

I held out my hand. "I'd at least like to know if the ring works."

Sam held my hand. I didn't feel any burning. Just a slight, enjoyable tingle. Excellent.

She jerked her hand away. Seeing me in all my glory really seemed to make her nervous. "Now you know."

"Indeed." I put the shirt back on. Time to test out the ring. "Okay. Hand of God me."

Sam turned a bit stiff. "Here? In the parking lot?"

I shrugged. "Sure. Nobody's around."

"All right." She put her hand on my chest. "Bartholomew, I want you to squawk like a chicken."

Squawk like a chicken? Really? "That's the best you can come up with?"

"I don't want to ask you something big. What if the ring doesn't work on this?"

True. She could have me run through the store flashing my privates at old ladies.

"So? Squawk. I order you."

I felt a sudden force rise up inside me, trying to will me to comply. I felt a chicken squawk crawl up my throat. With some force, though, I successfully fought it off.

"Ha."

She smiled. Her hand grew so bright I had to shield my eyes.

"Are you jealous of Josh?"

Hey, whoa. That was powerful. And a dirty shot.

I wanted to answer. Just a simple slip of the tongue. So easy.

No. Demon up.

I bit down on my lip. "*Mmm.*"

Sam tried again. "Are you jealous of Josh?"

I shook my head no.

"You don't want to tell me?"

"*Hm hum*," I said, without opening my mouth.

The brightness in her hand disappeared, leaving my eyes to readjust to the darkness.

"It works. That was the strongest I've got."

"That was a low blow," I said.

"Does that mean you liked it?"

I thought about that for a second. "Kind of, yeah."

She arched an eyebrow. "Can't say I'm surprised."

Inside, Sam got caught up looking at handbags, so I left

her and searched for some towels on my own. I decided against whatever designer crap they had and went with some Batman beach towels.

"I always thought of myself as more of a Superman guy," a voice said to my side. "That prodigal son thing always struck a sentimental chord for me."

Nicholas. I almost called Sam over to see if she could make him squawk.

"Can I help you?"

"Thought I could help you." He looked at the Ring of the Gods. "That's what I'm here for. Whatever you need, you come to me. This running around and stealing business is just going to make people angry."

Shocker. Nicholas shows up *after* his help might have been welcomed. I glanced down at the ring. "As you can see, we're getting on okay without your help."

"I stopped by your condo earlier. Certainly didn't look like you were getting on okay."

The revelation made me feel somewhat violated. "I've got that under control."

Nicholas played with his red tie. "You do now. Consider it a… friendly gesture on my part. To help solidify our partnership. I even got all the stains out."

Partnership? Same old Nicholas. The second he got the Shard, I'd get my ass shipped down to the Ninth Circle, only he'd be the one taking me to town instead of Lucifer. He'd probably make Judas and Cassius have a tea party with me down there. At least he got all the stains out.

"I appreciate that. I do. But if I need your help, I'll call you."

Nicholas looked into one of the bathroom mirrors for sale and messed with his hair. "Fair enough. So how goes progress?"

"We have a lead or two," I said, intentionally playing coy. If I gave Nicholas too much information, he might decide to cut me out of the entire equation and go straight for the Shard. One can take the son of the devil at his word only so far.

"Care to elaborate?"

I shook my head. "Not really. I don't want to jump to any conclusions. You understand, I'm sure."

Nicholas grinned. He knew what I was doing. "Sure."

"Hey, Bartholomew?" Sam asked from the next row over. Glancing back, I saw her enter our row. She froze at the sight of Nicholas.

"And who is this dashing young lady?" Nicholas stepped forward, extending his hand. "Pure as the winter's snow, you are. If you want to stay that way, I'd recommend keeping better company," he said, winking at me. "This one will only bring you down to his level."

Sam hissed. "Stay back, son of Satan."

The woman actually hissed. So absurd.

Nicholas acted taken aback, putting on a hurt face. "Did… did you just hiss? People do that? I only wanted to introduce myself."

Sam clenched her hands into fists. "Don't come any closer or I'll send you back to Hell."

"Scary," Nicholas said, waving around like he had jazz hands. "And how are you going to do that?"

Sam smirked. "Step closer. You'll find out."

I had to hand it to the almost-angel. Sure, she was pretty worthless when it came to the nitty-gritty, but seeing her go up against Nicholas impressed me. I didn't think she had it in her.

Nicholas laughed. "I like this one, Bartholomew. She's got some pluck." His face hardened like a Greek statue. "Tell you what, sweetie. I'll let you have this round because I need my associate here," he said, placing a hand on my shoulder, "to finish whatever job you two are doing. Then, if I'm feeling generous, I won't invite Saddam, Stalin, and a cadre of other assorted monsters of all shapes and sizes to violate every hole in your body for a millennium. Okay?"

I winced. "You don't want that, Sam. That's no fun for anybody."

Sam's face turned as white as a piece of paper. Her body trembled, but her gaze remained fixed on Nicholas. She didn't budge an inch. "Why not go for two millennia?"

"Whoa." Nicholas looked completely taken aback. He pointed at her. "You. You're… something special. Most angels don't have this much chutzpah. Tell you what, sweetie. When you get down to Hell, I'll keep you all to myself." He looked over at me. "Let me know when it's done."

I nodded and, before I could blink, Nicholas disappeared. Sam didn't move.

"Look at you being a bad ass."

She didn't respond.

I moved closer to her. "You all right?"

She closed her eyes for a moment, probably to get her bearings. "Yeah. Get your towels and I'll see you in the car."

We rode north on I-85 in silence for almost thirty minutes. The only sound was the music of some pop star that made a deal with the Devil for fame on the radio. I figured Sam still had to be shaken up after that encounter. It's not every day the son of the Devil threatens an almost-angel with a gangbang featuring Joseph Stalin and Saddam Hussein, or even with himself. At least he hadn't thrown in Hitler. She really would've been in trouble then.

She nibbled at a fingernail. "I should have known."

"Known what?"

"That you'd work some kind of angle with them to get free of this deal."

I turned the radio down. "Listen to me. I hate Nicholas. He's a snot-nosed little brat. He kidnapped me the other day and said either I agree to help him get the Shard of Gabriel or he'd pour holy water down my throat and kill me. I think I made the right call, to be honest. Mind you, this offer came *after* he'd doused my feet in holy water so I couldn't walk."

"You should've told me." Her tone sounded less defensive.

She had a point. I probably should have.

"Would it have helped matters any? And don't lie. I'll know. Would it have been of any help for you to know that?"

She sighed. "No. It probably would've made things worse."

"Exactly. That clown is my problem, and when the time comes, I'll handle him."

"Okay. I believe you. You hate Nicholas." Her voice sounded hollow, like she only agreed with me to shut me up. The worst part? I actually wanted her to believe me. I hated that.

"Can I have a cigarette?" she asked with a sigh.

I glanced at her for a moment, wide-eyed. "Really?"

She nodded. "I could use one."

I laughed to myself. *You and me both.* "I'd say yes, but I just got this car today. As a rule of thumb, I try to enjoy the new car smell as long as I can." Especially now. "Never know when a minion is going to attack you and leave it in shambles or someone, and I'm not going to name names here, wipes demon guts off her hands on the floorboard."

She smiled faintly. "That's true."

The rest of the drive went by without interruption. I stopped to refuel, but other than that, the quiet couldn't have been more uncomfortable if one of us confessed we'd been having an affair. With a parental figure.

When I pulled up in front of her apartment complex, Sam remained in her seat, staring at the floorboard. I felt the engine's low rumble through the steering wheel.

Sweet Claudette, how tender you are.

"I want you to take the ring off," Sam said.

"After all we went through to get it? Why?"

Sam nodded. "Right now I don't know what to believe. Josh said I risked my very existence working with you, and I'm afraid he might be right."

"A. Don't listen to that douche. And B. What would taking off the ring accomplish?"

She held up her hand. "I have to know. For sure."

She wanted to Hand of God me again. "You're being ridiculous, you know that?"

Not to mention, she might ask me if I was jealous of Josh again. I really didn't want to find out what my answer would be.

She smiled. "You're a demon. Why should I believe you?"

I shut up. I'd hammered that point home to her a few times already. Now it was my turn to trust her. She could do anything to me without this ring. If she wanted me to speak in iambic pentameter for all time, I'd have to. But, much as I didn't want to admit it, I needed her right now. Neither of us could pull off our quest without the other. I ground my jaw and set the ring on the dashboard.

Sam nodded. "Thank you," she said, placing her hand on my chest. It burned. "I order you, by the power of God, to tell me the truth about you and Nicholas."

I didn't even try to fight off the urge. I just let the truth spew from my lips. I told her that no, I didn't want to get the Shard of Gabriel, then screw her over by giving it to Nicholas. I also told her that yes, I really did think he was a massive turd. I also told her that while I did want to find a way out of this arrangement, it wouldn't come at her expense. She'd gotten me out of Hell in the first place and, much as it irked me being in debt to some pseudo-angel, whatever code I existed by wouldn't allow me to leave her to writhe for all eternity in Hell or Detroit or wherever she would end up if we failed.

"That's not how I operate," I said. "I let people damn themselves. I only give them the tools to do so. Maybe a little push as well, if they're having second thoughts. You get the point."

I hoped Sam had heard enough. I didn't want to keep playing Twenty Questions. It didn't suit me, being this honest and…forthright.

Sam sat there, nodding to herself. "Okay. I can live with that," she said, getting out of the car. "You can put your ring back on."

Twenty-Three

The Drought Ends in Quite Possibly the Worst Imaginable Way

With the weekend over, Sam and I discussed the best way to go about confronting Miss Evans, as she drove us to school while I set up my new cellphone. She thought it would be better to face her after school to reduce the possibility of people getting hurt if she decided to turn into the Cloud of Death. I thought she'd be less inclined to do that if there *were* kids all over the place.

"You say that, but she had zero problem making Casey explode in the middle of a museum or chasing us through downtown," she said.

"True. After school it is."

I left Sam to do some homework and searched for Monica, who I found in the commons area. I cornered her. "I know who Vixen is, so thanks for all your help. I'm not just saying that either. I mean it."

Monica arched her back, pushing her breasts forward. "Who is it, then?"

I smirked. "You don't know?"

"I just want to make sure you know."

Clever little demon. She'd never known, and now she

wanted me to tell her so she could try to pull some kind of power play. "That's not how this game is played. Ladies first."

Monica put her hands on her hips. "Whoever you think it is, you're wrong."

"Not the answer I was looking for. I may still wreck Homecoming for you, though. That sounds like fun."

"Great. I'm going to go ahead and say I told you so. So I won't have to later, when you're angry about being wrong and come crawling back for answers."

Monica started grating on me with this pussyfooting. "Tell me, don't tell me. I don't care. I've figured it out, so whatever."

The rest of the school day came and went without much trouble. I met Sam by her locker before going to Miss Evans's room.

"You ready?" Sam asked.

"I am. But I want you to stay back."

Sam gave me a *you've got to be kidding* look. "No."

"Yes. I can handle Miss Evans, but if anything happens to me, I need you to use your Hand of God stuff to get me out of trouble. Just hang out by the car, okay? If you don't hear from me in ten minutes, come in hands a-blazin'."

Sam bit her lower lip. She might not have liked my plan, but it was better to have her ready to pull me out of trouble than risk having no back-up at all. "Josh could help."

I put my hands on my ears. "You did *not* just say that."

"Okay, okay. Sorry. I won't say it again. But he could."

Sam put her science book in her locker. I went to confront Miss Evans, who sat at her desk, grading papers.

I closed the door behind me as I walked in. "Afternoon."

She looked up at me through her glasses and smiled. "Afternoon, Bartholomew. To what do I owe the pleasure?"

"Let's not play games, shall we? I've had about enough of people saying one thing and doing another."

Miss Evans stood, revealing a slit in her skirt that showed off her thigh. Ring of the Gods or not, I found it difficult to keep my eyes off her skin.

"All right. No more games. What do you want?"

"I know what you're up to. I want the Shard of Gabriel, or I'll send you back to whatever pisshole you came from."

Miss Evans closed the distance between us with a slow, seductive saunter, but her eyes went wide at the mention of the Shard. "Work, work, work. I'm disappointed in you. That's all you came in here for?" She took off her glasses. "To tell me to hand over something I don't have?"

I snorted. "We both know that's a lie. Quincy told me everything before I killed him. So. Give me the Shard, or I'll do the same to you."

Miss Evans stood a foot away, her legs spread, making her skirt ride up.

I gulped.

"I don't know any Quincy."

"We're past the point of playing dumb, Miss Evans. So just give it to me and we can both move on."

"I don't think so. I really don't have the Shard. But I'll tell you what I do have."

"What's that?"

A satisfied smile crept across her face. "You."

"Me?"

Before I could do anything, Tyler, Clayton, and Darrel appeared. They wrapped their arms around me, holding me in place. Miss Evans took the Ring of the Gods from me, immediately making my lust for her go through the roof.

"I was so disappointed when you had that necklace on. I knew my… feminine wiles weren't getting to you the way I'd hoped. I couldn't have that, which is why I sent your friend Quincy to kill you. I tend to get a little possessive when I see something I want."

Interesting. Most people coveted what they couldn't have. Miss Evans killed it.

She slid on the ring and held up her hand, evidently enjoying her new jewelry. "I didn't even know the Shard still existed, let alone that it was so close. That's wonderful news."

Miss Evans held my chin with her hand. The physical stimulation drove me crazy. I didn't care about Tyler and the Things being there. I had to have her. Now.

"When you do find the Shard, and I have no doubt you will…" She leaned in, a mere inch from my face. I could only think about sex with this mysterious creature. "I want it. And in exchange, I'll give you whatever you desire."

Miss Evans parted her lips, as did I. She slid her tongue into my mouth and *sweet holy Heaven must get the Shard.*

"And your friends. Kill them."

"Yes, ma'am." I needed more of her. Her scent, her feel, her touch consumed me. I moved in to make out with her some more.

"*Hmm,*" Miss Evans said, licking the saliva off her lips. "Yummy. Now, do what I ask and you'll get more of that… and then some."

She didn't have to ask me twice. Samantha and Josh were dead.

I grinned and acted like everything was normal as I approached Samantha. The stupid fake angel had no idea what I had in store for her.

"Did you get it?" she asked.

"Not exactly. She's not the one we're looking for."

"She's not Vixen?"

That sultry minx was most definitely *a* vixen, maybe even *the* vixen. I didn't care anymore. "Nope."

Samantha narrowed her eyes into accusatory slits. "Are you okay?"

"Never better. I feel like I could just float away."

"Float away? You sure you're fine?"

"Absolutely. Let's talk about it more at your place. I have some ideas I want to run by you."

Samantha opened her car door. "Did Miss Evans do something to you?"

Did she ever. I imagined how amazing violating her would be. "No. Just trying to look on the bright side of things."

"The bright side?"

"Yes. The bright side. You know, the opposite of dark?" I got in the car. "Am I not allowed to do that?"

"No, you can. It's just… weird coming from you."

I spent the ride back to Samantha's apartment thinking of Miss Evans's naked body writhing in ecstasy as I put my millennia-worth of sexual experience to work pleasuring her. I got myself so riled up I wanted to end Samantha right now, but I had to be smart about it. Taking care of her at her place would be perfect. No witnesses, no nothing. My horns almost came out, I felt so excited.

Miss Evans, you will be mine soon enough. And for all time.

My last visit to Samantha's apartment was a bit rushed, seeing that Marlon ripped out Josh's eye earlier that night. I hadn't really had a chance to see what her living space looked like. I saw a teddy bear sitting in a cushioned chair. Ridiculous. I did remember the overwhelming smell of vanilla candles from last time. This go-round, the aroma seemed every bit as pungent.

I made sure to avoid the crucifix set up on a bookshelf.

"Nice place," I lied. "I didn't really have a chance to notice last time I was here."

"Thanks." Sam set her book bag down on the table. "So what are these new ideas you have?"

Now was the time. I let my claws come flying out. My body burned with blood lust. Time to do what Miss Evans wanted. Kill Sam. Kill Josh. Get the Shard. With some luck, I could be inside her within the hour.

Samantha turned and gasped when she saw me.

"Bartholomew?" She glanced down at my hand. "Where's your... oh no."

I ran for her, digging my claws into her sides. She screamed in pain as she tried to break free. With her weakened, I could deliver the deathblow. I reached back, ready to rip Samantha's heart out of her chest.

"Why?" she asked.

"Why not?"

Samantha aimed her palm at me. A blinding light burst forth, throwing me across the room.

I didn't realize it until I woke up, but the bitch had knocked me out with her Hand of God special. I opened my eyes. I sat in a chair, wrapped in what looked like an entire roll of Saran Wrap. Samantha stood across from me, a stern look on her face. The wounds I'd inflicted had healed, and she'd changed into a pink V-neck.

"What did Miss Evans do to you?" she asked.

"She didn't *do* anything to me," I snarled. "She told me to get rid of you and help her get the Shard. Once that's done, I get to have her every which way I please."

Samantha leaned down to my eye level, her hands on her knees. "And how did she convince you to do all this?"

"She sealed the deal with a kiss. A glorious kiss that a poseur angel like you has never, nor will ever, experience."

I tried to free myself of my bindings and rip the skin off her face. Samantha picked up a spray bottle from the table and squirted me with it. I howled in pain. Holy water.

"Try that one more time and I'll make you kill yourself all over again."

"You deserved that." She set the bottle down on the carpet. "So. Miss Evans possessed you with a kiss."

"She didn't possess me. You think she could do that? To me?" I laughed, spitting bits of flesh out of my mouth.

Samantha paced around the room, muttering to herself. I couldn't make out what she said. Nor did I care. If only she would put her throat next to one of my hands, this could all be over.

The fake angel picked up her cellphone and called someone.

"Hey. This is Samantha. I know I'm not supposed to call, but I need help... Yeah. It's Bartholomew. No, not that. He's been possessed by something."

Who was she talking to about me? Josh?

"Get Josh over here. I'll do to him what I did to his dear old dad."

Samantha glared at me. "What? Nothing. He thinks I'm talking to Josh."

She wasn't talking to Josh? Who could she be talking to? She didn't have any friends I knew of.

Ah ha!

She was talking to an angel. A *real* angel.

"Which of those angel asshats are you talking to? Tell them

I said to piss off. Screw you and the halo you rode in on, dickhole."

Samantha covered the phone's speaker and gave me a flustered look.

"Do you mind? I'm on the phone."

I wiggled my hands. "Do *you* mind? I'm trying to kill you."

She sighed. "Sorry. Yeah, that's him. You want to say hello?"

"I don't want to speak to some shingles-infected angel. Tell that goody two shoes winged bastard that he likes dressing up in tutus and getting spanked by clowns."

Samantha went over what she knew about Miss Evans, and what I'd been acting like since this afternoon.

"Whoever's on the phone is literally blocking my cock right now," I said. "Hurry up and let me end you."

"What is she?" Samantha said into the phone. "Wow. That's not good. Can she turn into a deadly cloud of smoke? No? Dang. Okay."

I continued struggling to get free, but that Sarah Wrap held me in place like cement. I licked my lips. I could still taste Miss Evans on them. She tasted like… sex. Pure sex.

Samantha gasped. "I have to do *what* to him?"

"You're not doing anything to me. Not even if you put on a Miss Evans mask."

"Is there any other way?"

Of course there was. "Yeah. Untie me."

Sam ignored my helpful suggestion. "And this is authorized? You're sure? Yeah. I'll do it. I don't see that I have a choice." She sighed. "I don't know how. Very carefully, I guess."

Samantha got off the phone and stared at me.

"Bartholomew, I want you to listen to me."

"La la la, not listening." I wanted no part of what she had to say.

She picked up the squirt bottle. "You will, or I'll blind you."

I sighed. This sucked. "Fine. But I'm not looking at you while you speak." I gazed at the ceiling, imagining Miss Evans doing a striptease.

"Miss Evans is a succubus."

"A suck you *what?*"

"You've been possessed by a succubus. The only way to break whatever hold she has on you is to make sure you… copulate with someone before she has a chance to do it herself."

"Absolutely not." I threw my head back and forth. "I'd rather teach children about the virtues of abstinence."

"Sorry. I'm not too thrilled about this either, but otherwise you'll be lost to her forever." She held up her hand and placed it on my chest. "By the power of God, I order you to calm down and promise not to harm me."

My anger at Samantha subsided. I still wanted to dismember her, but the overpowering desire to do so went away. Now I only had a gnawing feeling in the back of my mind.

"Calm?" she asked.

"Sure."

"Okay. I'm going to cut you free now."

"If you must."

Samantha picked up a pair of scissors and cut my Saran Wrap shackles. She took me by the hand and led me into the bedroom.

I woke up the next morning, completely naked, and with a big black hole in my memory. Where the heck was I? The room smelled of vanilla, everything looked clean and orderly… clearly, a man didn't live in this room. So. Who was the lucky lady?

Maybe I finally banged a virgin.

I did feel oddly satisfied.

Sam walked in, pulling a gray shirt over her head. Music began playing in another room.

Wait.

Sam? I was in Sam's apartment? Even Sam's bed?

"Morning," she said.

I waved. "What am I doing here? Did we get blackout drunk or something?" My head felt like whipped butter.

"No, we didn't get drunk. You really don't remember what

happened?" She stuck out her lower lip. "I find that oddly offensive."

"I wish I did." I pointed at her. "Did we do something questionable?"

Sam shrugged. "If you don't remember, why does it matter?"

Aw, man, we did.

So many conflicting emotions ran through my body. Surprise, satisfaction, contentment, and, most of all, shame.

"I'd like to know if we did."

"Let's just say… Whatever happened, I did out of mercy."

"You gave me a mercy hump?"

"If you want to call it that."

That couldn't be right. "That makes no sense. If anything, I would mercy hump you. You'd need it a lot more than I would."

"You sure about that? Miss Evans possessing you doesn't ring a bell?"

"I vaguely remember being hard up for her." What in Heaven? Had I fallen into an alternate reality? "Wait. I was possessed?"

Sam pulled her hair into a ponytail. "Yep. I could only break the curse by… you know…" She waved a hand vaguely in the air. "…doing the deed before she could."

"Won't you get thrown out of the angel club for that?"

"I had it cleared beforehand. What's the phrase you used? Necessary evil."

I buried my face in my hands. "I feel so used."

Sam laughed as she finished her ponytail. "You feel used? I'm the one who had to sacrifice my body."

"How did we even do it? Why am I not burnt to a crisp?"

"I used protection." Her eyes widened. "Lots of protection. It was more awkward and workmanlike than fun."

I felt bile rise in my mouth. I've had women, and men, for that matter, beg me for a quickie to end their drought or whatnot, but I'd never had the tables turned on me like this, especially by someone who wanted to be an angel. I felt so ashamed. Hearing Sam singing Hall and Oates's *Maneater* in the next room didn't help. Miss Evans would have Heaven to pay for putting me in this position.

Twenty-Four

On My Best Behavior

"Never mind getting back at Miss Evans, at least for right now," Sam said. "We have bigger fish to fry."

I laughed. "Like finding Vixen before it's too late."

Sam gave me a quizzical look. "You really don't think it's Miss Evans?"

"No," I said, shaking my head. "She didn't mention the Shard until I did, and even tasked me with getting it for her."

We hung around the school parking lot, waiting for the opening bell to ring. I finished my fourth cigarette of the day, trying to smoke the taste of humiliation out of my mouth. Sadly, even more was on the horizon. I could only get back on track by tucking my tail between my legs and talking to Monica, who wore a particularly smug scowl as I approached her before first period.

"I told you," she said with a hint of condescension.

"How did you even know who I'd focused on?" I asked.

"Please. I can tell you which teachers, and yes, that's plural, are banging which students, or anything else shady that's going on here. I'm head cheerleader. I'm in the middle of *everything*."

"Then tell me who I'm looking for so you can keep on doing that."

Monica laid a hand on her hip and narrowed her eyes.

"Whatever. Saying the world's going to end is Heaven's version of crying wolf and you know it."

She had a point. Those touchy-feely hippies upstairs always overreacted, going on holy quests to restore the balance of things, or whatever issue caught their eye. "I agree, but that doesn't make this any less important."

"You have a week until Homecoming," she said. "All you have to do is make sure Jenny doesn't win and I'll tell you everything you need to know."

I groaned. "Fine. But I need something else from you, and this is non-negotiable."

I skipped English to avoid Miss Evans. With the Ring of the Gods in her possession, I had no defense against her wily succubus charms except for that large wooden tooth Remy had given me. Seeing how little the thing helped with Powell, I was pretty much defenseless for the time being. Sam broke the curse last time, but who's to say Miss Evans couldn't do it again and bang me on the spot, making me her bitch for eternity?

Sitting in the cafeteria, I played with my puddle of mashed potatoes. Josh walked by, glancing at me out of the corner of his eye. He must've been sticking around to make sure Sam was safe. If he only knew.

Something cold landed on my head and ran down my face. Milk. Clayton and Darrel stood behind me, smirking.

"Miss Evans wants to see you," Clayton said.

"I don't want to see her."

Darrel put his hand on my shoulder. "We're not asking."

I grabbed his hand and squeezed as hard as I could. He grimaced as the joints popped. As I stood, he fell to his knees. Darrel's eyes began to water.

"Cry," I said. "Do it. Cry like a little girl. Show everyone here what you're really made of."

"Please," he said. "You'll break my hand. We have a game on Friday."

"He's right, dude," Clayton said. "We need him. Go easy."

As if they had a chance to win on Friday. "Like you did

with me? I don't think so."

"Bartholomew," Kyle said.

I glanced back and saw him.

"Let him go. Come on."

"You're so lucky." I released Darrel, who crumpled to the ground, holding his hand.

Kyle motioned for me to follow him.

"What did they want?" he asked.

"That? Thing One and Thing Two wanted to sell me some Girl Scout cookies," I said. "When I said no, they tried to force my hand. I just turned the tables on them."

Kyle laughed. "Yeah, they don't hear the word *no* a lot."

We left the cafeteria and entered the commons area.

"Everything okay?"

Did he know about last night? "What do you mean?"

"From Friday night. Thanks for getting me in my car, by the way."

Ah. So much had happened since then. "Yeah, everything's fine. Do you remember anything?"

He shook his head. "Only the things I want to forget."

"Come on. You don't want to carry those images around in your head for the rest of your days?"

Jenny stood by her locker, putting away some books. To get what I needed from Monica, I'd have to do something I hadn't done since I'd accidentally told Galileo the world was round—apologize. The revelation almost cost him his head. He was pissed, to say the least.

I told Kyle I'd talk to him later and approached Jenny. I had to walk past Miss Evans's class to get to her, which worried me a little. The closer I got to that room, the more I wanted to go in and rip her clothes off, but I kept to the opposite side of the hall and went by without my libido going haywire.

Jenny slammed her locker shut. She seemed disgusted by the sight of me.

"What do you want?"

"I'm… I came to…" This would be a lot harder than I'd thought.

"Has anybody told you that you don't look as ridiculous as you normally do without that massive necklace around your neck?" She turned and walked away from me.

I jogged to catch up. "Thanks for noticing."

"So what did you come to do? All I'm hearing is stammering and white noise."

"I wanted to, you know, what's the word I'm looking for here?"

Jenny's forehead creased as she raised her eyebrows. "Apologize?"

I snapped my fingers. "Yes. That word. I wanted to do that."

She slid her thumbs under the straps of her book bag. "I'm all ears."

"Didn't I just do it?"

"No, you just asked me what word you were thinking of."

Bless it all. I thought I'd found a way to do this and not have to actually say that word.

"Good try, though," she said.

"Okay, okay. I'm... sorry. For everything. Getting mad at you, accusing you of spreading rumors about me, the whole nine yards. I was way, way out of line. I'd still like to go to Homecoming with you, if you're interested." That sucked. My chest wanted to explode.

Her face scrunched together as she thought it over. "I guess you're forgiven."

We rounded a corner, entering the math and science area of the school.

"Excellent. And Homecoming? I have a tux and everything." Never mind I already owned the tux; she didn't need to know that.

"Maybe. Make it through just one week without embarrassing me and I'll think about it."

I'd take that as a yes. "Good. I know I can be a bit of a troublemaker, but I think I can go a week without being knee deep in some shenanigans."

"I hope so, because I'm serious. And don't think I won't know, either. I have eyes everywhere," she said with a wink. "This is my class."

I said goodbye and watched her take a seat. In a week's time, at the most, we would know Vixen's identity. I just had to make it until Friday without stirring anything up, which seemed easy enough... even though I'd almost broken Darrel's hand a few minutes ago. I could do this. Sam could do her Hand of God thing and make it impossible for me to do anything bad. Five days was nothing.

My loins stirred. A powerful sexual being approached. I turned and Miss Evans stood in the hall, a wry smile parting her lips.

Forget five days. I wouldn't make it five minutes.

TWENTY-FIVE
OPENING THE FLOODGATES

"You've been avoiding me all day," Miss Evans pouted. "Are you trying to hurt my feelings?"

I shrugged and took a step back to ease the sensual hold she had over me.

"Not really, no."

She matched my retreat with an advance, making my libido flare up again. Times like this, I wouldn't have minded being a eunuch.

"Did you do what I asked? I've been aching for you to come back to me with good news."

"Yeah, about that," I said. "I—"

"He failed," Sam said from behind Miss Evans.

"Failed is a harsh word," I said.

The teacher whipped her head around. "How? Nobody has ever—"

"By the power of God, I order you to release whatever sway you have over Bartholomew and return his ring to him." Sam's hand glowed as she slapped Miss Evans across the face.

What a sight. I'd never had the privilege of seeing someone get the power of God bitch-slapped into them. Even the sound of the slap had a power of God feel. Truly a sight to behold.

Miss Evans stumbled back, her expression a mixture of

shock and fear.

My attraction to her dialed down to almost nothing. I smiled and held out my hand.

"The ring?"

She pulled it off her index finger with her teeth, then spit the ring on the floor. So hot. I knelt down to pick it up. Miss Evans kneed me in the jaw. I flew back into the lockers behind me.

"Do you think Bartholomew here is the only one I can convince to end you?" She spat. "Maybe I'll see what your other friend thinks about the idea."

"Don't you dare." Sam raised her hand to slap Miss Evans again.

"You won't know when, but one of these days, I'll come for you. I'll pierce your chest with their fangs. Fill you with their venom." Her skin turned black. "You'll have precious few seconds left in this world. And my smiling face will be the last thing you ever see."

The teacher screamed in such a high pitch my eardrums vibrated. Wings ripped through her shirt and horns grew out of her forehead. She rose into the air and flew around the corner, bursting through a door.

Sam ran to chase her, but soon returned.

"She's gone. Miss Evans literally flew the coop," she joked.

I didn't laugh.

"I thought that was funny," she said in a disappointed tone.

I waggled my hand. "Eh."

Her gaze darted around me, probably checking for injury. "Are you hurt?"

"My head feels like it's been at an all-night rave, but I'll survive." I opened my hand to show her the ring. "I'm good. Um… gratitude for what you did."

I slid the ring back onto my finger.

"You're welcome?" Sam held out her hand. I took it and got to my feet. My hand tingled a little as she pulled me up. "You really stink at saying thank you."

The bell rang, so the two of us collected our bearings and went back to class while students wondered what happened to the door.

The rest of the day flew by in a whir. I talked to Jenny a little about Homecoming, but other than that, I kept to myself until school ended.

"Hey, killer," Tyler called out from behind me.

I didn't turn around.

"Killer."

I still ignored him.

"Bart. I'm talking to you."

A shocked silence fell over the hallway. I stopped walking and looked at Tyler. "Seriously? You're still on about that? That's so last week. Shouldn't you be engrossed in some new gossip by now?"

"Nope." He moved next to me, grabbing my arm. "We're going to take a little walk."

I chuckled. "You're not going to try and gloryhole me in the bathroom, are you?"

The students within earshot burst into laughter. Tyler's eyes darted back and forth. His face turned a fiery red. "Shut up."

The hallway complied.

"If I gloryholed you, you'd have no idea until it was all over," he said.

"Is it that small?"

The students broke out into a chorus of laughs again. Even I joined in.

"Stop laughing." Tyler seemed panicked. He pushed me. "I want to show you something."

"Do I need a magnifying glass?"

The students were in tears from laughing so hard. Tyler grabbed me by the jacket and pulled me outside.

I threw him off. "Hands off the jacket. You know what I can do to you."

A sneer crept across the quarterback's face. "And you're about to find out what I can do to you. Follow me."

I crossed my arms. "I don't think so. Last time we had a little meeting like this you tried to run me over with a car."

"Not this time. You'll want to see this."

I remained a few steps behind him as we walked until we were within sight of the main road leading into the school's parking lot. Darrel's Altima came into view. I imagined ripping the car to pieces with my fingers. Clayton hopped out of the passenger side and ran around to the trunk holding a knife.

Tyler grinned in that condescending manner only insecure bullies can master. "Now who's laughing?"

The Altima's trunk popped open. Clayton grabbed Sam by the hair and pulled her up so I could see her. He held the knife to her neck. They'd bound her hands and gagged her mouth.

I broke out in a giggle fit. "You moron. Do you realize what you've done?"

The grin disappeared from Tyler's face. He didn't know how to react. "Wh… what's that?"

I stopped laughing. "You just gave me permission to kill each and every one of you. As slowly and painfully as I want."

I mimicked Tyler's condescending grin from a moment ago, scratching my cheek with one of my extended claws. Sure, I probably could have ended their lives and saved Sam, but these three were too stupid to do this on their own. No, they would lead me to Miss Evans and put me in a position to destroy all of them in one fell swoop.

The blood drained from the jockstrap's face as he stared at the sharp instruments protruding out of my fingers. I actually thought he might pass out. He backed away from me and toward the car. "Sam's life depends on you. Touch us and she dies."

"Touch you? In what way? In an… inappropriate way?" I broke out into another fit of giggles.

"Bring us the Shard, and she might not get hurt. Hell, she'll probably love whatever we do to her. We'll be in… touch." Tyler ran to the car, whose tires screeched as it barreled out of the parking lot.

I ran to Sam's car to follow them. I tried to open the door. Locked. I smashed the window and crawled in. I heard some fabric tear as I got into the car. *Another* suit ruined. I tried to hotwire the ignition, but after a minute of trying and failing, I punched the steering wheel. Too much time passed. No way I could catch up now.

I'd have to wait for instructions from them. Patience is not one of my virtues. Having the Shard right now would've been helpful, but I had no clue as to its whereabouts and Miss Evans, the little vixen, would probably spot a fake with ease. I could maybe succeed in taking down Miss Evans and her whipping boys without the Shard, but there was a problem.

I needed some help.

I called Remy. So what if Nicholas took care of Quincy? I wouldn't ask him for help. Ever.

Remy cackled over the phone. "I'm done helping you," he said. "You're on your own. Unless you want to negotiate some sort of payment?"

"What kind of payment?"

"Your new Benz, for starters."

I hung up on his gold-digging ass. No way he'd get his hands on Sweet Claudette.

I tried to think of anyone else to call, but any Hell-bound entities that could help would turn their backs on me when they learned I wanted to save an angel in training, even if part of the equation involved snuffing out Tyler and the two Things. I could only think of one person who might help me. Provided he didn't try to kill me along the way.

I knocked on Josh's door later that night. I found myself greeted with a pistol in my face.

I held up my hands. "You know bullets don't hurt me."

Josh lowered the gun, leaving the barrel aimed at my chest. "No, but it can ruin your suit."

I pointed at the tear. "You're too late. This one's already ruined."

He raised the gun again. "Then another hole and a new stain?"

"Enough. It's Sam. The Things snatched her today."

Josh snorted. "Good job. I knew she couldn't trust—"

I fought off the urge to slam him against the wall. "I wasn't there when they took her, so you can shove that idea right up your ass."

Josh let the gun drop to his side. "Is this some kind of ruse to draw me out and kill me?"

"If that were the case, you'd already be dead. I need your help." I lit a cigarette. "Either you're in or out."

"Do you know where she is?"

"I have an idea. But we have to get moving. Now."

I needed a red herring to get Sam back, and I had an idea where I could find one. Her apartment probably had all sorts of goodies hidden in there, all of which could probably serve as a nice decoy for the Shard of Gabriel. The girl would have to live with me breaking into her place, though.

I extended my claws and used one of them to destroy the deadbolt on her front door. Josh and I walked on in.

"I'll check the bedroom," I said, heading in that direction.

Her bedroom looked neat, with the bed made up and that wretched vanilla aroma invading my nostrils. I checked her dresser first. Mostly just shirts and underwear. I found an old photo of Sam at the bottom of the underwear drawer. She looked the same as she did now, surrounded by her family. Everyone seemed happy, mugging for the camera. Even Sam. Still, I could see the pain in her hollow eyes. This must have been taken shortly before she croaked. I put the picture back and continued looking.

The rest of the dresser drawers contained nothing but clothes. Shame. I really thought I'd find a sex toy in there. I checked the nightstand next to her bed. Just a pen, some paper, and a Bible. Gideons and angels are the only ones who keep that book in a drawer next to a bed. One of these days, I'd replace every copy in this apartment with *The Exorcist*. See how Sam liked that.

I found a couple of boxes under the bed. One overflowed with books, including the *Harry Potter* series. Thankfully, the *Twilight* books were nowhere to be found. The other box had a few water guns. Hmm.

I picked one up and shook it. Full. I sprayed a little water on the back of my hand. It burned a bit. Yep. Holy water. Thanks to the ring, my hand didn't feel like it would melt, but it still hurt. I stashed the gun in my jacket.

I had pretty much torn through Sam's room without any luck until I searched in the closet. On the floor, behind a shoe rack, I found a small, locked wooden box. I destroyed the lock and opened it.

Unbelievable.

I should've been furious. All this time, the tease did nothing but lead me on. I'd wondered why she always said we were after someone who wanted the Shard of Gabriel, and not the Shard itself. Now I knew.

"Hello, my precious."

I held in my hand the bane of my existence. The reason I'd fallen out of favor and been sentenced to eternity in the Seventh Circle of Hell.

The Shard of Gabriel.

And Samantha kept it hidden in her closet the entire time.

TWENTY-SIX

TEACHER'S PETS

I gazed at the Shard's jagged edges, a rough contrast to the smooth, green glass that made up the surface. The entire Mirror of Gabriel must have been a sight to behold. I never got a chance to see it during the War for Heaven. Now, I held a piece of it in the palm of my hand. The wisdom of God. If I looked into it, all my questions would be answered and I'd know how to get out of this whole mess without a hitch. I couldn't wait any longer. I had to use it.

"Bartholomew?" Josh asked. "Find anything?"

"No." Blast it all. No questions right now. Not with Josh around. I jammed the Shard in my pocket and went into the den.

Josh held the wooden knife he and Quincy both tried to kill me with. I stared at it.

Josh stashed the knife under his shirt. "Figured it might come in handy later."

I bet.

"Good idea."

I'd used Frady-McNeely's online directory to find out where Miss Evans lived. I told Josh my plan to get Sam back on the drive over to Miss Evans's house. Provided that's where they were, I'd be the one to knock on the front door and talk to the succubus, now that I had immunity to her wily charms.

"What do I do in all this?" he asked.

"You get to be Sam's knight in shining armor."

Josh looked like he fought back a smile. I'd figured that would make him happy. It would also probably win him some brownie points with Sam, but whatever. If she got to crushing on him too hard, I would remind her he merely served as a pawn in my master plan.

Miss Evans lived in a small cottage house nestled between clumps of trees. A very quaint home for a succubus that probably had preyed on people for centuries. I guess people might've gotten curious if she lived in some kind of sex mansion. Two cars were parked in the driveway. The Altima and a Toyota, which probably belonged to Miss Evans. What a bunch of idiots, leaving their cars parked out front. Did none of them realize anyone could find Miss Evans's address online?

Lights were on in a few of the windows, so somebody had to be home. Hopefully, that included Sam. I really didn't feel like searching all over Raleigh for her tonight.

"Let's get our Peeping Tom on, see if we can't figure out what's what," I said.

We crept under one of the tree branches and gazed through the window into the dining room. The room was empty, except for a glass vase with flowers in the middle of the table. A figure moved past the window, making Josh jump. Miss Evans. She wore Tyler's football jersey and nothing else. Josh's heavy breathing misted up the window.

I moved him back a little. "Down, boy. You want to give us away?"

"Sorry," he said, trying to get a glimpse past me. "I can't help it. There's something about her. She's so hot."

"She's a succubus. Her only goal in life is to suck people in with her sexuality and swallow their souls. So try thinking of your grandmother naked next time you see her."

Josh wrinkled his face. "My grandmother's dead."

"Even better."

Miss Evans passed by the window again. I instinctively held my arm out in front of Josh so he wouldn't press his face up against the window. She disappeared up the stairs.

"Okay," I said. "My guess is she's getting gangbanged up there, which means Sam is most likely in the house somewhere."

"How do you know?"

I tried not to roll my eyes. The folly of youth and inexperience got me every time.

"Because she and her three little boy toys wouldn't be getting freaky here unless they had Sam nearby. For all I know, they're up there making her watch."

Which would be an interesting way to try to corrupt an angel. Or at least torture one.

I pulled out my cellphone and dialed Miss Evans's number.

She answered on the third ring.

"My call almost went through to voicemail. I figured you and your harem would be more attentive than that, considering the stakes." I knew full well they probably needed a minute or two to untangle themselves.

"Well, I'm here now," she said. "Do you have what I want?"

"You have Sam?"

Miss Evans moaned. "Can we keep her? She's so virtuous and pure. I can't believe you haven't sullied her by now."

"Who says I haven't?" I covered the speaker with my hand and waved to Josh. "Let's go back to the car."

We moved toward Sweet Claudette, staying in the shadows as best we could.

She laughed. "Please. We both know that's a lie. Do you have the Shard?"

"I do." We stopped at the Benz. I didn't want to open it or do anything to give away our location.

"Good. Meet me at the state fairgrounds near the clump of trees next to Carter-Finley Stadium. One hour. Can I trust you to come alone?"

"Of course you can trust me." I wondered if Miss Evans really was dumb enough to trust me. I hoped so.

"See you there." She hung up.

I unlocked Sweet Claudette and we slid inside.

"What's the plan?" Josh asked.

"We're going to hit them while they're getting in the car.

They should be vulnerable, then."

Josh squeezed his hands together. "Why don't we just burst in there?"

"Since I doubt you can pick locks, the only way that would work is if you were the decoy, and you being alone with Miss Evans will end with you becoming another of her sex slaves." I followed the headlights of a car that passed by us, which left a glare in my eyes. "I learned that one the hard way. Nobody can handle her raw sexual power."

He rubbed his forehead. "You did okay a minute ago. Do you have something that can protect me?"

I held up my ring finger, gazing at the Ring of the Gods. "I'm not giving you this."

Josh gave me pleading look. "It would be so perfect, though. You could sneak in back, take care of the guys, grab Sam, then get out. Boom. We all go home."

I scratched my head. "You don't want to be the one to rescue her?"

"I'm helping, aren't I?"

I leaned my head back against the headrest. Josh's plan was risky. And stupid. This also meant if anything went wrong on my end, he'd probably wind up dead.

"Let's give it a shot." I opened my door.

If I rescued Sam, but intentionally let Josh die, she would know—and promptly boot me down to the Ninth Circle—but this plan was so insane the chances of us pulling it off without a hitch were next to none. That was the beauty of it. I wouldn't have to try to get Josh killed. He'd probably do it himself.

I reluctantly gave him my ring so he could withstand the onslaught of hormones Miss Evans would unleash on the poor mortal. I hoped that if he got eaten, the ring wouldn't be digested.

Josh rang the doorbell. When she answered, he would tell her his car broke down and ask to use the phone. Very original, but, hey, he'd be a distraction alive or dead, so it made no difference to me.

I crept around to the back of the house. The lights mostly focused near the front door, making it easier to move around unnoticed. It would've been embarrassing if some neighbor saw me creeping around and called the cops. I extended a claw and waited. I peeked just enough into a window so I could see Miss Evans with only one eye. How virtuous. She wore white pajama pants complete with a matching white shirt. Guess she knew to not answer the door wearing Tyler's jersey. When the succubus greeted Josh, I went to work, picking the lock. I eased the door open, stepped inside, and softly closed it behind me.

I must've been in the den. A television sat in the corner, a burgundy couch tucked against the far wall, above which hung a painting of people participating in an orgy back in medieval times, which totally clashed with the rest of the room. But, no Sam.

I dashed across the entrance to the hallway, knowing Miss Evans would notice me if she turned around. I didn't see Sam in the kitchen. I could see through the kitchen and into the dining room. Not there either. Maybe they really did have her up in the bedroom, making her witness the depraved sex acts of a succubus and her three teenaged lovers.

Or maybe they left her in the trunk of the car. Bless it. This was a bad idea.

I crept back into the den. I'd have to pass by Miss Evans to get upstairs. I motioned to Josh with my hands and pointed outside. I hugged the wall as the Succubus turned around to see what Josh looked at. I counted to five and peeked around the corner. Her back was to me again. I moved toward them as quietly as possible.

"Maybe you can help me. Could you take a look at it?" Josh asked her. "I'm not really sure how to change a tire."

"I don't know. It's kind of late and I have papers to grade."

I made a choking move with my hands, hoping he would get the idea that I wanted him to fake choking to get her outside.

"Please. I don't know who else to call," he said.

No!

I pointed at him and made the motion again. His eyes lit up for a second. He got it. Sadly, Miss Evans did too. She began to turn her head toward me when Josh started coughing. He leaned down, a hand on her shoulder. The hand wearing the Ring of the Gods. If she noticed it, game over.

"Are you all right?" Miss Evans asked, tending to him.

Josh coughed even harder, moving away from the front door. Miss Evans took the bait, moving out onto the porch to pat his back.

I rushed upstairs and into the bedroom. What I saw made me want to rip out my eyes.

Tyler, Clayton, and Darrel were all naked, spread-eagled and gagged with their hands bound above their heads, an image that I knew would haunt me for some time to come. The three of them made sounds to warn Miss Evans, but the gags cut down on the noise.

Sam sat, leaning against a wall, tied up with rope but still clothed. She'd been gagged with a blue bandana.

Sick bastards. They wanted her to see this orgy of terror.

I cut her free with my claws and removed her gag. She collapsed into my arms.

"Thank you. You have no idea the things they made me see."

"I can imagine." Actually, I'd seen worse. A woman fooling around with a centaur and a chimera. I'd never get that image out of my head.

"How did you find me?" she asked, her voice breaking.

"You're at Miss Evans's house."

She massaged her wrists, rubbed raw by the rope. "Oh."

The guys kept trying to alert the succubus. Tyler got the bright idea to bang his head against the wall. I hoped it wasn't loud enough to tip her off.

It was.

TWENTY-SEVEN

ROLLERCOASTER OF DEATH

Miss Evans's succubus wail made Sam and me cover our ears. Sam fell to the floor in agony, forcing me to drop my hands from my ears and pick her up. The wail felt like a million needles stabbing my head all at once. Much as the pain ate away at me, we had to move. Thanks to Sam being zero help, I bore the brunt of the monster's shrieks as I cradled her in my arms. My hands burned from touching her skin, but I gritted my teeth and tried to think of anything besides the all-enveloping pain.

"Are you strong enough to Hand of God Miss Evans?" I asked.

"What?" Sam asked.

Great.

I staggered out of the bedroom and headed down the stairs. We needed to get close enough to Miss Evans so Sam could Hand of God her ass.

She crashed through the front of the house in full succubus regalia: dark, scaly skin, horns, wings, and a tail. She was the size of a garbage truck. Miss Evans shrieked as she flew at us. I panicked and tried to run back up the stairs, but I didn't move fast enough. She scooped us up with her scaly feet and crashed through the rear of the house.

The succubus picked up altitude as we flew over some trees.

"What's it doing?" Sam asked as the three of us moved higher and higher. She struggled to get free.

"Best guess? It's going to drop us from a height that makes us go splat."

"Can we not do that?"

"Ask Miss Evans with your Hand of God. See what she says." I didn't know what we could do to get out of this if the Hand of God didn't work. The healing stuff wouldn't save us if we were already stains on the road, and I doubted Miss Evans would let us go out of the kindness of her heart. This might suck a little.

So, Bart. How did you end up back in Hell?

I got dropped from hundreds of feet in the air by a flying succubus.

Ha, ha. Loser.

The jokes about being killed by a bird would be nonstop. Especially from Hitler, who'd make at least a million Eagle's Nest jokes about it.

Sam tried to order Miss Evans to set us down, but the almost-angel had a hard enough time hanging on to the succubus.

"I can't get a good grip," she said.

I had an inappropriate response, but now wasn't the time. I remembered the water gun in my jacket. I pulled it out and shot at the foot holding me. Her scales sizzled and smoked where the holy water landed, loosening the grip around me. I grabbed one of the talon-like toes before I fell.

I swung myself on top of the foot and reached out to Sam. She tried to take my hand. I'd almost reached her fingertips when the succubus did a corkscrew. My feet scraped against the top of a tree as I tried to hang on.

I stuck out my hand for Sam to grab again.

"You're flexible," I shouted. "Think long."

Sam reached for me again. I leaned toward her and wrapped my hand around her wrist. I pulled as hard as I could, freeing her from the talon's grip. My sizzling flesh almost made me lose her. A razor-sharp claw snagged her thigh as she escaped, leaving a gash the length of her leg. Sam and I glanced at each other, then at her bleeding leg. A stream of blood soaked through her jeans.

"Come on." I crawled out of the foot and took hold of the base of one of her wings for support. When I left the safety of her foot, Miss Evans dipped and drifted to my side as my weight unbalanced her.

"Let's see if the angel has wings," the succubus said with a hiss. She went up in the air, increasing her speed as she climbed. I held onto the wing as my feet dangled in the air. I'd be toast if I lost my grip on Miss Evans's scales. Sam's screams let me know she hadn't fallen off yet.

"I can't fly," she said. "I'm not even a real angel yet."

The succubus laughed. "Pity."

"Set us down," I said to Miss Evans. "Or it's holy water in the eye."

The succubus hissed and went into a dive. I lost my grip on the wing and almost fell, but I grabbed her tail at the last moment. The wind buffeted my face. Lights approached. Miss Evans took us straight into oncoming traffic on the Beltline. Those drivers would have one heck of a story to tell when they got home, provided their brains could process everything and they didn't convince themselves they saw nothing more than a balloon or floating teddy bears.

Miss Evans wagged her tail back and forth, trying to make a car hit me. Drivers honked their horns at us, as if that would deter a succubus. I yanked up my feet as I barely missed the cars. I almost smashed into a SUV, but managed to push myself off the side of it, which, at sixty-five miles an hour, was easier said than done.

Sam screamed again. If I hadn't also been struggling to stay on, I'd have told her to quit acting like a girl and nut up. A car clipped her feet. We wouldn't last much longer out here. At that moment, I kind of envied Josh, hanging out at Miss Evans's house, wondering where we'd flown off to.

"Face palm her," I said.

"I can't." One of her hands lost its grip, but she quickly latched back onto the succubus.

I crawled up the tail, dodging cars as they sped by, and

planted my feet on her wings. I wrapped an arm around her neck and pulled out the water gun.

"You asked for it," I said. "Suck on this."

I shot her in the face with holy water. Miss Evans screamed, but didn't seem inclined to take us down. I kept squeezing the trigger. Her molten scales left a smoke trail that smelled like a combination of raw eggs and canned dog food. I turned my head so I wouldn't have to inhale it. I felt a tap on my shoulder. Sam.

"Glad you could make it," I said.

"Shut up." She laid her hands on both sides of Miss Evans's rib cage. "By the power of God, I command you to set us down safely."

Her hands lit up. The succubus turned so sharply to the left I almost tumbled off. I continued shooting the holy water in her face. She landed on top of a parking deck. Sam and I rolled off her back onto the concrete.

"You didn't say anything about leaving you alone after landing," Miss Evans said. She snapped at Sam, sinking her teeth into her shoulder.

The angel yelled out in pain.

I ran up and tried to shoot Miss Evans in the eye, but the water gun was empty. Stupid toy.

Sam's hands glowed so brightly they nearly blinded me. She grabbed the succubus's head, which lit up from the inside.

Miss Evans howled, letting go of Sam. The teacher's scaly head kept glowing, as if it were heating up. She moved away from us, shrieking and shaking her head back and forth, like she tried to get the light out of her.

I helped Sam to her feet and watched Miss Evans writhe in pain. I took no small amount of glee in the sight.

Her head suddenly exploded. Succubus brains landed on my suit, but I didn't care. So many had already been ruined at this point, what was one more?

"I didn't know you could do that," I said.

"Only if I'm touching the thing," she said. "Otherwise, the best I can do is knock it out."

I was still impressed. "The name's Sam," I said. "Samantha if you're nasty."

She grinned, then held her hands up in front of her. "Hell hath no fury, right?"

"You know what else hath no fury like a woman scorned?"

"Still me. That S&M orgy was repulsive."

"Good answer, but no." I fished around in my pocket for the Shard of Gabriel. "Me. Look what I found."

I showed her the Shard. She went rigid and the air turned stale around her, as if she'd been told her parents died in a horrific plane crash.

"What are you doing with that?" she asked.

"Josh and I went to your place to see if we could use a red herring for the swap with Miss Evans. Instead, I found the real herring. Were you ever going to tell me you had the Shard?"

Sam reached for the Shard, but I jerked my hand back.

"If I had, you would've used it for your own personal gain. Am I right?"

Indeed. If I'd known before now, I absolutely would've used it for my own demonic purposes. I lowered my head. I didn't like being called out.

"Right."

"So, that's why I didn't tell you."

"Why the charade, then? Why not just use the stupid thing to find out who wants it? We wouldn't have had to go through all this stuff, like a succubus trying to take our heads off by flying us into oncoming traffic."

"Because—"

I waved her off. She'd have said anything at this point to calm me down. I looked into the Shard. "Who is trying to get their greasy little hands on you?"

Before the answer could formulate in my mind, Sam slapped the Shard out of my hands, breaking the connection. The glass skidded across the pavement.

"They'll know," she said as she ran over to pick it up.

"How? This is ridiculous."

"Whoever wants the Shard has had it before, but only briefly. They figured out a way to track it. If we use the thing, they'll know, and they'll know where." Sam moved toward the deck's stairwell. "We have to go. Now. Before they show up. I'll explain more, but we have to go."

I followed Sam down the stairs and out onto the sidewalk. I called a taxi to pick us up. While we waited, Sam explained how she came to possess the Shard, and the homing beacon. After I'd lost it, in a rare act of cooperation, Hell returned the piece of the mirror to Gabriel. Lucifer worried some other demon would get the same idea I did. But Gabriel was ambushed and temporarily lost the fragment.

Insert joke about not using the Shard here.

Before Heaven got it back, the tracking spell had been placed on it. The allure was addictive, something I understood better than most. Gabriel knew whomever stole the relic wouldn't stop looking for it, so he'd put Sam into action. She'd tracked the suspect to Raleigh on her own, but the two of them got into a scuffle, and Sam realized she didn't have the ability to do this on her own.

"I needed help. My people didn't know who to ask, so I went to the only thing that did."

"The Shard," I said.

"That's why you were attacked right after you got topside," she said. "Whoever had it last knew you'd been chosen, putting us both in danger."

"Thanks again for that horrible Tony Stewart shirt, by the way."

"Sorry. I was at a gas station. They didn't have a lot to choose from."

"Why not meet me when I got topside?"

"I wanted to, but I had to make sure whoever wanted the thing couldn't find me. By the time I could, you'd taken care of things on your end."

"That's how I roll," I said with a wink. "If this person or whatever knows where it is, why aren't we being chased right now?"

Sam pointed above the parking deck. "Speak of the devil."

I had to squint, but I saw it. The Black Cloud of Death. I could see it only when it passed under the lights.

She pulled me back into the shadows. "That thing only knows where the Shard was used. It can't track us now."

The smoke-thing left after another minute. I squeezed my hand into a fist. I wanted to fight the mist machine, but I knew that wouldn't be the wisest course of action. The taxi arrived shortly after and took us to Sweet Claudette. Josh sat on the trunk.

"What are you doing?" I asked the little pissant before unlocking the car. "Don't sit on Sweet Claudette. You have any idea what this baby cost?"

I handed Sam one of the vials of angel goo for her shoulder.

Josh slid off the trunk. "Nope. Don't care, either. What took you guys so long?"

Sam rubbed the healing ointment on her wounds while she regaled Josh with the story of how she destroyed Miss Evans.

Josh looked like he wanted to kiss her. "You're so badass."

"Aw." Sam blushed. "That's sweet."

Gag.

"What about Tyler and the two Things?" I asked, changing the subject. "Anything happen with them?"

"Come see for yourself."

We walked to the house, which looked like a tornado ripped the place in two. Even the fire department had arrived. Tyler, Clayton, and Darrel, still in their S&M getups, rolled around on the grass across the street in the fetal position, crying. Some firemen stood to the side, probably trying to figure out if they should even touch these kids.

"Miss Evans," Tyler said. "No."

"It happened a few minutes after you guys disappeared," Josh said. "The firemen and ambulance arrived, then the three of them stumbled outside in those outfits. Next thing I know, they're acting like babies calling out for their mom. I kind of feel sorry for them."

The sight of these three reduced to leaky faucets would've been hilarious if they weren't so pathetic. Actually, no. I take that back. It was still a laugh riot.

"Will they ever recover?" Josh asked.

I laughed. "I hope not."

"They'll sort of recover," Sam said. "They'll stop crying and everything, but they'll never be the same. For the rest of their lives, there will be a massive void in their souls that nothing can fill." She tapped me on the arm. "That's why I did what I did with you. Once the bond is sealed, it never goes away. These three are going to just drift through life, their entire existence an open wound."

I clapped my hands together. "Serves them right."

Sam smacked me. "They didn't know any better. She lured them in, just like you. They're victims. Have some sympathy."

This girl needed to stop calling me out. It drove me nuts. I decided to not even respond.

"Give me the ring back," I said to Josh.

He pulled it off his finger and handed it to me. I slid the ring back on. With Miss Evans out of the way, I just needed a plan to wreck Jenny's chances at Homecoming Queen. I had an idea, but things would get nasty. Really nasty.

There was nothing quite as destructive as a rumor that'd gone viral.

Twenty-Eight

THE RUMOR MILL

Only one rumor had a chance of crippling Jenny McPherson's chances at Homecoming Queen. Not that it bothered me, but if this rumor gained traction, it could have a devastating effect, much like the rumor about me did.. Of course, while it could be painful for her in the short term, she might also win a ton of support. Either way, I had to take that chance.

I approached Monica at school the next day, feeling pretty confident about myself for coming up with this idea.

"Word has it Miss Evans is a no-show today," the cheerleader said as she texted away on her phone.

"And that means what to me?"

Monica didn't take her eyes off her phone. "Just sayin'. She's not around."

"Great. I want you to do me a favor," I said.

"You keep coming up to me in crowds like this, people are going to start talking. A rumor that you like me and not Jenny won't do the trick. You need something better."

"I know, and I have it. Honestly, I can't believe you hadn't thought of it yourself."

"Maybe I have." Monica's eyes darted up to meet mine. "Maybe I just wanted to see if you're as good as you like to think you are. Or maybe I wanted to see how serious you were about learning Vixen's identity."

"Or maybe you just want to play some silly game with me."

"That's also possible." Monica shook off what I'd said, returning to her cellphone.

"Listen. I need you to tell your cattiest friends that Jenny slept with a teacher."

The cheerleader's eyes looked so bright and wide I thought she'd won the lottery. "I wonder where you got that idea."

I grinned and stuffed my hands in my pockets. "Sometimes, they just come to me."

"Just be careful. It could backfire."

Kids could be cruel. Sometimes even worse than demons. With this rumor, Jenny would be torn to shreds.

"I doubt the story will stick for long, but it should ensure she doesn't become Homecoming Queen."

"You got it."

I clapped my hands together. "We'll soon find out."

I started to leave, but Monica grabbed my shoulder.

"You need a backup plan. I told you, Jenny is crafty. This whole thing could easily play out as a non-starter." She moved in and gave me a hard, cold, closed-mouth kiss. The whole thing felt more like a fare-thee-well smooch than anything passionate. "Remember that."

Before lunchtime rolled around, most everyone at the school heard the rumor that Jenny had an on-going affair with one of the male teachers at Frady-McNeely. I'd hoped the kids gravitated towards Coach Mort, but most of the speculation centered on Mr. Dawson, a math teacher.

I found Jenny sitting alone in the commons area, working on some Calculus.

"The answer is George Washington," I said.

She looked up and halfway smiled. "Thanks, but I still have to show my work."

"Just draw a wig, an apple and some wooden teeth."

The smile broadened. "Excellent."

"What are you doing out here all by your lonesome?" I asked, sitting down next to her.

"I'm not really in the mood to be around other people. Someone's been spreading a rumor I've been sleeping with a teacher, and it caught me off guard. It's awful that someone would try to be so hurtful, you know?" She turned the page of textbook. "It hurts. It really does."

Well, at least I could tell Monica that Jenny could be gotten to. "That's terrible. Do you have any idea who would do such a thing?"

"I have an idea. Most of the people who've told me about the rumor said a cheerleader told them, so my best guess is it came from there." She tapped her pencil against her Calculus book. "I never did anything to them, but whatever. If they want to be cruel, that's their prerogative."

"Yeah, that stinks." I sat there for a moment in silence. Then I had an idea. Who said Monica could be the only one doing the torturing? She'd been holding Vixen's identity over my head, and even forced me to slander Jenny. Sometimes I really loved being a demon. "Are you planning on getting them back? Because I could help you with that."

Jenny shook her head. "It'll blow over soon, I'm sure. I mean, if you can survive being called a murderer, I can get through being called a slut."

"True," I said. "I'm just glad the teachers and staff had enough sense to disregard it as a rumor and didn't call the cops on me. I wouldn't have survived being driven away in a police car." Though it might have made me popular among the burnouts, but nobody liked them. After a while, the combination of drugs and self-loathing in their systems became toxic. And deadly. Most burnouts never lived to see thirty.

Jenny closed her book and notebook. "I don't know that anybody would be able to show their face around here again if that happened."

She stood up, and I followed her lead. "I'm off to class."

After she left, I walked around the halls, killing time until my lunch period ended. My cellphone vibrated. I'd gotten a text from an unknown number.

I know you have the Shard of Gabriel. I want it. Or else.

Ridiculous. I knew responding would be a bad idea so, naturally, I responded.

Sure, just show up in your true form and I'll be more than happy to hand it over.

I wanted a cigarette, but I'd smoked my last one this morning on the way over. The phone vibrated again. I had another message from *Unknown*, whom I assumed was the Black Cloud of Death. Part of me wondered how a cloud could send text messages, but then I remembered it had the ability to possess people. Maybe even go a step further and become a person. For all I knew, it could be standing right next to me.

Soon.

Great. I loved ominous threats. As if *Unknown* expected me to spend my time in a perpetual state of fear, waiting for the other shoe to drop. I will admit it didn't help that this happened while I was out of cigarettes, so when the day ended I felt a bit on edge.

Josh stood with Sam by her car. I gave him a sideways glance. I half expected him to try to stab me with a shiv.

"I see everybody's all buddy-buddy again," I said.

"I need to talk to you," Sam said, shifting her weight back and forth.

"Did you get some texts from Unknown too?" I asked.

She nodded.

"How did the thing even get our numbers?"

"Same way you found Miss Evans probably. The school directory."

I glared at her.

"What? We had to when Quincy enrolled us."

"You couldn't provide false information?"

Sam's face dropped. "I guess so."

Great.

"What do you make of it?" she asked.

I wanted to say Vixen, or the cloud or whatever, just wanted to be a blowhard and puff out their chest. I wanted to say that, but I didn't believe it. The texts did bother me. A little.

"Have you had a chance to put the Shard somewhere safe? And by safe I mean *not* in the place I found it?"

"Not yet."

Leave it to a pseudo-angel not to treat the situation as dire.

They always had to look at the bright side of things.

"Don't you think that might have been a good idea?"

"Don't get mad at her," Josh said.

As if I wanted to get into another pissing contest with him at the moment.

"Let it go, man. If you want to ask Sam out, then ask her out. We don't have time for this chivalry act right now."

"I don't want to ask her out," Josh said. His voice didn't sound defensive. At all. Not even a little bit.

"Be nice," Sam said.

"What would be nice is if you'd treat this a little more seriously and stop being so happy and cheery." It was unnecessary and counterproductive. Nobody needed to be happy all the time.

Sam grabbed me and pulled me out of earshot of Josh.

"You think I'm not doing that? I had to watch a succubus and three of her victims engage in some pretty depraved behavior last night. It still triggers my gag reflex." She swallowed, probably trying to force back some bile. "Not to mention that Miss Evans tried to take a chunk out of my shoulder. I'm *sorry* if I'm trying to stay positive. But at the rate we're going, we'll be out of the healing ointment, and then where will we be? Up... poo creek."

"Language," I said.

She scowled at me. "You may be used to this kind of stuff happening to you, but I'm not. So I'd appreciate whatever compassion you can give me, okay?"

She looked like she tried to fight back tears.

A small part of me wanted to put my hand on her shoulder, but self-control won out.

"Okay. But Vixen looks like she's making her move." I made sure to sound calm. "Can you think of somewhere safe we can hide the Shard until things cool down?"

After a moment, she smiled. "I can think of one."

The weather forecast didn't call for rain but, judging by the movement of the dark clouds in the distance, it headed our way. Provided they actually *were* storm clouds. I thought about making Sam take us to my place so we could use Sweet Claudette and get to a church faster, but honestly I had no clue when, or if, the Black Cloud of Death would strike, making time precious.

We passed a church about a half-mile from Sam's place. Sam brought the car to a stop in front of her complex. She hopped out, leaving the motor running. As soon as she disappeared into the complex, I crawled over into the driver's seat.

"What are you doing?" Josh asked.

"We need to get to the church and hide the Shard as soon as possible. I don't know about you, but I trust women drivers about as far as I can throw them."

"That saying doesn't really work for you. You're a demon, so I'd imagine you could throw one pretty far."

"Touché."

Sam appeared through the complex's main entrance. She stopped when she saw me in her seat, but changed direction and got in on the passenger side. She gave me a sideways glance.

"Bartholomew doesn't trust women drivers," Josh said. "But I do."

Sam kept staring at me. The box I'd originally found the Shard in sat in her lap.

"I'm not surprised you want to drive. But if something bad happens while you're behind the wheel, I want to be able to drive your new car next time we go somewhere. Deal?" She extended her hand.

"What's in it for me? What if something doesn't happen? What do I get?"

"You get to keep me out of your driver's seat."

"Weak. No deal."

Sam huffed. "Do we really have time for this?"

"I don't know. Do we?"

Sam made a sound in her throat that sounded a whole lot like a *grr*.

"Did you just *grr* at me?" I asked.

Sam made the noise again, nodding. "Forget the deal. Can

we go?"

I couldn't accept any bet that hinged on my Sweet Claudette, so I felt relieved she'd taken my baby off the table.

"Absolutely."

The clouds continued to darken as I drove us to St. Anthony's. I glanced up to make sure there weren't any weird formations, birds, or Clouds of Death coming after us. A few minutes later, I pulled to a stop in front of the church. Sam and Josh hopped out. I elected to stay in the car.

Sam closed the door and I watched her walk into the church, her ass moving back and forth like a metronome, keeping the beat. She'd already slept with me once out of pity. Maybe I could convince her to do it again, this time out of lust. Or as a poor life choice. I needed a chance to redeem myself. No way I'd brought my A-game last time. Maybe our tumultuous affair would get her booted from the angels' team. That wouldn't be the worst thing that happened.

I tapped my fingers on the steering wheel. I flipped on the radio to a classic rock station. I was more partial to contemporary pop, mostly because we'd ruined it for everybody. People like Jimi Hendrix were graced by you-know-who, but we tried to make sure talents like him lasted only so long before drugs or alcohol got the better of them. Each year, Hell dug its claws deeper into the music industry, killing whatever "art" the medium possessed.

Sam and Josh got back in the car. I put the gear into drive and sped off to my place.

"Everything safe and sound?" I asked.

"Yep," Sam said. "I don't think even you can get to it now without bursting into flames."

"Tasty." I kind of wanted to test her theory, but not now.

Ten minutes later, I pulled the car over to the curb next to my building. Sam and I got out so she could take the driver's seat. We almost bumped into each other in front of the car. I stepped to the side and motioned for her to go on. She moved past me, then stopped.

"I heard a pretty vicious rumor about Jenny McPherson today," she said.

"Did you? What was it? I was kind of bogged down in

school work today." Tee hee.

Sam narrowed her eyes. She must not have bought my lie, but then again, I didn't really try to sell it.

"Would you rather I took her virginity, then ruined her?" I asked. "Because, believe me, that way would've been a lot more fun for me."

"Yeah, I know it would've been. I just hate that we have to hurt that poor girl."

I pursed my lips. "Indeed. A true shame on the level of, say, the Holocaust or Biggie Smalls being cut down in his prime."

Sam walked over to the driver's side door. "Go inside before you say something that's going to irk me."

I pulled my keys out of my pocket. "Love to, but I've been out of cigarettes all day. Need a refill."

Sam's face scrunched together as she glared at me. "That's a disgusting habit."

"Says you."

I walked into the parking deck and took a moment to gaze at my beautiful Sweet Claudette. She epitomized the best of what the automobile industry had to offer. I slid into her cushy leather seat, started the engine, and revved that baby up. The tires screeched as I drove out of the deck.

With the Shard dropped off at the church without incident, I relaxed. Things seemed to be getting easier. I decided to take the Benz on the Beltline so I could let my baby out to play a little. After passing a few exits, I pulled off on Lake Boone Trail to get some cigs.

I bought five cartons, immediately opening one of them and stashing a pack in my jacket pocket. I patted my cartons of cancer sticks as I laid them down on the seat next to me. My wonderful treats.

Sweet Claudette roared back onto the Beltline. The sun began to set, and the dark clouds surrounding the city made the sky look like a filtered version of night. I expected it to start pouring at any moment. Hopefully, Claudette and I would beat the rain and get back under the cover of the parking deck. I didn't want her getting wet.

The day turned even darker. I had to turn on my lights.

With this creeping darkness surrounding me, I should've been worried. I should've gotten off the Beltline. I did neither.
And that's when the Black Cloud of Death struck.

TWENTY-NINE
THE SHORT LIFE OF SWEET CLAUDETTE

Complete darkness enveloped the Benz. The second everything turned black, the car flipped on its side. At eighty-miles an hour, Sweet Claudette's frame screeched against the road as I barrel-rolled across two lanes of traffic. My head jerked forward when another car slammed into mine. The airbag went off, hitting me in the face like a high-powered air rifle projectile. Claudette and I continued flipping. Everything happened so fast I didn't even have a chance to lament what had befallen my new car. Sweet Claudette and I rolled down a hill. We must've been off the Beltline and in some grass. All I could focus on was the sound of metal crunching.

The Benz and I came to a violent, upside-down halt as a tree trunk pierced the passenger side of the car. I tried to take stock of everything. Windows shattered; the engine wheezed as it died. Fiery blood burned in my mouth. I spit out pieces of glass. My body felt like I'd been put in a blender. Blood ran down my neck. The screaming sensation in my bones let me know I'd probably broken a few. Everything spun. I unbuckled my seatbelt and tried to move, but I couldn't.

I should've known.

My horns had come out and lodged in the roof. Destroying my week-old, two hundred thousand dollar car with me in it tended to unleash the horns. I wiggled my head around, trying to create some space in the roof to get my horns free. I moved my noggin in a circle, then pulled my head down. They came loose. I crawled out of the gaping hole where my passenger window used to be and sat in the grass outside. When the spinning in my head let up, the rain began.

I reached into the door's container for one of the vials of healing ointment. I lifted my hand to find it covered in goo. None of the vials survived the wreck. I scooped up as much as I could and rubbed it all over myself. There wasn't enough to completely heal me, but enough to get me in basic working order. Thankfully, I hadn't broken the plastic seal on the cigarettes, so the ointment hadn't ruined them. I tapped the box against the palm of my hand, then pulled one out and lit it. I took a deep, long drag. I needed to see the full extent of Sweet Claudette's damage, but first I needed a few more pulls on the cigarette, for courage.

I fell to my knees at the sight of my dear, dead Sweet Claudette.

I couldn't find one inch of her that wasn't dented, shredded, or mangled. The roof had collapsed under the weight of the rest of the car.

My baby. My beautiful baby.

"Why?" I asked, pounding my fists into the ground. "She didn't deserve this."

I understood going after me, but Sweet Claudette? I hadn't even hit one hundred miles an hour with her yet. If I'd had a human heart, it would've been broken right now. I took one last drag, then flung my cigarette in the grass. I felt too sad to keep smoking.

Flashing red lights glared off the Benz. I looked back and saw an ambulance approaching. They couldn't see me like this, with my horns still out. I pushed myself to my feet and stumbled into a patch of trees, hoping they wouldn't try to find me. The rain hid my tears from sight. The last time I'd cried was in 1588 when Heaven saved Great Britain from the Spanish invasion with the Protestant Wind. I'd spent over a year helping set that up, and those douche nozzles upstairs wrecked the entire thing. That one should've been my big break. Instead, I ended up a cautionary tale. A joke. *Bite off more than you can chew, end up like Bartholomew.* Even rhymed.

I had to get out of here. Now. I pulled my phone out of my pocket. The cracked screen gave me a moment of near-panic before the thing lit up. I called Sam.

"Bartholomew? What's going on?"

"The thing... it... it... killed Sweet Claudette," I said through my tears. "Struck down in her prime by a monster."

"Are you okay? Where are you?" Sam sounded panicky.

"On the Beltline. Not sure where." My brain felt like a stampede trampled it to death. "Ambulance here."

"I'm on my way. I'll look for the flashing lights." Sam hung up.

I held the phone to my ear for another moment. I couldn't find the will to move.

Something landed on my back, knocking me face-first into the ground. My head jerked back as someone grabbed my horns and yanked. Kyle knelt down in front of me, grinning like he'd gotten away with murder.

"Surprised?"

A bit, actually. I tried to speak, but the combination of spaghetti brains, my head wanting to be removed from my body, and the grief over Sweet Claudette made it almost impossible.

He slapped me. "Answer me."

"Uh... yeah." I forced out the words.

Kyle motioned to whoever held me down to ease up a bit. Then he kicked me in the face, making my teeth vibrate.

"You killed my baby," he said, then glanced at the person behind me. "Well, one of them."

"Huh?" I had no idea what he meant.

Another flick of his hand and his flunky jerked my horns so hard I ended up being brought to my feet.

Kyle moved past me. "Come on. We don't need an audience."

I still couldn't see the person behind me, but the flunky led me through the trees and down to an abandoned side road. We approached a beat-up Toyota.

"You... how?"

Kyle laughed. "I got a phone call telling me to be here at this time and whoever called promised… satisfaction… for what you did to my darling Miss Evans."

The flunky threw me against the car. I slid down the wet metal to the pavement. The flunky revealed herself to be the Goth girl I'd seen Kyle making out with.

"She… you were under her spell?"

Kyle shook his head.

"As bright as you like to think you are, you really are an idiot." He put his arm around the girl. "No, Miss Evans, much like my new protégé Ursula here, was part of my harem."

I didn't understand. Kyle ran the succubi? "What?"

Kyle stomped on my face, driving my horns into the car and forcing me to look up at him.

"We've traveled the world forever, leeching off an international buffet of horny people who didn't have a clue. Like Tyler. Clayton. Darrel. We made a nice living out of it too. Miss Evans was one of my most prized girls."

The football players? "But… they bullied you."

Kyle grinned, revealing sharp, spiked teeth. "Nope. I knew what you were the second you walked into Casey's house. You only saw what I wanted you to see."

"So you're a… pimpubus?"

Kyle glanced at Ursula. Both of them nodded and smiled.

"I like the sound of that. Yeah. You could say that. I'm a pimpubus." His eyes turned black. "Where's the Shard?"

I laughed, spilling blood out onto my chin. The smoky smell wafted into my nostrils. "Gone. Hidden. Safe."

"And where would that be?"

I wiped some of the blood off my chin, then flicked my hand. "Church."

Kyle stared at me for a moment. He probably tried to figure out if I was bluffing. I used my peripheral vision to see if anyone could stumble on us, but I saw only trees. I hoped Sam knew she'd better move her cute little ass.

"You're lying," Kyle said. "You wouldn't let it be stored in a spot where not even you could get to it."

"*Onward, Christian soldier.*"

"Ursula, let's make our friend here a little more presentable for the rest of the world. He can't walk around in public with those things sticking out of him." He grabbed one of my horns. "The mortals would piss themselves."

"You got it, baby," she said, taking hold of the other.

I screamed as they pulled my horns out of the car door. Then, they each placed a foot on my arms and used all their strength to pull my horns to opposing sides. I almost wished they poured holy water down my throat instead. I bet it would've hurt less. My brain felt like it was being ripped in two. Red lights flashed through the trees, but the pouring rain and sirens drowned out my shouts. I felt my horns fracturing. They snapped with a loud crack. What remained of them pounded in my head. My ears rang. The world seemed like a flushing toilet all around me.

Kyle dangled a horn in front of my face.

"You took what was most precious to me," he said. "Now I've returned the favor."

Kyle and Ursula danced around, throwing the horns up in the air and catching them.

"Look." Ursula held the two horns in front of her chest. "Diamond cutters."

A demon's horns were more than just a symbol that we'd fallen from Heaven. Many of the original demons, like myself, wore them as a badge of honor. To us, they were like a cooler version of the halos angels wore. Yes, we had to hide them while topside to conceal who we really were, but that didn't temper our love for them. Some people defined themselves with a mustache, or baldness, or an unhealthy fondness for Elvis Presley. Our horns defined us. They let everyone know who we were and what we were capable of. Without them, demons had no definition. We didn't belong in Hell. We didn't belong anywhere. We technically might not have even been demons anymore.

I felt as if both my honor and demonhood were stripped away all at once. I still had all my strengths, but my identification with Hell was gone. Horns didn't grow back, so losing them undid my connection to Hell for eternity. From now on, I could no longer call Hell home. And the worst part? I would still be expected to finish this crap with Sam. Just because I'd lost my horns didn't mean Hell wouldn't come calling if I failed.

I lowered my head. My will to exist vanished.

"Just do what you want and be on your way."

"What's that?" Kyle asked.

Ursula held a horn up to her ear, like a hearing device. "Speak up."

Kyle pushed the end of my horn under my chin, forcing my head up.

"You heard the lady."

"Finish it."

Ursula laughed. She wrapped her arms around Kyle and jammed her tongue down his throat. Even when I'd been busted trying to get my hands on the Shard of Gabriel, I'd still had some fight left in me. I'd endured the Seventh Circle. Now? The fight drained out of me. I didn't see the point anymore.

"We have one last thing we want from you," Kyle said. "Ursula here needs to take possession of someone before she can fully transform into a succubus. And guess what? You're it."

Ursula slowly ran my horn down the middle of her chest, then used it to trace the curvature of her breasts. When they'd still been attached to my body, I'd relished the opportunities to use my horns like that.

"I'm so nervous." She giggled. "It's my first time."

Under any other circumstances, that would've been music to my ears. She leaned down in front of me and grabbed my face with her hand.

I refused to lock eyes with her. The succubus-in-waiting forced my mouth open, then kissed me, massaging my tongue with her own. I barely noticed. My head still felt like such a swirling mess of pain and emptiness. She pulled back, licking her lips.

Nothing happened. I didn't fall under her control.

"What's going on?" she asked. "Is he possessed? Can I have him?"

Kyle knelt down in front of me, his teeth showing under a nefarious grin. "I don't know. He should be crawling all over you."

I should be, but the Ring of the Gods kept her patented succubus seduction technique at bay. Not that I really cared at this point. I didn't have the energy to fight back and, even if I did, I wouldn't have wanted to.

"Is it the horns?" Ursula asked. "Is that it?"

"I don't know," Kyle said.

A bright light illuminated the ground. Lightning. Another flash. Strange, I didn't hear any thunder booming over the rain. Kyle fell to ground, out cold. I glanced up to see Ursula rushing toward Kyle, screaming. Her screams turned into tearful wailing as she cradled him in her arms.

THIRTY

TALK TO THE HAND (OF YOU KNOW WHO)

Ursula screamed. "You bitch."

I lifted my head to see Sam, hands still glowing. She looked down at me with pity and sorrow in her eyes.

"You killed him." Ursula, not yet a full succubus, let her skin melt away to reveal her scaly form. She didn't have wings, and looked to be maybe half the size of Miss Evans.

Sam took hold of Kyle and Ursula. A beam of light moved under their skin, tearing the two to pieces. They exploded, the rain slashing through their remains as if they were dust.

Josh rushed over and helped me to my feet.

Sam stared at the stubs where my horns used to be, frowning. She reached out to touch them, but stopped herself.

"Come on," Josh said. "We need to go before anyone sees you." He glanced at my broken horns. "Love the new look."

Sam took out the two vials of healing ointment I'd given her earlier. I couldn't be sure, but I think she used the remaining contents on me. Losing my horns left me so broken and disoriented, I didn't even notice if the stuff helped or not.

Josh helped me down the abandoned road. We turned toward the Beltline and moved through the trees. Sam had parked her car on the shoulder. I fell into the back seat and closed my eyes. When I opened them, we were moving down the road. For all I cared, Sam could've dumped me on the unpaved shoulder. I wasn't much use to anybody.

"Hello, 9-1-1?" Josh said into his cellphone. "I'd like to report a theft. Yes. Someone stole my car." Josh gave the 9-1-1 operator the make and model of Sweet Claudette. He glanced back at me. "What's the license plate number?"

"Tem... temporary." I reached around and got hold of my wallet, then flung it at Josh.

He flipped through my wallet, found the tag information for Sweet Claudette, gave it to the 9-1-1 operator and hung up.

"That takes care of the wreck. You should have another Sweet Claudette in no time."

I reached into my jacket and pulled out my cigs. I popped one into my mouth but felt too weak to light it. "Ligh... lighter."

Josh glanced back and understood what I tried to say. He popped in Sam's car lighter and waited.

"You're not smoking in here, are you?" Sam asked. "I am not okay with that."

I forced out a small laugh. "M... medicinal."

"That's a load of bull," she said. "And you know it."

"Come on," Josh said. "Look at the guy."

"Fine." Sam sighed. The window by my head rolled down. I couldn't believe this ancient piece of metal with four wheels had power windows. "Just blow it outside."

Josh grabbed the lighter and held it to my cigarette. I inhaled. My body felt a little more at ease. I put another cigarette in my mouth, and used the one I smoked to light it. Two for one, baby.

"Unbelievable," Sam said.

Josh winced. "Two? Really?"

The smoke and nicotine seeping into my body immediately made me feel better. I still couldn't move around a lot, but they at least took the sting off the horns. The healing ointment helped some, but aside from numbing the pain, it didn't do much. It couldn't make them grow back. Nothing could. I must've looked more busted than Humpty Dumpty.

I closed my eyes and imagined voluptuous, naked virgins dancing to the tune of *Hey Mickey*. "Take me home. I want to get drunk."

I gave Sam the code to get into my parking deck and she pulled into a spot marked Compact, giving us less room to get out and making things that much more painful for me. I banged against the car next to me as they tried to help me out. Every time my body bumped into something, pain like a sonar ping moved throughout my body.

Sam and Josh propped me up as we walked out of the elevator and toward my condo. A couple of feet away, I noticed someone jimmied the door.

"What now?" I asked. "Can't I just cease to exist in peace?"

Sam leaned me against Josh as she held her hands out in front of her.

"Stop being a baby." She carefully pushed open the door. Her coach-speak didn't work. I still felt like being a baby.

The door creaked and a man called out from inside, "Come on in. We won't bite."

He had a strong Southern accent. A familiar accent.

Josh and I followed Sam inside. Arthur Powell leaned against the kitchen's island, drinking a glass of wine. My wine. He must've noticed me glaring at him.

"Surely you don't mind me partaking," he said, waving the glass.

I spit on the floor. I'd worry about cleaning it up later.

Powell sandwiched himself between two men, neither of whom looked very large or imposing. The pair wore matching red bowties around their necks. That Powell would bring muscle with him that didn't even look like muscle made me curious.

"Josh, call the police," Sam said. "Report a break-in."

I propped myself up against the wall, freeing Josh to take his phone out of his pocket. He pressed the digits nine, one, and one.

"You sure you want to do that?" Powell asked. "You hit send, my friends here are going to get angry. I love them when they're angry but, hey, that's me. I like a good tussle."

"I don't like them regardless," I said, feeling a sliver of strength returning. My anger at Powell gave me something to focus on besides my missing horns.

Arthur smirked. "You don't look so good. Give me back what's mine and you won't look any worse for wear, you have my word on it."

I raised my hand and extended my middle finger. I could almost see the heat emanating from Powell's henchmen. The televangelist took a sip of the wine and motioned for them to back down.

"I like your spunk, I really do," he said. "I don't want this to get ugly. Just give me back my ring and I won't devote myself, my ministry, and my viewers to destroying all three of you."

The healing goo fixed my exterior wounds a while ago, and now seemed to be strengthening me internally. I forced myself off the wall, struggling to maintain my balance. Things still felt a little wobbly. The rumors were true. Losing the horns messed with my equilibrium.

"Not happening," I said.

Powell finished off his wine in one giant gulp. "Just remember. You chose this."

He nodded at his henchmen. Their chests heaved up and down as they drew in huge breaths. The pair grew in size, as if they inflated themselves. What on Earth were they? Their shirts began to stretch and tear. Their skin went from pale white to deathly gray. The bowties ripped in half, falling to the floor.

"Um, Bartholomew," Sam said.

"Don't look at me."

As the henchmen's eyes glazed over, I tried to figure out their origin. Voodoo had zombies, Christianity had us and those silly angels, ancient Greece had the Olympians, Zoroastrianism the Amesha Spenta, Sumerians the Annunaki, but these guys? Who knew? Maybe they came from another dimension, but the possibility of cross-dimensional mythological creatures would've been too complicated to think about, even if my horns were still attached. Their bodies got so large the shirts ripped right off, breaking my train of thought. They destroyed my kitchen island with one flick of their wrists. One less obstacle between us and them. And one more thing for me to fix in this blessed place.

"They're like gray Hulks," Josh said.

The wood, silverware, and everything else in the island flew at us. Small pieces of wood lodged in my chest. Sam and Josh shielded their faces with their arms, which were covered with splinters. I pulled a fork out of my shoulder, the tines drenched in black blood.

Sam's hands lit up as she used the Hand of God. The light surrounded the three of them, but nothing happened. They didn't go to Purgatory. She thrust her arms forward. The light surged forward, throwing the henchmen and Powell back against the kitchen counters, smashing the wood and granite to pieces. If this roughhousing went on much longer, my apartment would be in as bad a shape as Sweet Claudette.

Josh pulled Quincy's knife out from under his shirt and flung it at the intruders. It flew straight into one of the henchmen's eyes. We all stopped for a moment to see if it actually hurt the thing. The henchman wiggled the knife back and forth, trying to remove it as optic fluid leaked out of the socket. The knife finally came out, with the monster's deflated eyeball attached to the end. Both the knife and the eye landed on the floor with a wooden, squishy thud.

My water gun lay on the back of the couch. I stumbled over, grabbed it and aimed at the henchman's eye socket. A stream of holy water flew across the condo, splashing all over his face.

With the exception of water spilling out of the empty eye socket, nothing happened.

Of course the holy water didn't do anything. Since televangelists are able to use the perks of being associated with God without any strings attached, it would figure their henchmen had the same deal.

Powell laughed. "Bart, Bart, Bart. Holy water only works on the damned, and to Heaven, we're nothing more than simple, God-fearing creatures."

"Not anymore," Sam said, sending another flash of light in his direction.

The force of it sent the buttweasel through the kitchen wall and into my bedroom. So much for only needing a new carpet and renovations to the den. Now I'd have to remodel the whole friggin' place. Or get a new one, which would be easier. The henchmen looked through the hole in my kitchen at Powell, who lay on my bed, out cold.

"Boss?" the one with both eyes asked.

With his back turned, I snuck up behind him. I glanced over at Josh and motioned for him to do the same with One-eyed Jack. One more step and I'd be within reach of the henchman's head. Josh stopped to pick up his knife. Using his foot to keep the eye in place, he pulled the knife off. Josh, being Josh, used a little too much gusto, dinging it against the refrigerator and making just enough noise to catch the attention of the henchmen.

The monster missing an eye smashed his hand across Josh's face, knocking him several feet back. I lunged at the other one, nails extended. I dug my razor-sharp claws into the henchman's neck. The flesh tore apart between my fingers. The thing's throat gave way and I ripped it out. The gaping hole in the throat spewed black bile everywhere as the henchman fell to the floor, dead. I threw the mangled flesh at the other one and ran around behind him.

I tried to wrap my hands around his neck and remove his head, but the thing proved too strong. He easily pulled one of my hands back, so I did the only other thing I could think of. I plucked out his other eye with two of my claws before he threw me off. The blind henchman stumbled around the kitchen, howling. He bumped against the window frame, holding his hands over his empty eye sockets.

"Do it, Sam," I said.

Sam's hands lit up, and the Hand of God pushed the henchman out the window. Considering the damage already done to the place, a smashed window didn't matter at this point. It would've been like crying over a broken fingernail during the Apocalypse.

Josh picked himself off the floor and joined us by the window in time to see the henchman revert to his human form.

"Isn't that going to raise a few alarms?" Josh asked. "Especially since it's kind of obvious which window he came out of?"

I shrugged. The henchman's death did answer the question of whether or not to get a new residence. "This place is in

Quincy's name."

"There is a way we can kill two birds with one stone," Sam said, nodding toward the bedroom where Powell remained down for the count.

"You've never been more attractive to me than you are right now," I cooed.

"I bet you say that to all the girls," she said.

I dialed 9-1-1. The operator answered on the third ring. Not very responsive for an emergency phone number.

"Yes, there are several men screaming at each other in my building. Sounds like a lover's quarrel. I'm really scared. I tried to tune it out, but then… oh, I don't even want to imagine what happened next."

"What happened next, sir?" the operator asked.

"I heard a loud crash, then a thump on the sidewalk below. I hope they only threw a chair or something out the window. I don't want to meddle, but they were interrupting my cartoons."

I gave the operator my address and we scooted across the street to watch the fireworks.

"Maybe I should become a missionary in the Sudan or something," I said. "Just disappear from everything. Maybe die of Ebola or the Hanta virus."

Sam smacked my arm. "Will you stop feeling sorry for yourself?"

"No."

"Seriously," Josh said. "It's even getting on my nerves."

"Like that's going to make me stop."

Thirty minutes later, the police carted Powell off in handcuffs on suspicion of double homicide. He screamed and shouted that he'd been framed, and that the Lord would clear his name.

The silly goose. I'd teach him to mess with me.

THIRTY-ONE

SYMPATHY FOR THE DEMON

I swallowed my self-pity about being hornless, or at least tried to by focusing on my anger. Few things drove a demon like anger. Except I wasn't a demon anymore. Or was I? Maybe I could refer to myself as a rogue demon, beholden to no one. That actually sounded pretty sweet.

I packed a suitcase full of clothes for school and grabbed my tux, which somehow survived the demolition of my place. I wanted to stay in a hotel, but Sam insisted I stay with her. Josh went home to ice his face, which had a baseball-sized bruise on it.

"You want to sex me up, don't you?" I asked, carrying my stuff up the stairs to her apartment. "That's why you don't want me to stay in a hotel."

She sighed. "Please. You weren't even that good."

Ouch. I'd figured as much, since I'd been possessed at the time, but her words still hurt. "You did not just say what I think you said."

Sam crossed her arms. "In case you didn't hear me, I'll repeat. I said you weren't. That. Good."

So much for that famed angelic compassion. What hurt worse, she had only Coach Mort to compare my performance to.

"Well, it couldn't have been that good for me either, because I don't remember it. So there."

"Of course you don't. You were possessed." Sam unlocked the door and walked in. She didn't look the least bit amused by our conversation. From what I could gather, she hadn't been all that amused when we slept together, either.

"That's beside the point," I said as I entered her apartment.

Sam tossed her keys on the coffee table. "Is it?"

"Yes." At least, I thought so. "You can't hold being possessed against me. I demand a do-over."

Sam snorted. "Absolutely not. You know better than that."

I took in a deep breath of her vanilla candles. "I can't have you going around telling people I'm terrible in the sack. Haven't I suffered enough already?"

Sam flipped on the lights in the den. "I'm sorry you lost your horns. I really am. But you're not getting a do-over."

I set my suitcase down next to the couch. "I'm assuming I don't get to sleep in your bed?"

Sam shook her head. "You can make do with the couch."

"Wonderful." So much for finding some kind of silver lining in this whole mess. No horns, no sex, no nothing. Just work. *Give me an office, a beer belly, three kids, and I'm the average middle-aged male.*

The rest of the week passed without any drama, a more than welcome change. I even began the slow adjustment from being a "Hell-bound" demon to "rogue" demon. That change wouldn't happen overnight, but maybe I'd survive this whole ordeal. Josh stayed home from school so nobody would ask any questions about the massive bruise on his face. Sam even made him promise to skip the Homecoming game Friday night so he could rest up for the dance on Saturday. If he'd been a real man, he would've ignored Sam and done what he wanted. Someone should've probably told him a girl wasn't going to respect someone whose nose was up her ass, but that someone wouldn't be me.

I spoke to Jenny after school on Friday, asking if I needed

to be with her at the announcement of the Homecoming King and Queen during halftime of the game that night.

"Did you get nominated for Homecoming King?" she asked.

"No." I probably would have, if not for that rumor about me killing Casey. Stupid rumors.

"Then clearly you're not popular enough to be up there," she said with a wry smile.

"Clearly." I would enjoy trying to get under her shirt tomorrow night. Maybe I'd even get inside her pants. One could only hope.

Sam waved at me. Time to go. She wanted to bring Josh a milkshake from Cook-Out and check on him.

"And see how he looks," she said.

"Admit it. You just don't want to go to the dance with someone who has an alien growing out the side of his face."

She turned the car onto the main road outside of school.

"You got me," she said flatly.

"You vain, vain girl. Would they approve of such behavior high up yonder?"

"As opposed to going with you? I doubt they'd mind."

She picked up a couple of cheesecake milkshakes for Josh and herself. I abstained, choosing to smoke instead.

"Please crack the window," Sam said. "I don't want this tasting like black lung."

"Why? It would probably improve the taste."

She glared at me. I gave in and cracked the window, exhaling my sweet, smoky nectar outside.

When we got to Josh's, I had the unbridled pleasure of knocking on the door, as Sam had a milkshake in each hand. Josh still looked like he had a purple monster trying to hump his jaw.

"Oh wow." Sam scrunched her face up. "How do you feel? Does it hurt to move?"

Josh shrugged. "It hurts to live."

Truer words have never been spoken.

Sam handed over his milkshake and took a seat next to him on the couch. She eyed the bruise with tenderness, like she'd instantly morphed into a protective den mother. I tried not to make a joke about her maternal instincts.

"Sure you don't want me there tonight?" Josh asked, wincing. "This mystery vixen could show up." He looked over at me. "Can you even do this without your horns?"

Sam spoke before I could open my mouth.

"Bartholomew and I can handle it. You just rest."

I smiled and winked at Josh when he looked at me. "Yeah. We got it. You... rest."

"Just get better," Sam said, placing her hand on his.

Josh shot me a sideways glance, as if to say he'd won both the battle and the war because of Sam's gesture. Whatever. I tapped my watch.

"We need to go if we don't want to be late, Sam."

I stood and smirked at Josh, who looked crestfallen.

"Enjoy the milkshake," I said.

"Enjoy not being Hell-bound."

My chest sank. Dealing with this internally was one thing, but having it thrown in my face hurt my feelings, even if the kid did have a point. I really didn't know how I would... perform without my horns.

Sam and I arrived at the football field an hour before game time. Coach Mort paced around the parking lot, holding a clipboard. He saw Sam and made a "check" motion.

"Looking like a million bucks," Mort said with a twinkle in his eye. "I see you brought the boyfriend with you. What's up, my man?"

He held up his hand for me to high-five, but I gave him a look that told him to back off.

"I'm not her boyfriend."

What a buffoon. Had Mort acted this stupid in high school? Sam must have been *really* naïve.

"Okay man, that's cool," he said.

"I'm going to have a smoke," I said, leaving Sam alone with him. She probably didn't want me to abandon her right then, but I also hadn't wanted her to put her hand on Josh's. The angel, and me too for that matter, needed to learn that actions have consequences. No matter how petty those actions might seem."

"Don't walk away so disappointed," Lucifer called out to me. "Just because you lost your horns. Women lose their breasts to cancer every day, yet they fight on."

I turned to see him standing in Coach Mort's spot. He even had the man's gym coach outfit on.

"Go on into the locker room, get changed and warmed up," he said to Sam, patting her on the rear with the clipboard. She didn't seem to notice Coach Mort's transformation, or care about the sexist gesture. The big man had a knack for concealing himself from people. It was probably the greatest trick he ever pulled.

"What do you want?" I pouted.

"You know what I want."

"I don't have it."

"You don't have the Shard, you don't have your horns... I bet you don't have your dignity, either."

I raised my eyebrows. "What can you do?"

Lucifer changed the subject. "So, how are things going with you and tight-ass? And by tight-ass, I mean she has a tight ass, yet at the same time is a tight-ass because of her affiliation with you-know-who. It's a dual meaning."

Oh. Is it?

"Great," I said. "So happy you asked."

Lucifer took a step back. "Do I detect sarcasm?"

I smiled. "From me? Never."

"Remember. I'm keeping an eye on you."

I held up two fingers to my eyes, then pointed them at Lucifer. "I'll be sure to keep two on you."

"I hope you don't fall flat on your face trying to strike out on your own."

"You'd like that, wouldn't you?"

"Say what?" Coach Mort had returned. "Son, I don't think I like the direction this conversation is going."

"Never mind," I said, waving him off and walking away.

I lit a cigarette as I walked around the school grounds. I didn't want to be the first one into the stadium for the game. I could hear the shouts of the football teams warming up, but I had no desire to sit there and watch them. Plus, they didn't allow smoking in the stands.

Monica walked toward the gym wearing a bodysuit. Part of me wondered if she had any panties on underneath. I was sure she did, but that didn't stop me from imagining otherwise.

I flicked the cigarette and reached into my pocket for another. I looked up to see Nicholas, holding a cigarette between his fingers. I jumped back.

"You and your dad both. Can't you just text me or something?"

Nicholas laughed under his breath, twirling the cigarette between his fingers.

"You know we like to kick it old school. So you saw Dad? How is the old son of a bitch?"

"Same," I said.

Nicholas held up the cigarette. "How long has it been since you had one of these?" he asked.

"You literally just saw me smoking one." Idiot.

"Interesting." Nicholas ran the cig under his nose, taking an audible whiff. "You just smoked a Red Circle?"

My eyes flew open. Red Circle. I snatched it out of Nicholas's hands. The cigarette smelled like all the worst parts of Hell rolled in smoking paper. Fantastic. I'd had one before, as a reward for helping Rome get sacked. I would've traded sex with a thousand virgins for a pack of those beauties.

"By the gates of Hell, how did you get this?" I asked.

Nicholas chuckled. "Dad has crates of them lying around."

He held up his Zippo, which had a peace sign on it, and lit the cigarette for me. I inhaled. Every molecule of my body buzzed with delight. A kitten prancing in a field couldn't have felt better than I did at that moment.

"Exquisite," I said, exhaling through my nose.

Nicholas held up an entire pack. I felt a slight bulge in my pants.

"These are yours, if you can tell me when I can get my hands on the Shard."

I took another drag on the Red Circle. "Soon. Very soon. Trust me."

Nicholas's light-hearted face turned cold. "I *don't* trust

you."

"Like I told you before. You aren't the only interested party. By tomorrow night, your main competitor will be out of the way, and it will be all yours."

"Why not just give me the Shard and I'll get rid of the other party myself?" Nicholas asked.

"You could, but the competition… it's different. I don't exactly know what it is. Do you want to fight some third party we have no intel on, especially when it could destroy me instead of you?"

Smoke escaped from my mouth as I spoke. Every color I saw took on an extra pop as the cigarette's goodness ran through my body.

Nicholas leaned against one of the trailers used as a classroom, since the school's population had outgrown the main building. His eyes darted back and forth, like he tried to calculate the odds. He nodded.

"You've got a point. But," he said, moving in close. "I won't be coming after you if this thing goes tits up. I'll be coming after your angel friend. Let the boys have a run at her, like they did with you."

"That could be fun."

"After they're done with her, they'll come after you. If you think losing your horns is a fate worse than death, you're very, very wrong. Remember that." He tossed the pack of Red Circles on the ground.

I knelt down and cooed over the pack. Such a beautiful sight. I picked up the cigs, then stashed it in my jacket. When I looked up, Nicholas had disappeared. That whole family needed to learn how to properly say goodbye.

Thirty-Two

The Worst Homecoming Floats of All Time

With fifteen minutes until game time, I took a seat in the bleachers near the marching band, the only students who actually sat in the stands and watched the game. Everyone else just hung out behind the bleachers and socialized. Jenny and the other Homecoming nominees stood by on the track and Sam was cheering, so I had nobody to talk to. With starting quarterback Tyler off at the loony bin, at least the game would be a hoot.

Jenny locked gazes with me and waved. I grinned and waved back. She looked amazing in her outfit. The wardrobe wasn't anything special, just tight blue jeans and a low-cut, green, long sleeve shirt, but the clothes hugged everything just enough to show off her tight body, but not so much that she looked like a dime-store hooker. My gaze kept wandering over to Sam, who rocked her cheerleader uniform. I tried not to think of her as a sex object as the game began. I didn't want to give her the satisfaction.

The first half of the game flew by. Without Tyler in at quarterback, Frady-McNeely got steamrolled. The backup, a sophomore, got sacked six times in the first half, en route to a

28-0 deficit. That kid was lucky his head didn't get snapped off. I clapped at the players as they walked past me toward the locker room, applauding their good effort. Three or four of them thanked me with a one-finger salute, the sweeties.

The marching band stepped onto the field to play the school's fight song as the cheerleaders thrust their pom poms in the air. When the song ended, the principal made his way over to a makeshift podium and addressed the crowd.

"Good evening, everybody. Let's give our football team another hand for that great show of... sportsmanship in the first half," he said into a microphone.

There were scattered claps. I even belted out a half-hearted shout. I glanced down at Sam, who looked like she tried to stifle a laugh as she stood with the other cheerleaders.

"This year's Homecoming Dance has a special theme," the principal said. "Awareness. Not necessarily the major issues, but ones that tend to get overlooked by the mainstream. That doesn't mean they aren't important, though."

The first float that rolled out onto the track featured a small child holding a baby, with the sign *Being a teen mom is not the bomb* painted on the side. The girls on the float alternated between speaking on phones and gossiping while dealing with baby dolls wrapped in blankets. The rest of the night could turn out to be one of the all-time worst, and it'd still have been worth it to see this cavalcade of good intentions gone wrong.

The next float stuck with the baby theme. It featured a gnome that looked a lot like Admiral Ackbar from *Star Wars*, holding a bottle of beer. The slogan for this one? *Just say gnome to Fetal Alcohol Syndrome.* I bit down on my knuckle to keep from exploding in laughter.

Sam caught my eye. She must've been looking at me to catch my reaction. The angel shook her head, but her lips betrayed the slightest hint of a smile.

The next float had the slogan *We're bullish on bullying.* Every boy and girl on the float looked either very scrawny, overweight, or had acne visible from thirty yards away. I bet their float was nothing more than a cry for help.

The last float had to have been mandated by the school. I'd

heard there'd been a case of arson here last year. I guess the school wanted to keep the memory of the tragedy fresh in people's minds, because this float simply said that we needed to *Kick arson's butt.* It featured students crying over a burnt-out building. *So* touching.

The floats came to a stop behind the principal, who clapped and smiled at the students as they waved to the crowd. The entire scene felt so… tacky. I started to get a bad taste in my mouth.

"Aren't these floats beautiful?" The principal beamed. The students voted on which of these *fantastic* floats looked the best earlier in the day. I abstained, choosing to point and laugh at the ridiculousness of it all instead. The principal pulled out two envelopes from his jacket. He tore one of them open and read from the piece of paper inside. "And the winner for best float… *Kick arson's butt.*"

The band played some congratulatory music as the kids on the arson float cried and hugged each other.

This time, I shook my head at Sam.

I know, she mouthed.

Once the students composed themselves, the principal held up the unopened envelope. "And now, the moment we've all been waiting for. At least during halftime. Not to denigrate the football team. We love our boys."

The principal cleared his throat. The crowd remained silent, amplifying the awkwardness of his words. He introduced the three finalists for both Homecoming King and Queen, but since the king finalists were either in the locker room or the nuthouse, a la Tyler, he'd announce that one first. He opened the envelope and read Tyler's name.

"Unfortunately Tyler can't be with us tonight, since he's out dealing with some… health issues," the principal said. "Get well soon, buddy. We're all rooting for you."

The principal proclaimed that in his stead would be the runner-up, Rob Nelson, a defensive back on the football team.

Next, the principal called the three finalists for Homecoming Queen up to the stage: Jenny, Monica, and some junior I'd never seen or heard of before. I figured they'd thrown her in so it wouldn't be such a senior-dominated affair.

"These three young ladies exemplify everything that makes Frady-McNeely one of the best schools in the state. And the winner is..." the principal said, opening the envelope.

In an effort to draw out the suspense, he looked at the name of the winner for several seconds, which naturally felt like several hours. Since Vixen's identity hung in the balance, it seemed more like years. I almost tore the bleachers out, I felt so nervous and excited.

Monica squealed as the principal called out her name. She hugged Jenny and the other girl, then stepped up next to the principal. The demoness wrapped her arms around him, and then fussed with her hair, so that her crown would fit perfectly on her head. The principal held her hand and led her to the arson float, so they could take a victory lap around the football field.

I glanced at Jenny, to see how she'd taken the loss. She appeared sincerely happy for Monica, which didn't come as a surprise. Jenny was a genuinely good person, and I would genuinely have a great time trying to round the bases with her tomorrow night.

Monica climbed onto the arson float and waved to the crowd, holding a bouquet of flowers the arson students gave her. They hopped off the float, leaving her alone on it. Which is when the entire arson prevention float went up in flames.

Thirty-Three

A Burning Ring of Fire

The crowd screamed as flames engulfed the float, and Monica with it. They ran for the bleachers' exits, trying to get as far from the fire as possible. These people acted so insane, I bet they believed the fire would jump across the track, set the *metal* bleachers on fire, and burn them alive if they didn't get away. Usually, one or two people would try to help in a situation like this, but nobody did. Not one person. Truly a proper display of humanity at its finest. Pride overcame me.

"Bartholomew," Sam said.

Sam's voice broke me out of my watching-the-ants-flee trance. I sprang from my seat and ran for the float. I knew Monica, being a demon, would be fine, but that didn't mean I wanted her to languish in the fire for hours. Funny, of all the souls here, only the rogue demon came to the rescue.

"Can you help her?" Sam ran beside me.

"She's okay. She's a demon, remember? Fire flows through her veins."

"So, she's not hurt?"

"Don't be daft. Her uniform, however…that probably went up in a second. All that polyester." I eyeballed her outfit. "Speaking of, you might want to keep your distance in that thing."

Everyone cleared out after a couple of minutes. I heard the faint sound of sirens in the distance. The fire department would be here soon. The fire started dying down once it destroyed most of the float. I walked closer.

"Unless you want the firemen to see you in the nude, you might want to come out."

Monica emerged from under some debris, naked and covered in soot. A hot look for her.

"What happened? One minute, I'm queen of the universe and the next, it's like I'm back home."

I waved away a floating piece of debris. "It is an arson float. In my opinion, they were asking for it."

Monica scowled at me. "You really think this was an accident?"

Sam and I exchanged glances.

"Not really," I said. "Ironically, I think it *was* arson."

"Good to know you're not completely clueless. Your precious Vixen did this."

I removed my jacket and handed it to Monica, hoping she wouldn't get too much soot and ash on it.

"Thanks," she said, wrapping it around her body. Shame. I wouldn't have minded seeing her naughty parts a bit longer.

I saw some woods past the football field.

"We could get you to your car through there," I said.

Monica widened her eyes at me, like I'd just said she had bad breath.

"Why don't you pull around front and pick me up?"

"Because, smart girl, look out in the main parking lot. It's swarming with people who saw you get burned to a crisp."

Monica looked toward the parking lot.

"Right. As much as I'd like to show off the girls, I don't think that would go over very well."

We walked down the track toward the woods as the sirens grew louder. Sam stuck her hands in her pockets.

"How are we going to explain that you survived the fire without a scratch?"

Monica buttoned up my jacket. So much for navel-gazing.

"Believe it or not, this has happened before. Of course, those other times I got burned at the stake, but the principle is still the same."

The corner of Sam's mouth turned upward. She didn't fully understand.

"But everyone saw you get engulfed by flames."

Monica *tsked* Sam. "They'll believe it. Their minds won't be able to accept the truth. They'll convince themselves I got out in time. If you haven't noticed, people don't have a clue what's going on around them unless it slaps them in the face with a baseball bat."

The demoness did have a point. When recounting the story to others, people would just explain the whole incident as something they couldn't believe they'd seen. Their minds wouldn't let them even imagine they'd witnessed a demon survive a fire.

"I'll leave the details to you," I said as we entered the woods. "But there's still one last thing."

Monica glanced at me. "You want to know who Vixen is."

"No. I've thought it over, and I kind of just want to wait and find out who she is," I said with a little bit of sarcasm. "Then wing it from there."

Sam smacked me on the chest. "No you don't."

"Of *course* I want to know."

"We need to know," Sam said.

I cleared my throat, hoping Sam would get the message. She needed to shut her mouth.

"Why do you need to know so badly?" Monica asked, a wide-eyed look on her face.

"We've just been waiting so long," Sam said. "I'm dying to know."

"We both are," I laughed.

Let's all stop talking and just focus on business, please?

Monica took a deep breath, giving Sam a sideways glance. "Fine. You held up your end of the bargain. Jenny McPherson didn't become Homecoming Queen. Only fitting I hold up my end."

"Well, out with it," I said. "We've waited long enough."

Monica stopped, looking back and forth between us. "All right," she said. "It's not an absolute, but then again, what is in life?"

"Out with it already," I said.

Monica laughed. "Before I forget. That other favor you asked me about? You know which one I'm talking about?"

My head almost exploded like Adam Bomb from the *Garbage Pail Kids*. She had to bring that up now? "I will send you back to Hell myself if you don't tell us."

Monica smiled and crossed her arms. "Patience is definitely one of your virtues. Well, check your locker about the small thing. As for Vixen, it's—"

She started coughing into her hand. The suspense killed me.

"It's...oh, *that bitch*!" Her coughing became more violent. She opened her hand. She'd coughed up some black liquid. Her blood. "It's the goo—"

Before she could finish, the Black Cloud of Death appeared, narrowing itself into a long, thin line. The villain flew straight into one ear and out the other, then disappeared out of sight as fast as it had shown up.

"Monica?" Sam asked.

The cheerleader lost her balance and fell. I rushed forward and caught her, easing her to the ground. I moved the hair out of her face.

"Stay with us, Monica. Stay away from the fire. Stay away," I said.

Her eyes rolled back in her head. Her body became uncomfortably hot. I jumped to my feet and moved away. Fire engulfed her, returning her to Hell. She'd be topside again at some point, but not in time to help us and probably not in Raleigh. When the fire disappeared, only a scorched, ashy mark on the ground remained.

"Son of a bitch." I slammed my fist into a tree, making a crack in the trunk. The impact sounded like thunder. "Can one thing go right? Just one? Is that too much to ask?"

Sam grabbed my hand and pulled. "Not here."

She dragged me, literally kicking and screaming, to her car. As we drove past the flashing lights of the fire trucks, I missed the horns pressing against my skull, begging to be released, when I got angry. They always served as a reminder that I could either get myself under control or unleash the beast within. Now, I'd have to rely on discipline to keep my anger in check, which probably wouldn't work out very well.

"Every step of the way," I said. "Every step we've been stopped. I've had more success bedding nuns than I have on this thing."

"We'll figure something out. We're still here. That's got to count for something."

"Not much." I rubbed my forehead where the horns should've been. As angry as I'd gotten, what remained of them didn't even threaten to break out. I felt around for my pack of Red Circles... which were in my jacket. "Bless it. To Heaven with it all."

"What?" Sam looked in my direction.

"I left my cigarettes in my jacket." I threw my hands up. I finally got my hands on an *entire pack* of Red Circles, and they go up in smoke. Typical. "Seriously. Getting booted from upstairs felt pretty terrible, at least at first, but honestly? Right now I couldn't be more pissed."

Sam drove in silence for a minute, as if she didn't know what to say. "I'm sorry."

I waved her off. "Save it. I just want to get my claws on this Vixen and kill her as slowly as possible."

Sam sighed and brushed some hair behind her ear. "I think we're going to have to use the Shard to find her."

"And then, Vixen will show up in her Black Cloud of Death form. Which is all fine and dandy, except we still have no idea how to stop or kill it."

"Then we do it where we can dictate what happens and hope there's enough time to ask the Shard how to stop Vixen."

"Like where? A church? It'll just wait outside until we come out." What a terrible plan.

We turned onto Glenwood Avenue and headed downtown, which reminded me of my destroyed condo. Which reminded me of my destroyed cars. And my ruined wardrobe. I punched the dash, pulling back at the last moment so I wouldn't dent it.

"Don't take your anger out on my car," Sam said. "I have an idea where we can ask the Shard."

This should be good.

"If you say McDonald's, I'm going to move to Tahiti and

never come back. I'm just going to lie out on the beach every day in the buff, letting the native folk and bored tourists flock to me. It'll be like a rogue demon remix of a Jimmy Buffett song."

"We're going to do it at the Homecoming Dance."

"You and me? Not unless you don't mind Jenny being there."

"No, silly. We're going to use the Shard then."

Sweet music to my ears. I couldn't believe I hadn't thought of it. All those kids in their rented tuxedos and puffy dresses, just hoping to get past first base, and then, bam! Eaten by the death cloud, vanished without a trace. It would be like the Lost Colony all over again. When they had to move inland, as a joke I'd removed all evidence of where they'd gone, except for one cryptic word: Croatoan. I still got a kick out of all the fuss people made about that one to this day.

"Stop smiling," Sam said. She must've noticed how excited her idea made me. "Nobody's going to die at this thing."

My spirits sank. "Not even a couple of people?"

"Nope," Sam said, shaking her head. "Not if we can help it."

I narrowed my eyes. "You really do take the fun out of everything, don't you?"

"I try. And why do you care? You're not doing Hell's bidding anyway."

"Now you're just pouring salt on an open wound." Even without the prospect of a high body count, I would do my best to make the most of Homecoming. Mainly by doing my best to take the virtue of one Jenny McPherson. The only question was, where to do it. The gym? Library? Cafeteria, on top of stale square-shaped pizza slices?

I had it. The principal's office.

"How about we stop and get you some cigarettes?" she asked.

"It won't be the same."

"Come on. My treat."

We'd originally planned to ride to the dance in my Benz, but since I'd had two demolished on my watch, I felt I should wait on getting a new one and go in Sam's car. I caught some flak for letting her drive after my tirade about her staying away from Sweet Claudette, but whatever. No way would a third Mercedes be destroyed working this blessed job.

She rubbed the Shard of Gabriel with her thumb as she sat in the car, waiting for a stoplight to turn green. Glancing at the Shard made me feel homesick. Even when I tried to take over Hell with the Shard, it had still been home. Now I just drifted along, like dust in the wind. I shook my head. I needed to get my mind right.

"You ready for this?" I asked.

She stuffed the Shard in her small purse, which matched her wholesome pink dress that didn't have a hint a cleavage.

"Why not?"

We drove over to pick up Josh, who looked a lot better than he did the last time I saw him. His face still looked bruised and battered, but his tuxedo disguised whatever other injuries he had.

Sam winced at the sight of his face. "Oh, no. No. You can't go to the dance looking like that."

Josh patted himself down. "Like what? Did I do something wrong?"

Sam pulled a makeup case from her purse. "No, you're fine. I just don't want you looking like an ink cartridge exploded all over your face."

"That, and she doesn't want mom to get the photos and have a lifetime of memories of your broken face to cherish," I said.

"Ha, ha," Josh said, holding still so Sam could apply the makeup. "Did you find out who Vixen is?"

"Surprisingly enough," I said. "Vixen destroyed Monica before she could tell us."

Josh closed his eyes and shook his head. "You don't say. So what now?"

"We use the Shard to find her," Sam said.

Josh leaned back. "Is that smart?"

"We've got a plan. Sort of," I said.

"What is it? Get everyone at the dance killed?"

"It would have been." I pointed at Sam. "But she shot that one down."

Josh smiled at her. "Probably for the best."

"I thought so." Sam moved in close to Josh, rubbing a little more foundation on his face. "I think that's as good as we're going to get it."

Instead of a bruise, Josh looked like he had a very light hickey. The foundation also made that part of his cheek a lighter shade than the rest of it, like a big pale spot. I kept that to myself, hoping maybe one of them would notice, but only after the photos were ruined.

Jenny's family lived in a housing development that catered to the rich crowd. The Hyundai we rode in stood out, and not in a good way, among the high-end cars we passed, which included more than a few Benzes. I swallowed my envy and focused on the people standing outside their homes who eyed us as we approached, knowing we didn't belong among the upper class. I smiled and waved at them.

We stopped at Jenny's house—a three-story brick home with a massive window above the front door that revealed a large crystal chandelier inside. I liked stylish clothes and fast cars, but I didn't need a castle to show people I had money. Or power. I did that the old-fashioned way—with action. The stylish clothes and fast cars made me look good while I did it.

Jenny answered the door wearing a low-cut green dress with spaghetti straps. Her bra pushed up her breasts. I wanted to rip her clothes off right then and there.

"Hey," I said with a smile. "You look ravishing."

"Thanks. Let me grab my purse real quick," she said, disappearing into the house. "Come in if you like."

I heard her footsteps bounce off the wooden stairs. I stepped into the foyer and stood underneath the massive crystal chandelier. With something that large, I'd bet her dad definitely tried to compensate for some smaller things in his life, hint hint, wink wink.

"Nice place."

"Thanks," she called out from upstairs.

There didn't seem to be anyone else in the house. "No parents? I would've thought your mom would want to bombard us with pictures and your dad would want to give me a stern talking to about treating you nicely and having you home at a decent hour."

Jenny laughed. "Normally they would, but they're out of town."

Is that so? "So you're throwing the after-party here, right?"

"Absolutely," Jenny said with a laugh. "How awful was that fire last night?"

"Terrible. Just terrible. Do you know if Monica is okay?" I wanted to see what the common folk had to say about things.

"I don't know. They couldn't find any of trace of her in the fire, so I guess she got out. That's all I know. I thought I saw you trying to help?"

She saw that?

"Sort of, but it's like you said. She's nowhere to be found. I guess she's okay."

"Hope so. Anyway, I thought you were very brave." Jenny appeared and started her trek down the stairs. The heels gave her calves sleek definition. She looked so good, I swear she walked down those steps in slow motion.

I stepped closer to her. "You really do look radiant."

Jenny blushed. "That's very sweet of you to say."

I moved past her and opened the door. "After you."

"Such a gentleman." She smiled and placed a hand on my chest.

I held my breath for a moment. Usually an above-the-tuxedo touch wouldn't get me very excited, but this time was different. This time, the girl doing the touching wore a black ring in the shape of a snake on her thumb.

THIRTY-FOUR

LEAVE ROOM FOR THE "HOLY" SPIRIT

How had I not seen this coming?

My mind felt like someone poured it into a pan, then fried it in grease. Jenny was Vixen? She had to know about me. Had to. And here I'd been impressed that she'd seemed so genuinely happy for Monica last night. Of course she'd been happy. By setting the arson float on fire and destroying Monica, she'd guaranteed herself the Homecoming Queen crown, regardless of the vote. Diabolical. Just diabolical.

I wanted to bed her now more than ever.

"So, with Monica missing, does that make you Homecoming Queen?" I asked. Surely she didn't want the Shard just so she could win the crown. She'd pulled that one off on her own.

She shrugged. "I think so. The principal called me this afternoon to talk about the whole thing. I told him it didn't feel right, but I would accept in her honor. You have to have a Homecoming Queen, right?"

"Right." I had to play it cool. I couldn't let on that I knew about Jenny. I also had to figure out a way to keep the others from finding out too soon. I helped the little vixen into the seat behind Josh, then got into the seat next to her. I hoped neither Josh nor Sam would see the ring, since they were up front.

I kept to myself, for the most part, on the ride to school. I didn't want to blow my cover. The mix of shock, awe, and attraction intoxicated me. If I opened my mouth, who knew what would come out? Probably something an overexcited sixteen-year-old would say.

Jenny put her hand on my arm. "You okay?"

"Yeah, you've been awfully quiet," Sam said.

"I'm fine," I said. "Just thinking about some things."

"Like what?" Jenny asked.

Like what color underwear you have on. If it's cotton or silk. Thong or edible. How easily it will tear away from your supple body. Not to mention, how you hoodwinked me into thinking you were just some sweet, nice girl and how hot that deception makes me, regardless of virginity.

"Nothing really."

"Obviously it's something," Sam said. "You're not the quiet type, unless you're smoking."

"She's right," Josh said. "Most of the time I wish you'd talk less, but tonight you really are a clam."

"So I'm not being talkative. I figured some of the people in the car would welcome that change, Josh."

Josh glanced at Sam. "He's got a point. And it is appreciated."

I'm sure.

Ten minutes later, we arrived at Frady-McNeely. Students walked past us in their cheap JC Penny suits, or dresses they'd gotten at Old Navy, or wherever people get cheap outfits from. I'd hoped one or two of them would've taken a cue from my wardrobe, but alas. Still, the ladies would surely only have eyes for me tonight, since nobody else would be wearing a designer Zegna tuxedo.

I opened the door for Jenny. She gave me her hand, the black ring a stark contrast against her ivory skin.

"Hey, you go on ahead," I said. "I'm going to have a smoke."

Jenny frowned. "Do you have to?"

She moved in closer, her lips a mere inches from mine. How I wanted to eat them up.

"I only ask because I was hoping to get close to you tonight."

"And you can't if I smoke?"

"Let's just say I'll be more... forthcoming... if you don't. I hate the smell."

This would be a tough decision. "Done."

"You two coming?" Sam asked.

We joined Sam and Josh and went into the gym, which was decorated with confetti, balloons, and about a thousand awareness posters on the walls for what seemed like every issue on the planet. I even saw one about blood diamonds. The minimal lighting made the place look more like a dance club than a ballroom, so any chance Josh and Sam had to spot the ring probably disappeared under the black lights. I still needed to warn them somehow.

"Can I get you something to drink?" I asked Jenny.

The vixen shook her head. "I'm good. I just want to dance and feel your body up against mine."

She led me out onto the dance floor to get down to LMFAO's *Sexy and I Know It*. Jenny sang along to the lyrics. She hiked up the hem of her dress and started grinding on my leg. She excited me so much my horns would've popped out if they were still there. I fought off the urge to take her into the bathroom, ram her up against a stall, and do her while standing in the toilet. I maneuvered myself to where I could make eye contact with Josh or Sam, who both stood off to the side.

"Your body is amazing," Jenny said, still grinding. She rubbed my arm. "Is everything this hard and chiseled?"

I grabbed a small chunk of her hair and pulled back with enough force to make her notice.

"You better believe it," I said, whispering into her ear. I nibbled on her neck. She shivered.

"Yeah, man. Hell yeah," some kid said at me.

I gave him a thumbs-up as I lightly bit her neck, which tasted like fresh peaches.

Looking toward the edge of the crowd, I made eye contact with Sam. I couldn't be positive with the lack of lighting, but her long face made it seem like she was upset. I tried to motion with my head for her to come out here on the dance floor. She put her hands on her hips in defiance. I stopped kissing and biting on Jenny and lifted my head.

I mouthed *Vixen* and glanced at Jenny.

Sam's eyes narrowed. *What?* I saw her say.

Vixen, I mouthed again. *Jenny. Vixen.* I couldn't tell if Sam understood what I tried to say.

Jenny put her hand on my crotch. "After they crown me, my first decree as queen will be to take you as a prize."

"I serve at the pleasure of the queen," I said.

She licked my face. "I want you to ride me like a four-wheeler on a dirt track."

Weird thing to say, but okay. Rolling with it.

"Excuse me," someone said behind me. I turned and saw the principal. "There's no need to act like that. This is a... family environment. I'm surprised at you, Miss McPherson."

"So sorry, sir," Jenny said. "I can do you next if you want."

She massaged my ear with her tongue. It felt fantastic, but also a little too... safe. I wanted danger. Or at the very least, some teeth.

The principal huffed and stormed off.

"What a prude," Jenny said. "His wife needs to blow him more."

My jaw almost fell down into her cleavage. Jenny must've really had to work hard to keep that good girl façade going.

"I love this side of you," I said.

The song ended and Jenny hugged me. "You only have to be as good as you want the world to think you are, and right now I don't care."

"What do you mean?" Monica was right about Jenny all along. Horns or no horns, I'd been an idiot.

She kissed my cheek. "Tonight, I become the queen for real. And you? Well, you know what I'm doing with you."

I smirked. "Yes, I do."

I didn't exactly know what she meant, but she had me so turned on part of me almost wanted her to succeed.

"I'm going to eat you alive," she whispered into my ear.

Martin Garrix's *Animal* began playing. Jenny immediately went back to work grinding on my leg. I searched the crowd for Sam or Josh, but couldn't find them. I felt a tap on my shoulder. Probably the principal again.

"Mind if I cut in?" Josh asked.

Finally.

"Only if the lady approves," I said.

Jenny grabbed my tie and pulled me close. Despite my excitement, I didn't appreciate her treating my tie like that.

"Hurry back."

I raised my eyebrows. "Will do." I turned to Josh. "Be cool, man," I said softly, making sure Jenny couldn't hear. "Whatever happens, just act natural."

"Are you okay?"

"Just be cool."

I hurried out of the crowd and found Sam. I took her by the arm as we walked out into the hallway.

"What's going on?" Sam asked, a little too harshly, I thought. "What are you trying to tell me? Rub in the fact that you and Jenny are sinning on the dance floor?"

"No."

"Whatever it is, I don't want to hear it. Some of us have work to do." Sam stormed back toward the dance.

I took her by the arms and turned her back toward me. "Sam."

She tried to break free. "No."

"She's Vixen."

That stopped her dead in her tracks. A wide range of emotions ran across her face, one after the other. Surprise, curiosity, denial, anger, and rage. Pain underlined all of them.

"How do you know?"

"The ring. She's had it on the whole night."

"And you chose right now to say something?" Sam shoved me. "You ass. Why didn't you tell us before we got to a gymnasium full of kids she could kill?"

I tried to keep my voice down. "If I'd told you in the car, she could have turned into the smoke thing and killed us all, then killed everyone here. And I'm sorry, but I've had my fill of violent car wrecks for a decade or two. I tried to tell you in the parking lot, but I couldn't shake her."

Sam arched an eyebrow. "Looks like you're trying really hard to shake her on the dance floor."

I rolled my head around. Of all the times to act like a crazy, insecure girl, she picked this one. "I don't want to tip her off. You think I enjoyed that little burlesque show we put on out there?"

Sam crossed her arms. "Yeah. I do."

"Okay. Maybe I did. But still. My intentions were pure."

Sam gave me a look that bored through my skull. They were pure. Purely seductive. Why dwell on the details?

"Don't you think you're focusing on the wrong thing here? Shouldn't we be trying to figure out how to stop Jenny?"

Why the jealous routine anyway? What did Sam care whose neck I nibbled on? She had Josh cooing all over her.

No longer on the offensive, Sam's body language eased up a bit.

"Fine. Any ideas?"

"I say use the Shard. It will draw her out, not to mention it's the only thing that knows for sure how to stop her. But we can't do it whenever. We need the perfect moment, because the second she goes up in smoke, it's on."

"What about when they announce her as Homecoming Queen?" Sam asked. "All eyes will be on her. I doubt she'd be willing to blow her cover with the entire school watching. At least, I hope she wouldn't."

She made a really good point. We agreed to reconvene out here during the announcement and use the Shard.

"Now let's hope she hasn't done anything to Josh," I said.

Sam punched me in the chest. "You left him alone with her? What if she makes him explode like Casey?"

I didn't say it out loud, but would that really have been so bad?

Thirty-Five

THE CROWNING OF THE VIXEN

Josh danced with Jenny to some awful contemporary pop song performed by a YouTube star. YouTube didn't seem like a big deal before my punishment, but now that talentless hacks got record deals off it, YouTube seemed like a whole new way to taint innocent souls who thought they had what it took to "make it." But tainting souls wasn't my department anymore. Sigh.

Vixen didn't grind away on him like she'd done with me, but she did turn around and bury her rear in Josh's crotch. His face seemed equal parts happy and uncomfortable. I hoped Sam noticed other people enjoyed being around Jenny tonight.

"You tell Josh what's up and I'll keep you-know-who occupied," I said.

"Try not to make love to her out there," Sam said.

"No promises."

Josh gave me a grateful look as I approached. I bumped fists to keep up the pretense this was all friendly and non-threatening.

"Wow, is she a wild one," he said, quietly enough that Jenny couldn't hear.

"You have no idea."

He stood so our shoulders touched. "Is that ring on her

thumb what I think it is?"

"Go talk to Sam," I said.

Josh nodded.

Jenny blew a kiss at him. "Thanks for the dance, sweetie."

Josh smiled and waved before disappearing into the crowd.

"I missed you," Jenny said, wrapping her arms around me. "Where did you and Sam run off to?"

"She wanted some advice on how to show interest in Josh while still being a lady."

Jenny's eyes narrowed. "Is that so?"

I laughed nervously. "It is. That girl has no idea what to do with a man."

At least, I hoped so.

The vixen licked her lips. "Good thing I do. They don't call me Vixen for nothing."

I tried to play dumb. "That's a hot nickname. How did you get it?"

Jenny ran her fingers through her hair, which left it looking just messed up enough to be sultry. Much as I wanted to destroy her, I still really wanted to bang her. Such was the demon's curse.

"You haven't figured it out yet?"

I wrapped my hands around her waist as a new song began. She shimmied down to crotch height, then sprang back up.

"My guess is you're a terrific lay."

Jenny kissed me, taking hold of my lower lip with her teeth. It snapped back into place when she released it.

"That's true, but you really don't remember me?"

"From where?"

Jenny pouted. "I remember you. From the museum. You didn't know Casey at all, did you?"

"Sure I did."

"Liar. You lie as easily as you breathe."

True. "Okay, so I didn't know Casey. Certainly not as well as you did, you little vixen."

Jenny smiled at the mention of being called Vixen.

"I don't think anybody knew Casey as well as I did. I knew him inside… and out. It's a tragedy. He cared about me so much. But once he found out the truth… What can you do?

What's one mortal measured against the world?"

"You sent Josh after me too, didn't you?"

Jenny licked her lips. "I had to, after Pierce failed to send you back to Hell. Then I met you, and you're so delicious, I decided to keep you for myself."

"That ridiculous charm I wore," I said. "How were you able to fight it off?"

"I couldn't at first," she said. "It made me throw up. But you don't survive as long as I have without being able to adapt."

I doubted she'd go into detail about that, so I decided to move on. "What about our date? How did you get to Josh?"

Jenny laughed, then licked my neck. "Did you actually see me reading to any kids?"

I hadn't. Sneaky, sneaky. "What are you? I have to know."

Jenny kissed my cheek. "Why?"

"Indulge me. We both know I'll be indulging every inch of you soon enough." I doubted that, considering the turn our conversation had taken, but I figured it couldn't hurt to keep her mind off destroying me.

"That's true." She gazed into my eyes. "Since you just have to know, I'm a Golem."

Ah.

That explained a lot. Golems were created from unformed material. Like smoke, or Silly Putty.

"I thought they'd all died out during the Roman Empire."

Jenny held up my hand while she twirled around me.

"They did. Except for me. I want the Shard so I can repopulate my race. I've been so lost without the Golem."

I almost felt sympathy for Jenny. Ever since my horns had been removed, I'd also felt lost.

"Surely this is about more than just getting some buns in the oven."

Jenny enveloped me in her arms, resting her lips on my neck. "Of course. It's about retribution against humans for exterminating us. But that part you'll have to see for yourself," she said, kissing my chin. "A girl has to keep a few things to herself."

"What about my car? Did you have to do that?"

Jenny laughed against my neck. "Collateral damage. You would never be mine with those horns and your blind allegiance to Hell. That's why I sent Kyle and his whore to relieve you of them. Now you're a free agent, able to play for any team you choose."

I thought about telling her the only team I wanted to play for let me sleep with virgins, but I kept that to myself. She didn't even apologize for Sweet Claudette.

The song came to an end and the principal took to the stage. The crowd quieted down.

"Welcome, everybody," the principal said. "Before we bring the Homecoming Queen and King up here for the traditional dance, I'd like to have a moment of silence for Tyler Walton and especially Monica D'Amico, who was... hurt in that awful, awful accident on the arson float. Get well soon, Monica." The principal closed his eyes, lowered his head, and placed his hand over his heart.

Jenny giggled. "If they only knew, right?"

"That you did in Monica yourself?"

Jenny ticked her head to the side, giving me a deadpan stare. "Of course. Monica, being the gossipy bitch she is, somehow found out the truth. And me, being the powerful queen I am, squashed her for it." She cupped her hand on my cheek. "At the exact moment I knew it would hurt you the most, my sweet."

"What about the fire? You knew it wouldn't hurt Monica," I said.

Jenny shrugged. "The fire is on you. I would've won Homecoming Queen, but you spread that rumor about me sleeping with a teacher and killed that." She moaned. "Yes, I know it was you. I'm not stupid. The float going up in flames ensured I'd become Homecoming Queen, since people won't be wondering why Monica didn't show up tonight to accept her crown."

One thing really ate at me, though. "But why? What's so important about Homecoming?"

Jenny kissed my chin. "This is high school. Everything takes on increased importance, even a simple case of spite. You of all... entities should know how much fun that is."

Indeed I did.

The moment of silence ended and most people in the gym clapped. The principal called Jenny to the stage to accept her crown. Tyler's replacement, Rob Nelson, followed her soon after.

For some reason, they played Whitney Houston's *One Moment in Time* for the pair to dance to. I waited for the dance to begin, so Jenny would be a little preoccupied, then I skulked out into the hallway, where Sam and Josh were already waiting.

"Took you long enough," Josh said.

I glared at him and decided to move on. "You got it?"

Sam held up the Shard. "Right here."

I motioned for her to go on and ask the thing how to destroy Jenny.

She took a deep breath and looked into the Shard of Gabriel. "How do we stop Jenny? Here. Tonight. As soon as possible."

A greenish light shone on her face as the Shard told her what to do. After several seconds, the light disappeared. Sam had the answer.

"Can I borrow it?" I asked. "Just for a second."

"Nope," Sam said.

I held my hands together.

"Please? Pretty please? I have to ask it something *super* important." Being able to use it at this moment was too tempting, too tantalizing for words. Surely I could ask it just one question?

"Really? What's super important?"

"The thing I have to ask the Shard." I fidgeted. "Come on. I even said please."

She put the Shard back into her purse. "You can do better than that."

"Yeah, I know," I said. "But—"

The three of us froze as hundreds of screams erupted inside the gymnasium.

THIRTY-SIX
A DEAL WITH THE SON OF THE DEVIL

We rushed into the gym, weaving around students running out. Using the Shard set off Jenny, just like we'd worried it would. Only we didn't think she'd have the gall to reveal her Golem form in front of the entire school. A ballsy move on her part.

She morphed into the black mist and twirled poor Rob around like a lasso. They came to a stop in the middle of the gym, about halfway between the floor and the ceiling. The smoke moved into Rob's body and he exploded into tiny particles. A red mist of blood rained down on us.

I looked down. Red spots speckled the exposed bits of my white dress shirt.

"There goes another one," I said. "I'm just going to start shopping at Marshalls."

The black smoke formed a smiley face as it caught sight of us. I motioned for Josh and Sam to do what they needed to do.

"I got this."

The cloud moved closer to me, making a smoky approximation of Jenny.

"The Shard," the cloud said in a very gassy voice. "Give it to me and we can kill the angel together."

"Wait, it's here somewhere." I patted myself down, then

pulled my pockets inside out. "I could've sworn I had it on me."

The cloud screamed and surrounded me. I felt myself being lifted into the air. The monster then tossed me around the gym. I crashed into the cinder block walls, the folded-up bleachers, and even slid into a group of kids, one of whom fell right on my junk. It did not feel good. I got to my feet, dusted myself off, and buttoned my jacket.

"I do love the rough stuff," I said.

The monster enveloped me again, but this time it tried to enter me. It bounced around, probing my body for an opening.

"No means no," I said.

Finally, Jenny gave up and morphed back into human form. "How?"

I held up the finger with the Ring of the Gods on it. "Always wear protection."

I glanced over at Josh and Sam, who struggled to break the glass to the fire alarm. Jenny noticed me looking at them. She ran at the pair. I dove, catching hold of her foot. She changed back into the smoke thing, freeing herself from my grip as she flew toward them.

Josh stood between Sam and the monster, holding his arms out, trying to protect Sam. Such a brave and stupid move on his part. The cloud picked him up and flung him onto the stage.

"Let's dance," she said, as she picked Josh up and spun him around the dance floor . It didn't take long for the Templar to throw up all over the place.

I rushed over to Sam. "What's wrong?" I asked.

"I can't get the glass to break," she said, trying to break it with her elbow.

"Hand of God didn't work?"

She stopped and lowered her head.

"I didn't think of that."

I smashed the glass with my fist.

"So this is what the Shard told you? Get Jenny wet? I was doing a good enough job of that on my own."

"Pervert. This kind of wet requires… a woman's touch."

Sam's hand glowed as she gripped the sprinkler system

lever, which lit up on contact. She pulled the lever.

Water poured down from the sprinkler heads. Drops of it burned as they landed on my head. I looked up and got some in my eye. That burned even worse.

"Holy water?" I asked, trying to shield myself. The Ring of the Gods kept my flesh from melting off, but it still felt like drops of scalding hot water hitting me. At least it wouldn't leave a permanent mark. I hoped.

Sam grinned. "Damn right."

"You're getting more PG-13 by the day."

Some of the other students still in the gym screamed in pain as the holy water seared their flesh. Guess there were more demons and Hellish beings in high school than I'd thought.

The Black Cloud of Death released Josh, who fell to the floor, out cold. A primal shriek made my eardrums ring in pain. The holy water tore through her amorphous form, disintegrating her.

"She's melting," I said in a high-pitch shriek. "Melting. Oh, what a world."

Sam put her hand on my shoulder as the monster's screams faded away, along with any trace that she'd ever existed. So much for the Golem. With the show over, the burning holy water returned to the forefront of my mind with a vengeance.

"I'll meet you outside," I said, running out of the gym.

I stood off to the edge of the crowd. The kids had a quiet sort of shock on their faces. They definitely couldn't comprehend what they'd just witnessed. Their brains would probably pass it off as someone spiking the punch bowl, causing a mass hallucination.

Sam helped Josh outside. I waved to them as I took out my cigarettes. Thankfully, they'd survived the sprinklers. I lit up.

"No smoking," the principal barked.

I exhaled a ring in his face. "Blow me."

The principal coughed as he meekly disappeared back into the crowd. Sam and Josh stood next to me. Josh bled from his head. I winced.

"You just can't help getting the shit knocked out of you, can you?" I asked.

"Guess not." He looked past me. "What's Gumby doing

here?"

"Huh?" I glanced behind me. Nothing.

"I think he hit his head a little too hard," Sam said, propping him up.

"That's surprising." I helped her keep Josh on his feet by taking his weight on the other side. "I figured he had a lot of padding up in there."

"I'm going to let that one slide," she said. "How did Jenny not make you explode?"

I wiggled the finger with the ring on it. "This thing is amazing. I could shower in holy water and come out with only minor burns."

"Sam's burning up the place," Josh mumbled. "She's so hot."

Sam blushed.

I tried not to laugh. "Is she? Would you like to do unmentionable things to her?"

He smiled and gave me a thumbs-up.

"Got yourself a real winner here," I said.

"Can we just get him to the hospital? Please? He's getting to be too heavy."

"You hear that, fatty?" I asked Josh.

Josh opened his mouth to respond but drooled instead.

Nicholas appeared out of the crowd. He looked at the drooling mess that was Josh and grinned. "Cute. He a pet of yours?"

Sam's face went blood red. "The Little Horn."

Nicholas made a mocking gesture with his hands. "The poseur angel."

"I know what you're here for. You can't have it."

Nicholas laughed. "Listen to that moxie. Bartholomew, you really are rubbing off on her, aren't you?"

"It happens." The idea occurred to me that maybe she'd rubbed off on me a little as well. I dismissed the notion as quickly as a fly in my face.

"Look, sugar tits. Your demon friend here and I have a deal. He gives me the Shard, I give him a spot on the High Council in Hell."

"Did you know he lost his horns?" Sam asked. She knew all

about Nicholas, since she'd forced me to tell her using the Hand of God. But he didn't know that.

Nicholas winced. "Say it ain't so."

"It's so," I said.

"That's a Greek tragedy."

"Yes, we're all quite torn up about it," Sam said. "The fact remains, he doesn't have the Shard. You should've made the deal with me."

"Maybe I'll just take it from you. Along with your arms. And your legs." Nicholas arched his eyebrows. His eyes turned a light shade of red. A few more seconds, and that famous temper of his would go off.

"Let's round the corner, shall we?" I asked. "Get some privacy."

We walked out of sight around the side of the gym. Sam and I set Josh down on the concrete, leaning him back against the school's brick wall.

He held up his hand, staring at his fingers like he'd never seen them before. "Pretty."

Nicholas glanced contemptuously at Josh, then back to me.

"All right. A deal is a deal," he said, holding out his hand. "I don't want to hurt your girlfriend here, but you know I will."

"That won't be necessary." The cherry of a cigarette glowed as someone inhaled.

I smiled. "Uh oh. You've done it now."

Lucifer stepped into the light, the smoke contorting around him as he moved.

"Hello, son. Keeping busy, I see."

"Sorry," I said. "I told your dad on you."

Whatever arrogance Nicholas possessed drained out of him.

"Dad, um... what are you doing here? This... totally isn't what it looks like."

Lucifer flicked his cigarette away.

"What does it look like?"

Nicholas's head tried to retreat into his body. His sphincter too, probably.

"I don't know. Just a few people having a friendly chat?"

Lucifer put his hand on his son's head. The touch let forth

a small scream of souls. It even wigged me out a little.

"You've been conspiring to get your paws on the Shard of Gabriel." He wagged his finger at Nicholas. "Your failures reflect very poorly on me. Makes me feel like I let you down as a father. Which, let's face it, I did, because I'm the devil. Doing something good just isn't in the cards."

I looked up at the sky. The old man did have a damn good point.

"But, Dad..." Nicholas pouted.

"Dad nothing. This is the last time you try to usurp my power, you understand? I'm sick of it. I've tried reasoning with you. I've tried bargaining with you. I've even tried grounding you. If you could only get something right every few millennia."

Nicholas trembled. "What are you going to do?"

"What I should have done when you were but a mere babe."

Lucifer bent Nicholas over his knee and started spanking him.

"Dad, please!" Nicholas cried out. "Not in front of them. This is embarrassing."

"No. You're going to learn your lesson."

Sam's mouth fell open. She evidently had no idea how to process what she saw.

Lucifer looked up and must've noticed.

"This... has been... a long time... coming," he said between spanks. He turned his gaze in my direction. "Thanks for the heads-up. Your punishment is rescinded. I can't do much else for you, since you lost your horns." Lucifer spanked Nicholas so hard he wailed. "I hear it feels a bit like being de-balled."

"You heard right." I'd probably have to join a bowling team so I could feel like I belonged somewhere now.

"Shame. Hate to lose one of my own. Even if you were more trouble than you were worth, but that's why I liked you."

I waved him off. "You're just saying that."

"I am." Lucifer dug in his pocket and tossed me his pack of cigarettes. "They're Red Circle," he said. "Consider it a going-away present."

I shook the pack to see how many remained. Almost full. "Nice."

"Remember, without your horns you're no longer under my umbrella. I can't help you, unless I want to."

"And we both know you'll only do that at a price."

Lucifer grinned. "Bingo." Nicholas tried to get free of his dad, but Satan held him down. "This is for your own good, boy."

I helped Josh to his feet.

"We should go," I said to Sam. "They're going to be here a while."

We returned to the crowd of people to the sound of Nicholas weeping between spankings.

THIRTY-SEVEN

EARTH ANGEL

Paramedics loaded Josh into one of the ambulances that had arrived. Sam and I followed him in the Hyundai to Wake Med hospital. After two hours in the waiting room, a doctor showed up, saying that Josh received a severe concussion, a few broken ribs, and a cracked jaw, probably from when Powell's lackeys beat the snot out of him.

"All you two can do, I'm afraid, is go home," the doctor said. "He's going to be here for a few days."

"Shucks," I said, snapping my fingers.

Though, I had to hand it to the kid. He'd definitely played through the pain.

Monday morning, Sam and I stopped by school. We had no reason to be here anymore, except I needed to pick up the favor Monica said she'd taken care of for me.

"Why are we here again?" Sam asked.

"Trust me." I fished out the DVD Monica put in my locker. I handed it to Sam.

"What's this?"

"Your own personal *Count of Monte Cristo*." I debated the

best way to word it. "Let's just say that if you ever want to get back at Coach Mort…" I gestured to the DVD, "now you can."

I could see the gears churning inside Sam's head. "So Monica—"

"Had a DVD of Coach Mort banging a student. It's where I got the idea for Jenny's rumor."

Sam cradled the DVD in her arms. I thought the tears would start flowing at any second.

"Thank you," she said. "This means… the world to me that you would do this." She turned around and threw the DVD in the trash.

I couldn't believe it.

"What the blazes are you doing? You literally just said how much it meant to you that I got this for you."

"And it does. But I can't do that to him," she said. "I'm trying to be an angel."

"Are you, though?" I asked.

"Well, archangel."

"Archangels can have a little fun."

"Regardless, I have to forgive him and turn the other cheek. We both know he'll get his in the end anyway."

"That's true. God's paybacks are the worst. Well… second worst. Or third. Whatever."

She threw her arms around me and hugged me tight.

"Thank you, though. Thank you so much."

Sam leaned in and kissed me on the lips. Not the cheek, mind you, but the lips. I felt a slight tingle down in my nibblies.

"That was a thank-you kiss. Don't go getting any ideas."

"I wouldn't dream of it."

We headed off to the hospital to visit Josh. I kept my fingers crossed that the extent of his injuries forced him to pee in a bucket. Sam and I walked down the hallway to his hospital room.

"Do you think Josh will have brain damage? Will he be able to talk right?" I asked. "What about reading? Will he have to relearn that?"

"Behave."

"I'm just saying. His brain could've been put through a cotton candy machine."

Josh slept soundly as we entered.

"Do not shout at him," Sam whispered. "For all we know, he might die if you scare him."

"Maybe I'll shine a flashlight in his face. See if that does him in."

Sam's eyes narrowed. "Stop."

"Josh," I said softly. "Wake up, little prince."

I moved in closer to him.

"Don't."

"Sleepy head," I whispered, next to the bed. I glanced back at Sam and smiled. My face hovered over Josh's. "There's a naked nurse in here."

Josh's eyes opened. He screamed when he saw me inches from his face.

"What the Hell?"

I fell back against the wall, laughing.

Sam flicked me on the ear. "You're so mean," she said, taking a seat on Josh's bed. "How are you feeling?"

"I've been better. Don't remember a whole lot."

"That will get worse with age, by the way," I said. They both shot evil looks at me. "It's true. Ask an old person their name. I guarantee you most of them have to look at their ID as a reminder. That's not mean. It's science."

"Out in the hall," Sam said.

"Yes, ma'am." I nodded to her and waited outside Josh's room. A couple of overweight nurses smiled at me as they passed by.

No thanks.

Sam tapped me on the arm. "He wants to see you."

"Why?"

"I don't know. But be nice, okay?"

Right. "I—"

"Promise."

"Fine. I promise." I sighed.

Josh propped himself up in bed. He seemed to at least be

somewhat coherent.

"Demon, you and I have some unsettled business."

I took a seat in one of the uncomfortable chairs. "We do?"

"You killed my father, remember?"

"I'd completely forgotten," I said, without a hint of sincerity. "What do you propose we do about that?"

"I wanted to kill you. Still do, sort of. But Sam talked me about of it."

That's so sweet. She really is an angel.

"All right."

"She reminded me I'd most likely be dead if not for you. So here's the deal. I don't like you. You don't like me. You cross me one day, we'll revisit this conversation. Until then, truce."

This kid and his hollow threat didn't scare me, but I promised Sam—wait. I'd promised her something? Sneaky devil.

"Okay," I said.

"Good." He extended his hand. I didn't want to, but I shook it. Stupid promises.

"Well?" Sam asked.

"Let's get out of here," I said, walking past her.

"Sure you don't want to read to some kids?" She caught up to me, a childish grin on her face.

I pressed the button for the elevator.

"No, but I wouldn't mind sneaking into the cancer ward to give some sickly lady a proper sendoff." I couldn't keep a straight face.

"That would probably be the most humanitarian thing you've ever done."

My smile immediately disappeared. "Forget it, then."

"Why not?" a man asked. He had a scraggly beard, wore Converse All-Stars, and had a *Frankie Says Relax* t-shirt on underneath a brown corduroy jacket.

The hairs on my body stood up straight. If I didn't already know him, I'd have assumed he worked at Starbucks or Trader Joe's.

"Gabriel. You lazy sack of cow dung," I said.

"Hello, Bartholomew. It's been a long time."

"Not long enough." Just being near him made all my pent-up anger boil to the surface. This was the angel who'd outed me to God as one of Lucifer's conspirators and had me expelled from Heaven.

"I won't be long. Just here for the last little piece of my mirror." He held out his hand.

Sam glanced at me, then reached into her purse and gave it to him. He held the Shard in his hands. I watched as it disappeared in a green haze.

"Couldn't get all the pieces back yourself?" I asked.

"I could've, but the Shard chose you. Just think. What greater hope for humanity than an angel and a demon teaming up to save the world. That's *Lifetime* movie of the week stuff right there."

"You shut your filthy mouth with that kind of talk." I wanted to punch that condescending grin off Gabriel's face so bad. His sense of self-entitlement disgusted me.

"Excellent work, Samantha," Gabriel said. "Really. The brass is very impressed."

"Thanks," she said.

I held my hand over my mouth.

"I wouldn't take that as a compliment," I said to her, loud enough for the prick angel to hear.

"I heard that," he said.

"Did you?" I asked loudly.

Gabriel looked like he tried to hide his enjoyment. "It's funny. They're even impressed with you, Bartholomew. You and Samantha make an excellent team."

What the who? The brass? Does he mean like the *brass, or a brass horn section?*

"Me?"

The angel nodded. "And, in light of the situation with your horns and all, they'd be willing to let you back into the fold on a probationary basis. That, and a massive attitude change on your part."

There was always a catch. Because I'd helped them in this interdepartmental operation, they were willing to consider letting me back in. Always a catch with these guys.

"Pass."

Whatever joy Gabriel might've been experiencing

disappeared.

"Excuse me?"

"I didn't stutter," I said. "I think I'm going to play on my own team for a while. See how that goes. Can't do any worse."

"Do you what you have to do, Bartholomew," Gabriel said. "But know that we're all rooting for you."

Rooting for me?

"The Shard may contain the wisdom of God, but with that wisdom also comes the compassion of the Almighty. Perhaps you were chosen for a reason."

"Whatever," I said with a shrug. "Go back to Starbucks and make some frappuccinos and listen to Emo rock."

I left him and Sam there by the elevator, the same shocked look on their faces. I took the stairs down to the first floor. What did that momma's boy mean, they were all rooting for me? Did they know something I didn't?

I patted the flask of bourbon in my jacket. I decided to take a trip to the cafeteria as I stepped into the lobby. Some bad hospital coffee would probably go great with this liquor. I strolled past the elevator as it opened.

"Hey," Sam said as she ran to catch up with me. "That was pretty gutsy. Stupid, but gutsy."

"Sounds like me in a nutshell." I showed her the flask. "Care for some coffee with a kick?"

"I could go for that."

We moved down the hallway in silence.

"He told you to stick with me, didn't he?" I asked.

"Maybe I volunteered to stick with you."

I stopped and turned to her.

"I can see that. All I've done is show you how to enjoy yourself in this cosmic joke of an existence. Only makes sense you'd want to keep learning from the master, now that I'm on my own and free of all rules and responsibilities."

She arched her eyebrows. "You think you're funny, don't you?"

I snuck a sip of my bourbon. "I know I am."

I held out the flask.

To my surprise, she took it. Sam got maybe a thimbleful of bourbon in her mouth before she started coughing.

I patted her on the back, telling her to take it like a man.

"You have to admit it," she said when the coughing subsided, "I'm much better at all of this than you originally thought."

"I don't know about that. You need to keep that ever-expanding head of yours in check. It gets too big, you might not be able to keep standing."

"You seem to be doing fine."

"Look at you with the burn."

We continued talking trash as we walked into the cafeteria to drink some spiked coffee. I didn't want to acknowledge it, but something about what Gabriel said kept gnawing at me. I felt like I'd exercised free will and rebelled against everything to go my own way, yet I couldn't escape the idea that I'd just followed the steps in somebody else's plan. Throw in Sam having a chance to decide Coach Mort's fate, and it made a little too much sense. Could everything I had done have gone according to a blueprint someone else had created? Someone who not only was a higher power than me, but a complete asshole to boot?

Nah.

ABOUT THE AUTHOR

Growing up, Ryan Hill spent his time writing stories instead of doing homework. This resulted in an obsession with being an author and a gross incompetence in the fields of science and mathematics. A graduate of North Carolina State University, Ryan loves the Wolfpack. Ryan also feels strange about referring to himself in the third person, but that hasn't stopped him from doing it this whole time.

Made in the USA
Columbia, SC
23 March 2018